THE F

Published by The Shollond Trust

87B Cazenove Road

London N16 6BB

England

headexchange@gn.apc.org

www.headless.org

Design by rangsgraphics.com

The Shollond Trust is a UK charity reg. no 1059551

ISBN: 978-1-908774-48-4

THE FACE GAME

Liberation without Dogmas, Drugs or Delay

D. E. Harding

The Face Game and its derivatives, described here for the first time, are relatives of the celebrated 'Games People Play' of Dr Eric Berne, and in their own way they are just as ingeniously and entertainingly dishonest. These 50-odd games comprise, however, a distinct family, whose function is to avoid Liberation or Enlightenment at all costs. How to become aware of and stop playing these games, thus achieving Self-knowledge and its fruits (heightened sense-perception, relaxation, spontaneity, openness, love), without the aid of dogmas or mind-changing drugs or indefinitely prolonged meditational practice, is the practical theme of this book. Here is made available something like the LSD experience at its best, without any of the risks, plus much else that is life-enhancing. The technique, though continuous with the great religious traditions, is a new and streamlined one that has already had remarkable success, especially among young people.

CONTENTS

Preface

The Face Game is the game of pretending to be a person. When we see Who we really are we stop playing the Face Game and begin living a game-free life, the fruits of which are love, joy and peace. This game-free life is also known as Liberation, Enlightenment, Salvation.

Douglas Harding wrote *The Face Game* in 1968 when he was 59. Up to this moment he had spent much of his adult life thinking deeply about his identity. Before he saw his faceless True Self in India in 1943, he had spent a dozen years thinking and reading and enquiring into the nature of what it is to be human. If anything, this enquiry intensified after he saw Who he really was. So by the time he wrote *The Face Game* he had spent more than 35 years deeply involved in self-enquiry. The Face Game, therefore, is the expression of a mature spirit, of someone who had for many years been profoundly committed to living consciously from the Truth. Reading this book, that maturity and depth shines out from every page. So does his skill as a writer.

After first seeing he was faceless, Harding had spent 20 years unable to really share the Seeing with anyone. Then in 1964 the secretary in his architectural practice saw, and valued, what he was pointing to. By 1968 Harding had shared facelessness with about 50 people who were, as a result, living consciously from their True Nature. *The Face Game* was influenced by this recent explosion in Harding's life—after so many years on his own with Seeing, he was now experiencing a fast-growing number of friendships with others who were also Seeing. This was an exciting, inspiring time both for Harding and for his new friends. The insights in this book reflect Harding's deepening awareness of the power of Seeing both in terms of psychological self-awareness and in terms of how the Seeing transforms relationships.

I once asked Douglas Harding about how he came to choose the subjects he wrote about. He replied that he didn't really choose—he didn't have a plan. Something would occur to him—would emerge spontaneously out of his True Nature—and he would follow it up and see where it led. Sometime around the beginning of 1967 Harding came across *Games People Play* by Eric Berne—Harding's wife had borrowed it from the library and Harding, seeing it lying around the house, had picked it up and read it. One thing led to another—reading Berne's book led to writing an article. In *The Face Game* article Harding introduced a new level to Berne's idea of psychological game-playing. In the world of Transactional Analysis, people were coming up with new games, one after the other, but Harding looked beneath all the games and identified a master game. It was a brilliant analysis and reframing of the whole idea of game-playing. Harding placed the Transactional Analysis attempt to liberate oneself from psychological games within the deeper context of spiritual liberation—the liberation from all psychology, the liberation from being a person. Harding sent his article to Berne in San Francisco who published it in the *Transactional Analysis Bulletin* in April 1967. It was the longest article published in the Bulletin up to that date, reflecting the importance Berne placed on Harding's contribution.

But then another idea must have occurred to Harding—emerging out of the creative Void within!—because he then expanded the article into a book: the book you now hold in your hands. But here's a curious thing. I met Harding in 1970 and became a close friend. I knew *The Face Game* article well—Harding had copies he used to give away to friends. In fact, in the early 1970s just about everyone in Harding's by then quite large circle of Seeing friends would have known about it. But none of us knew about the book by the same name. The first time I became aware of this book was when I was looking through Harding's papers and manuscripts some time after his death in 2007. What a surprise! A substantial, complete typescript, carefully bound in hard brown covers. A well-kept secret! I asked around and none of Harding's close friends knew about this book, including his second wife, Catherine. This is all the more astonishing because it is a very good book. It's not something you would want to hide away because it doesn't come up to scratch, or isn't finished. This is vintage Harding, a masterpiece. Why did he never mention it? Perhaps he was intentionally leaving it to be discovered later. If so, it could so easily have been neglected or lost. Anyway, it has now come to light, I suppose at just the right time.

The Face Game is a powerful, inspiring book. There are many, many jewels in it. I will not try to highlight them here but will leave you the pleasure of finding them for yourself. However there is one thing about the book I do want to mention. Harding accompanies his text with quotations from many great mystics from a number of traditions. Lots of quotations—how well-read he was! But he makes clear he is quoting these mystics not because he thinks of them as spiritual authorities but because he thinks of them as friends—fellow-travellers who discovered the same Jewel as he discovered. Harding is modest—he claims practically nothing for himself, referring anything of value, any achievement of his, to the Source, to the One that we all really are. But from my perspective, Harding's inclusion in his book of so many of the world's great mystics as friends is wholly appropriate. Harding stands amongst them as a friend. He is an equal in terms of the depth and maturity of his experience and the clarity and poetry of his unique voice.

I am happy to see this book appearing in the world. I hope it will inspire all who read it—inspire us to stop playing the Face Game and be Who we are.

Richard Lang

PART I

INTRODUCTORY

The unexamined life is not worth living.

Plato

To understand others is to have knowledge; to understand oneself is to be illumined.

Lao-tzu

Our self-knowledge is our beauty: in self-ignorance we are ugly.

Plotinus

You know the value of everything—except yourself!
The vital problem is to discover whether you are vile or fortunate.

Rumi

It is an extraordinary blindness to live without investigating what we are.

Pascal

All Christian religion wholly consists in this, to learn to know ourselves, whence we come and what we are.

Boehme

To understand everything except oneself is very comical.

Kierkegaard

I will see if I have no meaning, while the houses and ships have meaning.

Whitman

Who is it that repeats the Buddha's name? We should try to find out where this 'Who' comes from and what it looks like.

Hsu-yun

Forgetfulness of the Self is the source of all misery.

Ramana Maharshi

No age has known so much, so many different things, about man as ours; no age has known less than ours what man is.

Heidegger

1 LIBERATION WITHOUT DRUGS OR DELAY

On a winter night in London, a young woman and a friend of hers—a young man who had at one time been a monk—were looking at the coloured lights of Piccadilly Circus. The young man, entranced by the whole brilliant, mobile scene, filled with a sense of expansion and oneness with everyone and everything, kept exclaiming, "My God what a trip, what a trip!" In fact he was stoned, high on LSD, the drug lysergic acid diethylamide.

He turned to his younger companion, who had never taken drugs, and was astonished at what he saw. Her eyes, too, were shining. Her face wore all the marks of the very experience he was enjoying—a wide-openness and freedom and relaxation and unselective love. And she, too, was exclaiming, "Just look at those colours, those reflections!"

He found it surprising—even disturbing—that she should, seemingly, be enjoying all the delights of a trip at its rare best, without ever having touched the stuff. Even more surprising—and disturbing—was her explanation. She said that she saw clearly What she was, and this involved experiencing a world transfigured and glorified. Moreover she could see her true Self (or no-self) whenever she wanted to, and did in fact—she claimed—do so most of the time, with the result that she was practically free from fears, worries, dislikes, and moods in general. The simple childlikeness and radiance of her face, her tone of voice—everything about her gave authority to her words. In short, it really did look as if she was, at least in some measure, truly Liberated or Enlightened.

The young man had joined an order of monks and practised the prescribed meditation, with its rigorous attendant disciplines, precisely in order to become Enlightened. But the enterprise had not come off. Enlightenment in this lifetime was said to be very difficult and rare, even after decades of meditation—hours of it every day. He was warned that he might, indeed, have to strive for several lifetimes—perhaps hundreds or thousands of them—before seeing clearly what he was, and reaping the incomparable benefits of that seeing. And so, naturally enough, he had turned to the easy and swift way of reaping some of those benefits—the way of drugs.

And here was a young girl, who had practised none of the recognized meditations, who had read almost nothing about mystical experience or spiritual religion Eastern or Western, apparently dispensing with all the standard qualifications and enjoying instant Enlightenment! And certainly without benefit of acid or pot or any other chemical aid.

This story is a true one. We could cite other instances of how people on drugs have been astonished to recognize their own condition (at its very best) in others who, like this girl, have acquired the knack of seeing clearly What they are. "I could have sworn you were stoned" is a typical comment.

2 THE PURPOSE OF THIS BOOK

The practical implications of the foregoing are obvious, and make the writing of this book a necessary and urgent task. We intend to show that the quality of life enjoyed by this young woman need not remain a rare exception. We claim there is a third way—a Way of Liberation that involves neither the long postponement, frustration, psychological hazards, and practical difficulties of conventional religious training, nor the legal, biological, psychological, and spiritual risks of drug-taking. This third way recognizes and respects the aims and the results (in so far as they are at all achievable and positive) of the other two ways. It sympathizes, it is on their side. It says to the 'serious' acid-head or pot smoker (one who isn't merely after kicks or comfort, but aims to break through to some deeper and more real level of existence)—"Here is a more efficient way of winning the freedom and the insight you want." And it says much the same thing to the 'serious' meditator (one who isn't merely hooked on meditation, but interested in the Self-knowledge that is its goal)—"Here it is, *now.*" And it says to young people who are undecided, who are contemptuous of the values of the society they find themselves in, and are as yet uncertain whether to try drugs, or meditation (as generally understood), or perhaps both together, as a way out—"There is this third way, a way out of the falsity and hardness of the social game, and a way in to your own True Nature; and for you young ones it is comparatively easy and altogether natural. And its end-product is nothing less than the reputed fruits of the spirit—love, joy, and peace."

The present book, then, is about this third way to what Hindus call Liberation, and what Zen calls Enlightenment (or Satori, or Seeing one's Original Face), and what other spiritual traditions call Awakening, Illumination, Self-realization, or Mystical Union with God. It is also about the many games (the Face Game and its varieties, all of them dishonest and even desperate manoeuvres) which one has learned to play in order to avoid Enlightenment at all costs, and which one has to unlearn and break the habit of.

The unlearning—the Enlightenment technique described in the following chapters—is not always easy, but it is very simple. In some respects it is new. The perennial teaching of the great seers and sages is restated in a form and a language that are as free as possible from the traditional accumulations that have come to obscure its essence and hamper its working. Here is a thoroughly contemporary means to Self-knowledge and to its results—heightened perception of colours and shapes and sounds, spontaneity, openness, relaxation, serenity, love without any strings or preferences. These results are not to be aimed at directly, but are by-products of attention to what is given in ordinary, first-hand experience. Thus they owe nothing to the pharmacist and very little to the priest and the scholar. All that is needed is candour, honest observation, matter-of-factness. It is the simple, the all-too-obvious truth—not experiences, however beautifully mystical—which sets us free.

Seeing this saving truth—which is ceasing to play the Face Game and so seeing one's True or Original Face—does not have to go on being as difficult or as rare as hitherto. Who is in a position to say it could never become the norm, as upright posture and speech and literacy have in turn become norms? Already the technique we describe has, during the last four years and in a very limited test-field, succeeded in some fifty cases. The results have always been good, and in (say) a third of the cases very remarkable indeed.

Perhaps our most significant and encouraging finding has been how readily the *young* can opt out of the Face Game—or at least opt out long enough to catch sight of their Original Face, once it has been pointed out to them in a way they can understand. In fact, this is only to be expected. For the Face Game, though even more universal and respectable than alcohol, is a much more insidious narcotic: at first fairly soft, it becomes more damaging and addictive with every shot. Many young people are sensing this, and ready to try anything to free themselves before they are thoroughly hooked. Every year, every day spent playing the Face Game makes Liberation from it more and more difficult, and its symptoms—stuffiness, posturing, inefficiency, dulled perception, boredom, anxiety, lovelessness—more and more evident. Understanding this basic game (and fully understanding it is to begin opting out) is therefore an urgent assignment, and particularly so for anybody who feels inclined to try the drugs which can indeed give relief from play—intermittently, and with side-effects which can be more tragic than those of the Face Game itself.

3 THE BOOK'S PLAN

"The Face Game", comprising Part II of the book, is a somewhat expanded version of a paper which appeared in the *Transactional Analysis Bulletin* (the quarterly journal of the International Transactional Analysis Association) of April, 1967; it is reproduced here by permission of the Association and Dr. Eric Berne. Setting out briefly our main thesis, it describes how this universal game is learned in childhood, how it operates in society, how it is halted by Enlightenment, and what are the results of ceasing to play.

Part III, "The Games One Plays", is a detailed working out of the complex subgames and ploys of the Face Game, all of them normally unconscious, and between them extending over all aspects of our life. In each of the fifty-odd short chapters a subsidiary game is portrayed, together with its antithesis—that aspect of Enlightenment which is its remedy. Each chapter has a collection of relevant quotations taken mostly from the main spiritual traditions, and particularly from Vedanta, Taoism, Zen, Christian mysticism, and Sufism. This material is illustrative and no part of the argument: for throughout our study the appeal is always to one's own readily verifiable experience, and no reliance is placed on external authority, no matter how sanctified. The reader is invited to test everything for himself: he has all the data and equipment needed.

The purpose of Part III, as indeed of the whole book, is practice— the practice of radical Self-discovery, in which nothing is taken on trust from others. With this in mind, each chapter may be used as a kind of 'koan' or topic for meditation. Understanding this 'koan' isn't enough; in fact, it can't really be understood till its words are used as a springboard for leaping beyond words, to the position where its point is actually seen, and the game it describes—now seen through—is halted.

Part IV, "The Third-person World Game", is adapted from an article first published in the Saturday Evening Post's series *Adventures of the Mind*, entitled "The Universe Revalued". Its purpose is to facilitate an understanding of those chapters in Part III which touch on cosmological problems, and to contrast the world one *thinks* one lives in with the world one *sees* one lives in.

The Appendix is a check-list of Pointers to Enlightenment— simple devices which we have found effective as invitations to seeing What one is.

4 GAMES AND PROCEDURES

This book will probably be easier to read if one comes to it with some knowledge of the Perennial Philosophy—the mystical or spiritual element in the major religions. Even more helpful would be some meditational practice, such as training in mindfulness. However, these preliminaries may be dispensed with, especially in the case of young people, whose relative freedom from religious conditioning can indeed be a positive advantage.

What is rather important here is to have some acquaintance with Dr Eric Berne's *Games People Play, The Psychology of Human Relationships* (Deutsch, London, 1966). Our obviously heavy debt to Dr Berne, which is gratefully acknowledged, at least requires that our reader shall understand what is meant by the terms 'game' and 'procedure' in Transactional Analysis. Berne writes:

"A game is an ongoing series of complementary ulterior transactions progressing to a well-defined, predictable outcome. Descriptively it is a recurring set of transactions, often repetitious, superficially plausible, with a concealed motivation; or, more colloquially, a series of moves with a snare, or 'gimmick'. Games are clearly differentiated from procedures, rituals, and pastimes by two chief characteristics: (1) their ulterior quality and (2) the payoff. Procedures may be successful, rituals effective, and pastimes profitable, but all of them are by definition candid; they may involve contest, but not conflict, and the ending may be sensational, but it is not dramatic. Every game, on the other hand, is basically dishonest, and the outcome has a dramatic, as distinct from merely exciting, quality." (*Op. cit.,* p. 48)

A procedure, on the other hand, is a learned "series of simple complementary Adult transactions directed toward the manipulation of reality.... Procedures are based on data processing and probability estimates concerning the material of reality, and reach their highest development in professional techniques." (*Op. cit.,* p. 35)

Clearly to see the point of any one of these 'koans' is to see the point of them all; for this reason they may be tackled in any order, and it doesn't much matter if some of them are skipped altogether. On first reading straight through, in fact, they may seem repetitious. Actually, this is their essential message: they all point to the same conclusion—to the goal of Self-realisation. And the reader who is intent on this goal is not only likely to find all the 'koans' useful, but will probably find himself adding new ones of his own.

The games described in this book, and their prototype the Face Game, comprise a family related to, but distinct from, those described in *Games People Play.* They are the games *one plays oneself,* first-person games not (strictly speaking) to be detected in other people, though other people are certainly caught up in them. In this category of games it is always *oneself* who is dishonest and working for a concealed payoff, and *oneself* who needs curing. Others are seen to be all right. What is an underhand game in one's own case is recognized as a useful procedure in theirs. This distinction is crucial, but what we mean by it will become clear only as we proceed to studying the actual games and their antitheses.

PART II

THE FACE GAME

BUSHMAN ROCK PAINTINGS from the Drakensberg

Chia Yung went out to fight bandits, but was wounded and lost his head. Mounting his horse, he returned to the camp. The soldiers and people of the camp all came to look at him, and Yung spoke from his chest, "I was defeated by the bandits and they cut off my head. Tell me, in your opinion, does it look better to have a head or to be without a head?" The officers wept and said, "It's better to have a head." Yung replied, "I don't think so. It's just as good to be without a head!"

Luyichi (9th c.)

But then the worst happens. They take him by the hand and draw him towards the table; and all of them, as many as are present, gather inquisitively before the lamp. They have the best of it; they keep in the shadow, while on him alone falls, with the light, all the shame of having a face.

Rainer Maria Rilke

Alone, without form or face,
Foothold or prop, one goes on
To love That, beyond all creatures,
Which may be won by happy chance.

St John of the Cross

1 DEFINITION

The Face Game may be defined as the basic life game with which one surreptitiously fills in the time between childhood and Enlightenment or death (whichever comes first)—unless one happens to be a schizophrenic or retardate or primitive who hasn't learned to play. Its aim is to build and maintain a fictitious face here, where one has no face, in order to hide one's emptiness from oneself. Though (like all games studied in Transactional Analysis) it is dishonest and absurd, it cannot be called a bad and unnecessary game, provided play ceases between (say) the ages of 15 and 25.

2 BEFORE THE GAME

(i) Facelessness

Examples A newborn baby, a low-grade imbecile, an animal.

(ii) Facelessness—but self and not-self becoming distinguished

Example (a) Carlos (1 year 7 months) at a party is asked to locate various uncles and aunties. He points to each correctly. Then Uncle Roger asks him where Carlos is. He waves his hands—a gesture which seems to say he is *at large.* Anyway, Carlos cannot locate Carlos.

Example (b) Mary (3 years) is in the dentist's chair. Asked where it hurts, she replies: "At Auntie's".

Example (c) From the age of about 19 months to about 2 years, Carlos gets quite cross when he is referred to as a naughty boy or a good boy: he insists that he is *not* a boy.

Example (d) That even a child of 5 or 6 doesn't readily attribute to himself a face like the others, is suggested by the following typical conversation: "George, have you a brother?" "Yes." "Then he has a brother?" "Oh no."

(iii) The face found out there

Example Joan (2) is told to go wash. She proceeds to the bathroom and starts washing her face—the face in the mirror.

(iv) Facelessness found here

Example (a) Johnny (2 years 3 months) asks mother to make a picture.

She draws a circle for a face, and asks: "What next?" Johnny's trunk, legs, feet and hands are achieved, though not his arms. Next, he wants eyes, so mother draws two. But he insists on more and more till the whole face is covered with eyes. He then firmly declares the picture finished.

Example (b) Stephen (3 years 6 months), standing in the bath and looking down at his body, cries out: "Mum, I haven't got a head!"

Example (c) Paul (4 years) in the car, examining his hands, exclaims: "Look Mum, I haven't got a face!"

(v) Facelessness declined

Example "Mum, I wish he/she wouldn't stare at me so, and how I wish my nose/eyes/ears were as small/big/pretty as his/hers!"

Of these five categories, the fourth is specially interesting. Though probably no more than a passing flash of insight or a series of such flashes, this spontaneous discovery—that one's true Face here is "all eyes", or (better still) is missing altogether—is nevertheless a preview of Enlightenment, a little Satori. For Enlightenment is "becoming like a little child", and "seeing no more than an infant sees", and "seeing one's Original (featureless) Face", and "being headless", and realizing oneself as "all Eye and spiritual substance". Karen (9 years) wrote this poem:

Being Nobody

Have you ever felt like nobody?

Just a tiny speck of air.

When everyone's around you,

And you are just not there.

And this is what the sages say, rather less straightforwardly.

We suspect that this precocious Enlightenment is not at all rare. But in normal children it is certainly not a steady insight and is soon repressed. Before facelessness can establish itself, the business of hastily covering it up—the Face Game, in fact—begins. The reason the game starts so early in life, and is so little resisted, is that it is badly needed: it is an urgent face-making and face-saving contrivance. Rather as his sister has to cope with penis-envy, so young Stephen has to cope with head-envy. How awful to be the only child in the class whose head is missing! How disturbing to look at the spot one occupies and *always* find it quite empty, and oneself "just a tiny speck of air"—if that—in vivid contrast to all those splendidly solid and opaque people out there!

Fortunately, one's remedy is close at hand, and large doses of solidifying medicine are taken long before one notices the trouble.

The perennial Face Game is in full swing all around, and one has good reason to join in: its existential advantage is that it hides one's facelessness, this yawning void which threatens one's very existence. Shamefaced, our young Adam starts clapping on his figleaf mask almost before he has time to glimpse the dreadful nakedness it covers.

3 LEARNING TO PLAY

As a young child, one is faceless, and learning to pretend otherwise is a long and complicated task, starting almost at birth and hardly completed, till one's teens. There are three ways of learning the game, all necessary, and all thoroughly dishonest:

(i) Building a face here

(ii) Importing a face from elsewhere

(iii) Going out to find a face

(i) Building a face here

This way is non-visual, and builds on the foundation of touch, muscular activity and tension, sensations of heat, cold, pain, and so on. From birth, baby's face is kissed, patted, stroked, fed, washed, and generally worked on and fussed over, as if to make up for its inherent evanescence and to body it forth. In due course, there are added pastimes which are quite overtly face building:

Brow bender,

Eye peeper,

Nose dreeper,

Mouth eater,

Chin chopper,

Knock at the door,

Ring at the bell,

Lift the hatch,

Walk in.....

As mother repeats each line, she puts her finger (or baby's) on his forehead, eye, nose, mouth, etc., in turn. There are many similar nursery rhymes, and many nursery pastimes involving facial manipulation. For instance, this slightly gruesome one, played when the child is somewhat older: mother pretends to unscrew and wrench off his nose, which she then shows him (it's really the ball of her thumb, held between her first and second fingers); and he pretends to cry out in terror and anxiously explore his mutilated features.

Face-building goes on in the playground, where children 'pull horrible faces' or 'make faces' at one another or 'wipe their smiles off' and pretend to throw them at other faces. And in school itself: for example—"The teacher suggested the use of a playful game to direct the children's attention to their appearance. This technique increased their general awareness of their facial features..." The children tell each other how they look, the colour of their eyes, hair, and so on.

Teacher: "Let's pretend our fingers are motor-cars. Then we can take a trip round our cheeks..."

They then draw their faces as they imagine them to be.

These school-children were about seven years old. As one grows up, the need to body forth one's face, and the effort that is consequently put into it, increase rather than diminish. The site gets still more working over: witness the rituals of frequent washing, teeth-cleaning, hair-brushing and hair-patting, putting on and making up and repairing one's face (if female) and shaving (if male), fussing with spectacles, chin-stroking, nattering, smoking. (I just *must* have a face here for this great big pipe to be stuck in, for all this smoke to be billowing out of! What *could* this onrush of—otherwise pointless—chatter be coming from, if not a face?) It's as if one were H.G. Wells' Invisible Man, who gets by only through assiduous face-building, with dark glasses, hat pulled down, muffler pulled up.

How successful is this build-up? What sort of features does it produce, not in the make-believe of the Face Game, but in reality?

First, the result isn't opaque. However hard my parents and teachers and friends and enemies and I work on this 'face' here, it remains *for me* transparent, without the slightest mistiness. Joan washing in the mirror was right: *that* face was filthy. But *this* 'face'—one's own Original Face—is perfectly clean for ever, clean of dirt, of skin, of features, of itself.

Second, it is colourless. If someone daubs paint on my forehead, I'm the only one in the room who can't say what is the colour of the mark. What mark, indeed? What forehead?

Third, it is without shape and texture. At least it is so *now*, until time and motion and memory are brought in. For as soon as the fingertips stop exploring, both they and the explored features melt and merge. When I simply lay my hand on my 'face', practically no information about either comes through. Like Johnny's, the eyes can't be counted (what eyes?) nor the fingers (what fingers?), and this alleged face might be an inch or a mile or a light-year across, on the *present* evidence.

Fourth, it is essentially self-effacing, a perfectly empty reception-centre for *other* faces, mere capacity and nothing in itself. No matter what aches, itches, tickles, tastes, smells, tics, etc., are going on around here, they all leave the view-out-from-here as bright and clear as can be. How, indeed, could I receive your face, and keep my own? What confusion that would be!

In short (if we define a face as an opaque and coloured oval surface, simultaneously containing two eyes, two nostrils, one nose, mouth, and so on) this method we have been describing—the method of laboriously building a face here on non-visual foundations—is a total failure. Even the foundations are always vanishing. It is the gimmick of the Face Game to pretend otherwise.

(ii) Importing a face from elsewhere

What one needs but cannot make at home, one imports. This is where the mirror comes in.

At 1 $^1/_2$ to 2 years it is normal just to stare into the mirror, or to play with or 'talk' to the baby behind the glass, or to turn the mirror over in search of him. As the growing child learns to handle the mirror better, make faces in the mirror, wash in front of the mirror, and so on, he comes to regard the other child's face over there, behind the glass, as 'really' his own face right here, in front of the glass. This fiction is assisted by the Mirror Game, in which the child deliberately 'annihilates' and 'recreates' himself by bobbing up and down in front of the glass. The payoff is his magical power of rescuing his face from destruction.

But the face I make there, on the far side of the glass, has still to be brought across to me here. It's as if I reach out for it and draw it towards me, freeing it from the glass and turning it round and stretching it out as it comes, and finally clapping it onto my Facelessness. Now I am equipped to face the world—I think.

A desperate manoeuvre indeed! Only rock-bottom necessity could account for such tricks—tricks played on oneself. In fact, the Face Game (mirror subsection) feigns *seven* absurdities: that that two-eyed, opaque, coloured area over there is (1) myself, (2) looking at itself, (3) accessible to touch, (4) much bigger than it is, (5) present all the time, whether observed or not, (6) rotated 180°, (7) say 6 feet in front of itself.

To test how efficiently I am playing the Face Game, I look in my bathroom mirror. If I see a man in that second bathroom behind the glass, staring fixedly into my own unoccupied bathroom, then I am playing badly or not at all. If I simply see myself, I am playing well. In other words, I am living down my infant honesty.

(iii) Going out to find a face

If my face is really some way off, and I can neither (to be honest) build it up here at home by feeling it, nor fetch it home from elsewhere with the help of my mirror, then it seems I must go out in search of it. If *I'm* in no position to register my face, I must somehow get into the position of those who are.

To begin with, of course, this is impossible. As an infant, one is at first centred wholly upon oneself, observing phenomena from one's own unique, primitive, subjective point of view. Everything is as it is for me. But my gradual and many-sided development into a mature human being involves the growth of my ability to shift centre onto other observers and to contemplate myself as their object, from their point of view. This is the crucial move in the Face Game. Growing up is learning to play this game more efficiently, and this means learning to jump further and further out of my skin (imaginary, here) in order to view my skin (real, there). This is helped on by such children's games as Hide-and-seek and Can't-see-me. In the former, the necessary payoff isn't my 'success' in remaining hidden but my 'failure' to keep it up: the point of the game is *being seen*. In the latter, my satisfaction lies in my relief when father, having looked for me everywhere, including straight through me, suddenly ceases pretending I am invisible, and restores my status as a solid object after all.

The main trouble with jerking myself off-centre is that it grows increasingly difficult to get back. I do not need the gift that Robert Burns so craved—the gift to see ourselves as others see us: it's what all Face-game players are suffering from. My prayer should rather be for the gift one progressively loses by growing up—the precious gift of seeing oneself as one sees oneself, from one's own original centre and true home.

(1) Like baby Carlos at the party, I cannot pin myself down. Not yet shut up in a body, or imprisoned behind a pair of eyes, I am at large, unbounded. Faceless, I have no worries about how I look to others, so act unselfconsciously, naturally, spontaneously, and am no respecter of persons. I'm not in company; rather, the company is in me.

(2) But this innocent, jerk-free [1] phase is already passing, as I am increasingly aware that my parent is behaving and looking meaningfully in this direction—looking angrily or approvingly, lovingly or distastefully *at* something and not at nothing. So I begin to regard myself, though vaguely at first, as a solid and opaque object of some sort, through my parents' eyes. And thereafter all my self-awareness is apt to be, in effect, the Parent-in-me viewing the Child-in-me with anxious concern, from some station out there.

(3) Acting for the parents, continuing their function as face-makers are friends and relations and teachers, and indeed everybody I confront. As a boy, I find myself in company. This time, suddenly outfaced by a circle of faces, I start blushing and stammering. Those critical thought hiding masks—what do they make of me? They make me out to be a crest fallen little boy, and I adopt their view. No longer immense and free and nothing whatever like the folk around me, I now see myself through their eyes as one of them—and a small and inadequate one, at that. Such a come-down, such shrinkage, such vulnerability—no wonder I'm upset! The real wonder is that I take this cruel cutting-down-to-size as stoically I do. But at least I condense into a recognizable something, and not a faceless Nothing. That is the consolation, the payoff.

(4) A few years later, a very different person strides into the same room, one who has learned to play the Face Game rather better. This

---

1 This apt technical term is borrowed from Berne. A jerk is one whose built-in Child is over-anxious not to lose face in his built-in Parent's eyes. He lives off-centre, viewing himself from out there. Erratic, absent-minded, displaced in time and space, he overlooks the faceless here-now of present experience. Taking leave of his senses, he gets more and more out of touch with the world of actual sounds and colours.

time I make my appearance confidently (*who* makes this appearance, *what* it's an appearance of, I don't wish to know). Everything I say and do is to impress, not express. For I am right out there being impressed, and enjoying the spectacle of this splendid young fellow much more than the others are. In fact, they feel somewhat embarrassed; they sense the falsity of the game; it's horrid to see this recognition-hungry youth jerked so far off-centre, in order that he may be turned in upon himself instead of out upon them. Not yet hopelessly beside himself or self-alienated, he's obviously getting that way.

(5) Now quite grown up (though still just as Parent-dominated), I'm playing a harder Face Game than ever, but more subtly and effectively, and on a much larger field. Suppose my television face is familiar in a million homes. Now, at last, I'm surely winning. Imposing this carefully cultivated image upon so many viewers and so frequently, surely I am no longer a faceless nobody! And surely this huge expansion is a big step towards the reconquest of that worldwide empire I once ruled as an infant! (In fact, I never agreed to being cut down to human size, at all.) Even so, I'm losing. My appetite for recognition grows faster than the supply. Besides, for all my showmanship, the discriminating viewer finds me more hollow than ever. And hollow I am, for I have so lost touch with the faceless Child in myself, with that mysterious central reality of which all those screen-appearances are mere appearances, that I've lost my way back. I have gone on jerking myself out from myself till I am the shell of myself. I'm a fake, a mock-up. People sense my unreality.

(6) I can now play harder still, and go more obviously sick or mad;

or ease off the game and somehow get by till I die. Suppose I ease off, reconciling myself to losing not too much face in the process, to saving as much face as I can. Now I settle down to a comparatively Adult way of life, no longer quite so Parent-ridden, no longer quite so alienated from the faceless Child in me. This Adult existence is concerned with the 'processing of reality', which means the practical assessment and handling of my changing situation, *objectively*. And this means looking at oneself and others from all relevant angles in space and time; it is centrifugal and many-centred; its point of view is extremely mobile. The result is that worldwide observational grid which is the framework of civilization itself, with its inestimable benefits—and losses. Here, indeed, is where this great lifegame comes into its own. To be fully human is—for at least a few years of one's life—to play it. Society *is* mutual face-making and face-taking.

4 EXTENDED PLAY

This one short life is far from enough for the really keen player: to play the Face Game wholeheartedly is to try to play it non-stop for ever. This means giving it a religious turn and bringing God into it as star player, because (I tell myself) he alone is the eternally efficient face-maker and face-saver. My earthly parents did their best to help me find and establish my face, but much of the time they ignored or forgot me, or even deliberately refused to notice me. They had other business, and anyway they died. So also with my friends and enemies, my wife and children: they often overlook me now and their memory of my face will not outlast them. In the end, no amount of fame will impress my image upon the world. Hence my need for a Father in Heaven who "never slumbers nor sleeps", who will not for a moment forget my appearance through all eternity, who is so observant that he numbers the very hairs of my head. This is the God who, in the revealing words of the Psalmist, is "the health of my countenance and the lifter up of my head, who upholds me in my integrity and settles me before his face for ever": the God to whom I say, along with A 'Kempis, "If I be left to myself, lo I am naught and all infirmity. But if Thou behold me suddenly anon I am made strong and filled with a new joy."

But not even my Father in Heaven (supposing he exists there and is able and willing to contemplate my face for ever and ever) can make me a face *here*; at most he can help me overlook my facelessness by diverting my attention to himself. We shall see that there are, in fact, two sorts of religion, one for setting up the Face Game eternally and the other for stopping it now, and that their consequences in day-to-day living are as contrasted as their long-term aims. Certainly the Face Game (Religious Section) and the subgame 'Thou God Seest Me' extend, along with play, the problems and anxieties that go with it. To widen into the religious field what is essentially a pretence is to pretend on a cosmic scale, to play a still harder game, and therefore to land me in still more trouble.

Still it is a game, a pretence. Though some of its transactions help to keep things going, nearly all are also for face-building, and many only for that. Talk is for proving there's a talker, what's said being largely immaterial. The Face Game is maintained in full swing by the hidden advantages it yields. It papers over my deeply dreaded Emptiness; it enables me to avoid the true intimacy and love of which this Emptiness is the ground; it ensures that I shall be impressed with the way I impress others—the more people can be got to recognize this face and project it onto these shoulders, the more ungracious of me not to receive it here! If so many choose to make so much of me who am I to object? If all those folk acclaim my New Clothes, that's good enough for me! The Emperor would be a fool to disagree, on the flimsy objection that they are invisible here: I *must* be wearing them!

But these advantages are illusory. If this central Emptiness isn't acknowledged positively, it will make itself felt negatively, and in the end disastrously. Really to grow up, to be free and at ease and natural, to be quite sane, even to be quite practical, I must stop playing this game, while retaining as procedure the best of its hard-won techniques. To the extent that I go on playing at all, my objectivity is blurred, my world distorted, my game unconscious. Understanding it is the beginning of withdrawal from it.

5 FAILURE TO PLAY

Another possibility must now be considered. I may never learn to play the Face Game with any skill or conviction; indeed I may never get round to playing it at all. Having failed or declined to take myself at the world's estimate, I am liable to be labelled schizoid or schizophrenic. Understandably enough, the total discrepancy between the facelessness I find at this centre, and the facade which everybody out there seems determined to construct upon it, proves too much for me and for them. If, through parental neglect or deprivation, I have never been taught the game, or I am simply too honest to begin playing it, then I am mad in the eyes of regular players. And of course this non-player, despised, bewildered, despairing of ever being understood, hopelessly outnumbered and cut off, is driven to many ingenious and fantastic devices in order to maintain some sort of inner integrity, some secret defence against the imposition of that social Thing upon this non-social No-thing, some contrivance for keeping that face-in-the-mirror separate from its faceless spectator here. But who is mad, the player or the non-player of the Face Game, the sucker who declines the Great Con or the smart lad who falls for it?

Jung said that the schizophrenic ceases to be schizophrenic as soon as he is understood; and one method of treatment has been to adopt (with imperfect sincerity) the symbolic language of the patient. But if the therapist has himself opted out of the Face Game, he may (in suitable cases) do much towards healing the patient by

43

endorsing, with perfect sincerity and respect and even enthusiasm, the patient's view of himself. If I am a so-called schizophrenic, I may see myself as transparent, a vacuum, made of glass or air: people look right through me. I may declare that I am empty, unreal, unborn, non-existent, or dead. Or that I am weightless, discontinuous in time, headless, faceless, disembodied, lacking personal identity, at odds with what I see in the mirror, inviolate and untouched by the hateful self people try to impose upon me. Now all this is basically true, indeed obvious, to anyone who has ceased playing the Face Game; though the language runs wild, this is what he sees himself to be. Even if I claim to be Napoleon or the Virgin Mary or anybody else, the game-free therapist should have little trouble in cheerfully agreeing with me—on the grounds that one's true Self, being faceless and transpersonal and unconditioned, is the one Self (or No-self) of all. In fact, say the sages, one who clearly sees this essential identity is Liberated.

None of this denies that the schizophrenic is sick. And no wonder: the child who finds himself left out of the game everyone is playing is tragically vulnerable compared with the grown man who deliberately retires from it. One's central Void is ambivalent: it wears a powerfully malevolent as well as a beneficent aspect. When ignored and repressed (as by the 'sane' player) it progressively undermines happiness and sanity; when recognized, but without understanding and full acceptance (as by the schizophrenic non-player), it doesn't produce happiness and true sanity, but much misery and fear. The schizophrenic's emptiness and facelessness may accordingly be experienced positively, as the most precious possession to be guarded from all invasion; yet also negatively, as a terrible threat only to be averted by constant assurances from other people that he is something and not nothing. Paradoxically, these people prove his existence (disappearing when alone, he needs to be seen in order to be), yet they deprive him of it (of the invisibility which is his secret refuge). He may have his unloving parents to thank for this, especially if they overlooked and ignored him, failing to define him or to indicate what he was to be. They failed to give him his face. Whatever the reason, he never learned the game. And, non-players are liable to punishment. He is subjected to psychiatric diagnosis and treatment, hospitalization, and so on.

Nevertheless the type of schizophrenic we have been describing does fill a negative role in the game, as a (more or less) non-playing participant. His abnormal sanity, and insanity, can only be understood as occurring in the social milieu as a whole. It isn't that he's sick and others aren't, but that the sickness is transactional, inseparable from the to-and-fro of the game for which all share responsibility. His cure, accordingly, is transactional too: he has to understand the game, the therapist to stop playing it. *He* isn't cured—*they* are.

6 HALTING PLAY

Traditionally, Liberation or Enlightenment seldom descends out of the blue upon anyone. Nor is it likely to be had by reading books, or by much thinking about it, or even by solitary do-it-yourself meditation. After due preparation, it is *transmitted* from master to disciple. It is easy to see why. Essentially transactional, a social infection, the Face Game is very catching; and so is ceasing from the game catching. In the company of hardfaced players one plays one's hardest. In the company of non-players—young children, some primitives, idiots, and animals—one abates one's play and doesn't bother to put on special faces. In the company of a sage, one may find oneself temporarily defaced altogether—so infectious is his *darshan*. (In fact, it is nonsense to talk of his Enlightenment as *his:* it is *everybody's*. When one sees one's true Face here one is seeing the true Face of all.)

If I am opting out of the Face Game, some of the people around me are already tending to follow, though their initial response may well be to step up their play in self-defence. Precisely how does my ceasing play necessarily involve them, and maybe help them to do the same? There are three transactional stages.

(i) PARENT-Child—FACE TO FACE

Suppose I'm sitting facing you and playing the game. Then to me the set-up appears symmetrical: I count *two* of everything—two pairs of eyes, two mouths, two noses, two faces. I regard us as similar, face to face. This means my attention is split, one part *seeing* your face there, the other *thinking* my face here. The result is that I glimpse rather than see your face. And certainly I don't *take on* what I see of it. I've a perfectly good one here of my own, thank you! So *I throw your face back at you* (that's exactly how it feels and looks from here) making it almost impossible for you to refuse delivery. This is what your Parent, and we your Parent's surrogates, do for you: our wearing faces practically ensures you shall wear one, which in turn practically ensures that people around you shall wear theirs. Thus we switch roles, face-making and face-taking by turns, and the game recruits its teams of new players.

(ii) CHILD-Parent—NO-FACE TO FACE

Now suppose, while still sitting facing you, I upset this familiar and fairly stable relationship by withdrawing from the game. Then the set-up becomes for me asymmetrical: this time I count *one* of everything—one pair of eyes, one mouth, one nose, one face—all yours and none mine. I notice that we are totally unlike and indeed incommensurable, no-face to face, my absence to your presence. This means my attention is undivided: childlike, I'm going by what I *see* here and now, and am not *thinking* things into it. The result is that I really do see you, maybe for the first time after years of mere glimpsing; I receive you as you are given, vividly and without subjective distortion. And, even more vividly, I really do see Myself, as this perfectly empty Receptacle open and waiting for you, as this perfectly clean Mirror held up to you, as this perfectly blank

Screen on which you are now starring. For the moment, I am wholly occupied with you as you are, wholly replaced by you: that's not merely how it feels and looks from here, but the way it actually is. I can find only your face, nothing added this side of your skin (not even distance) and nobody here looking at it. Having so strikingly what I lack so totally, you are truly welcome here. I'm absolutely delighted to *take your face off you!*

(iii) Adult-Adult—FACE TRADING

Now suppose you say Yes to this warm invitation, and cheerfully give what anyway I take. (It shouldn't be too hard now—after all, I've done a good half of your job for you!) Then you, in turn, are defaced and absent; you are wearing my face, as I am yours. Changing places and trading faces, at last we know where we are with one another: our relationship is easy and stable. There is no *confrontation* (note the hostility and defiance that word implies); we are no longer opposite each other, no longer *opposed* (note as before). Quite the reverse: we are complementary, in fact united. This is the only fully Adult-Adult relationship, when the Child is liberated in us both and makes true intimacy possible. Here is the only love which has no strings attached—because there's nothing here to tie up to.

But this happy issue is rare. The last things one normally wants are relief from one's face, game-free intimacy, and the love that is candid and ungrasping. The common response when one's play is threatened is a negative one, which we must now consider.

7 UNDERCUTTING THE GAME'S PAYOFF

The fact that the Face Game is a game in the technical sense (as defined in Transactional Analysis) is confirmed by what happens when Mr Black refuses to play it with Mr White and/or threatens the concealed advantages which Mr White is getting from the game. In that event, White is likely to attempt various face-saving manoeuvres. If these fail, he suffers a kind of despair, in which distress and resentment are mingled. The following are illustrations.

(i) Successful Resistance

Black declines to go on playing faces with White, and (unwisely, in this instance, not to say impertinently) tries to explain the game and why he's pulling out of it. White neatly sidesteps the danger of Self-examination by dismissing Black as (a) clever-clever, or (b) incomprehensible, or (c) conceited, or (d) paranoid, or (e) blasphemous, or (f) any serviceable combination of these. Anyhow, the upshot of Black's well-meant efforts is to provoke White to play still harder. If Black's retirement from the game is too blatant, he may have to pay for his indiscretion with his job, his liberty, or even his life.

(ii) Breakdown Threatened

(a) Or it may be that White, the face-saver, is cut in the street by Grey, or ostracized by Green, Brown & Co., or put into solitary confinement, or subjected to brainwashing techniques aimed at the confusion and destruction of his image of himself. All mean loss of face, accompanied by distress, with the threat of a breakdown. Any falling-off in White's reputation or public face is liable to have a similar effect.

(b) Suppose White smokes heavily. Now the payoff in such games as Alcoholic and Chain Smoker isn't the imbibing itself, but rather the imbibing *head* it gives one at the time, plus the thick head it gives one the morning after: thus ingeniously one avoids a worse fate—headlessness, or facelessness. One's mouth may be like the floor of a parrot-cage, the top of one's skull may be coming off, but at least one's head *exists;* and, so far from being empty, it's bursting! Supposing, then, Black tries, by *direct* persuasion or treatment, to get White to give up smoking. The expected resistances, the distress, the tendency to relapse, naturally follow. When the cigarette goes, the 'cigarette holder' is in danger, and sucking sweets does little to fill the gap. And even if White does manage to give up the habit, he's in the market for another, possibly worse, face-making game.

Instead, Black may try the *indirect* method, and somehow draw White's attention to his blind fear of his facelessness, which lies at the root of the trouble. This may lead to panic. But honest Self-seeing is his only radical cure. Once White starts dropping out of the Face Game, he is likely to stop playing Chain Smoker quite naturally, without despair or distress, because the hidden reason for it has vanished. Our observations, so far, are that smokers who see their facelessness immediately feel less urge to smoke; and if they don't cut out tobacco altogether, at least they cut down their consumption drastically.

(iii) Breakdown

(a) In our experience, when White is becoming (however dimly) aware of the game, and of Black's reasons for ceasing to play it with him, his attitude to Black changes dramatically. It is liable to degenerate into a curious mixture of sulks, apprehension, and fascination. He tries to avoid Black, but makes sure that his efforts are unsuccessful. Their friendship seems at an end. (In fact, if all goes well, it is now really beginning.) A correspondent reports: "I reread your (Face Game) article many times.... and it had a curious effect on me, in this way. I was very nervous for a time, and couldn't read the material without getting upset, edgy and irritable. I believe that it was your emphasis on the truth and of course this would mean me giving up something comfortable. This disturbing feeling is present now as I write."

(b) Normally, the Zen monk goes for his daily interview with the Roshi quite willingly, but when he gets to the verge of Satori he may have to be carried, struggling, into the Roshi's presence, which he would give anything to avoid. In general, the disciple who is about to see his Original Face (i.e., his facelessness) meets with unexpected and formidable resistances. His bafflement, as he confronts this barrier, is matched by his joy and relief as he breaks through to Satori. The denser the barrier, the clearer the Original Face is likely to be, when at last it shines forth.

8 THE ORIGINAL FACE

'Seeing one's Original Face' is one of Zen's synonyms for Enlightenment. It refers to the famous occasion when the monk Ming begged Hui-neng (637-712), the real founder of Chinese Zen, to initiate him into the central Truth. The advice Ming got was to calm himself, to stop all his craving and cogitation, and *see:* "See what at this very moment your own face looks like—the Face you had before you were born." It is recorded that Ming, perceiving at last What he really was, wept and sweated. Saluting the master, he asked what secrets remained. None whatever, was the answer. Now he was at their Source, and had them all.

One's Original Face is absolutely featureless. The *Heart Sutra,* which reduces Mahayana Buddhism to its briefest essence and is daily recited in Zen monasteries, having begun by stating that one's form, *here,* is void, and that one's body is just emptiness, goes on to declare that there is no eye, no ear, no nose.... Understandably, this bald announcement perplexed the young Tung-shan (807-869); and his teacher, not a Zenist, also failed to make sense of it. The pupil surveyed the teacher carefully, then explored his own features with his fingers. "You have a pair of eyes," he protested, "and a pair of ears, and the rest, and so have I. Why does the Buddha tell us there are no such things?" All the teacher could do was to refer him to a Zen master. This advice Tung-shan followed, and in the end became a master himself—the founder, in fact, of Soto Zen. The occasion of his Enlightenment was when he happened to see his reflection in a stream. In our terms, he located his human face down there below the surface of the water, and his non-human, featureless, Original Face above it. He looked at himself as if for the first time, and took seriously what he saw—at its true face value—instead of playing games with it.

Daito Kokushi (1281-1377), Japanese National Teacher and Rinzai master, says: "The 1700 koans, or themes to which Zen students devote themselves, are only for making them see their Original Face. The World-honoured One sat in meditation in the snowy mountains for six years, and saw the morning star and was Enlightened, and this was seeing his Original Face. When it is said of others of the ancients that they had a great realization, or a great breaking through, it meant they saw the Original Face.... When thought is put down, the Original Face appears."

Other schools of Buddhism, as well as Taoism, Hinduism (Advaita), Islam (Sufism), and even Judaism and Christianity, have their versions of the Original Face. One of the teachings that, occurring in them all, can claim to be universal and perennial, amounts to this: *my cure is ceasing to overlook this Spot I now occupy.* I have to *see*, not just acknowledge, this Void that lies here at the Centre of my world—and is filled with that world. It isn't that I must *become* as faceless, as incorporeal, as much at large, as I was in the cradle: I have to see that I have always been like that, and always will be, whether I trouble to notice it or not.

And, after all, only this makes sense. The game-free baby is so obviously in the right. If ever I doubt my facelessness here, I have only to invite you to come right up to me here and check it. Well before you arrive at this Spot, you have lost my face: its place has been taken by other things, and in the end by no thing. To find it again you have to retire to that region, a few feet from here, where I keep it—in you, in your camera, and in every polished surface.

9 WHO SEES HIS ORIGINAL FACE?

It is practically certain that, throughout history, only a very small proportion of the human race have seen their Original Face—after childhood. Yet, according to one Zen tradition, nine out of ten are capable of doing so. Evolution will probably go on, and the exception today is liable to become the rule tomorrow. All sorts of factors are combining to strip the great spiritual traditions of their accumulated overburden—dogma and ritual and custom and organization in all their sacred variety—and expose the simple, unhallowed common ground they rest on. Now that the religious safeguards against seeing one's Original Face are wearing thin (religion itself playing a diminishing role in the Face Game) it is no longer so easy to pretend that seeing is intrinsically hard and reserved for some spiritual *élite*. In short, the conditions are ripe for Liberation or Enlightenment, on a much larger scale than ever before.

Our own very limited observations tend to confirm this view. They comprise about fifty cases of clear seeing spread over the last four years, plus one case twenty-six years ago. Ages have ranged between sixteen and sixty, about half have been women, intelligence and education have been above average, religious and social backgrounds have varied very widely. Most seem to have had fairly stable and mature personalities, not caught up in serious games. (In fact, ability to see—ability to stop playing the Face Game—increases with ability to stop playing other games.) Perhaps the majority have been interested, to some degree, in Self-knowledge, but less than half had practised much meditation before seeing. The truth is that none of these people appears to have enjoyed any special quality or advantage—except exposure to infection. Given the right set-up, facelessness is catching. We have observed that anyone who sees clearly and steadily helps people around him to see, quite apart from any conscious intention to influence them. Thus the whole tendency is centripetal and exceedingly 'democratic'—a chain-reaction is indeed possible—and mercifully relieved of any central guru or teacher.

Significantly, young people can usually see very easily, provided they are interested enough to look. New to the Face Game, they can still take brief rests from play. Seasoned players find this very hard. On the other hand, when at last they do see, they are apt to value their seeing: they are more aware how much they need it.

Though there are well-known accounts of people seeing their Original Face without any preliminary training, either spontaneously or as soon as it was pointed out to them, this is comparatively uncommon. (But not at all puzzling to the Hindu or Buddhist who believes in karma and rebirth; these doctrines imply that some people must be on the brink of Enlightenment, thanks to the practice they have put in during past lives. Thus no-one can be sure he is not perfectly ripe for Enlightenment.) In any case, something like training is indispensable—sooner or later, before or after. On the whole, one gets what one pays for in this life, though there are alternative modes of payment. It's like buying a television set: one may take delivery now and pay over the next two years; or one may save for one year, put down half the price on delivery, and pay off the balance over the next year; or one may save for two years and purchase outright at the end. In the last instance, though viewing is postponed, the set is one's own for keeps; in the others, one's viewing will cease and the firm will distrain if one fails to keep up one's instalments. It is all-too-possible, if one's seeing has arrived very naturally and unexplosively and without effort, to undervalue and neglect it, with the result that it fades away—though in fact it remains perfectly accessible. It may be said that the more earnestly seeing is desired and prepared for, the more stable and profound and life-changing it turns out to be, and the more energetically it is pursued to full maturity. There are, however, so many seeming exceptions to this rule that one can never be sure, and each case of seeing should be taken for what it is—quite unique.

10 WHAT ARE THE RESULTS?

Attaining Satori, or seeing one's Original Face, is nothing like so final, nor so difficult, nor so exciting, as people imagine. Suzuki, exhausting his vocabulary of deflation, describes it as matter-of-fact, prosaic, non-glorious, grey, extremely unobtrusive, unattractive. It is noticing what is clearly the case, not having wonderful feelings about it. Nor are its results necessarily much more startling. The literature on the fruits of Enlightenment confirms our own findings, which nevertheless show some interesting peculiarities. Here we shall merely summarize what we have observed in the cases we have studied at first hand, where the Original Face has been clearly and indubitably seen.

The seeing itself is a very precise, unmistakable, all-or-nothing experience, renewable at will. One cannot half see one's facelessness, nor can one see half of it. Either one does or one doesn't see one's Original Face, and to doubt the validity of one's seeing is (while it lasts) quite impossible. Also, one's seeing friends aren't easily deceived: they can tell the imagined from the real thing.

The fruits of seeing, on the other hand, though sometimes spectacular and always beneficent, are comparatively ill-defined and variable. Each case has special features, hardly one exhibits all the signs we list, and old habits die hard. We may conveniently sort our findings under the headings Child/Adult/Parent, which are the individual's 'ego-states' as defined in Transactional Analysis.

(i) Child

This clear seeing is the reactivation of one's implicit Enlightenment as a young child. It is one's built-in Child finding himself again, and the result is childlikeness. Awkward, self-conscious behaviour is replaced by carefree naturalness, ease, spontaneity, relaxation, playfulness. Movements become more graceful, the voice less harsh. In time, the complexion clears, lines smooth out, the expression becomes open and innocent. An uncanny knack of doing and saying the right thing, on mere impulse or whim, may develop. The entire personality is rejuvenated, and social relationships improved all round.

So far, perhaps, all this might have been expected. What did surprise was the sudden sharpening of the senses. (R.G., walking out into the garden, after seeing for the first time, insists that these roses must be a new variety: he has never seen such red ones before. It is only when we draw his attention to other flowers, and he notices that they are equally luminous, that he will admit his mistake.) Similarly, food is more tasty, shapes stand out more sharply, textures have more feel, music is more alive and rousing. One feels one is reborn into a new and more brilliant world, and enjoying everything for the first time. Actually, such results might have been foreseen. They are inevitable directly the absent-minded Jerk in us collapses and we attend to what is actually present, to the here-now in which our senses operate, clear of conceptual fog. When this thought-up face here is wiped off, it's as if a filthy window were cleaned after many years, revealing a forgotten landscape.

The profoundest, most satisfying result is Intimacy. All other kinds of so-called intimacy are by comparison fugitive and incomplete. Inevitably! So long as I'm in, you're out: there's no room here for two of us. So long as this Spot—my here-now—accommodates my face, it cannot accommodate yours: I stand in your way here, refusing Intimacy. But when it sees itself as mere room-for-you, you are more than welcome here; whoever and whatever you are, you belong here, here is your home. This is indeed more than Intimacy. It is Union. And this is the natural state of the Child in every one of us.

(ii) Adult

We did not foresee increased efficiency. Ostensibly, turning away from the surrounding world to its Observer here at the centre, would be likely to put one out of touch with 'reality' and unfit one for ordinary living. In fact, the reverse happens. Now, one really looks at people, really listens, is really interested. There is a general increase in objectivity, open-mindedness, good-humoured tolerance, and equanimity. And, so far from one's work slackening off, it gets done more accurately, quickly, and creatively, as if it were doing itself; with the welcome bonus that more leisure is available for the deepening of one's Self-realization. (H.S. reports that her typing is much faster and more accurate. J.L. reports likewise, independently. One of the first results of T.Y. seeing her Original Face is greatly increased confidence and efficiency while driving, to the astonishment of her instructor. V.S. is startled to find how interesting household chores have now become, how boredom is a thing of the past, how calmly she copes with the children.)

More important still, one is happy to remain anonymous, because Anonymity is one's real Nature. Craving recognition is craving recognition of one's *face,* and when that goes recognition-hunger goes too. The paradoxical consequence is that one is now truly recognizable and recognized. No longer caring about—in fact, welcoming—loss of face, one is genuinely respected.

In short, outer 'reality' is most successfully processed by attending primarily to the inner Reality which is doing the processing. Only Enlightenment is quite practical.

(iii) Parent

Seeing What one really is, being at last Oneself, releases unsuspected springs of compassion, tenderness, love. It is truly unselfish, for the Self it uncovers is no personal or private possession, but that boundless Clarity, that Expanse without divisions or edges (there are scores of names for It), which is the Unity and Ground of all.

But—"teach us to care, *and not to care."* The detachment is crucial. One who goes on seeing his Original Face without much effort, habitually, enjoys people just as they are and has no urge to improve them. This is the place, in fact, to make an important correction. So far in Part II, the Face Game has been described (necessarily, as well as for easy exposition) as if it were a game *other* people play. And so it must seem, till one stops playing it oneself—more or less. Then it becomes plain that this is precisely the game that others *cannot* play! It is essentially a first-person game—a game in which (it is true) others are caught up, but which they are never observed to play on their own account. On the contrary, *their* game, if they played any, would be to pretend that they were faceless! Only *this* one, the first person here, is faceless, and only this one can play the game of pretending to be otherwise. They all carry perfectly good heads on their shoulders, and any plot of mine to decapitate them would be both ridiculous and impertinent. The last thing I'm required to do is deface them. I cease playing the Face Game only when I cease suspecting others of playing it!

The traditional way of stating this paradoxical but fundamental truth is to say that the sage does not see himself as enlightening others, but as Enlightened by them. Utterly alone and unlike all creatures, his emptiness needs filling with their forms, his colourlessness needs painting with their pigments. Only so is he one with all the world.

There is a less happy alternative. If one's seeing is immature, one can be tempted to set up as a spiritual teacher and collect a following. Then one will soon find oneself deeply involved in the Guru-Disciple game. This is quite the most satisfying way of avoiding Enlightenment, under cover of working specially hard for it. (Master: "I'll make you free—but not yet, nor from me." Disciple: "My true guru, at last!") This elegant game is a variety of Berne's 'Gee you're wonderful, Professor' and 'Peasant', in which the patient so admires the doctor and so treasures his prescription that he can't bear to trust the pharmacist with it; so the medicine is never made up, let alone taken.

11 CONCLUSION

Resting from the Face Game—seeing one's Original Face—is the rediscovery of the natural Child-in-oneself and his release from the Parent-in-oneself. This rectifies the functioning of one's Adult, so that all three begin to work harmoniously.

Normally, the perfecting of this inner harmony takes much time and dedicated effort. Seeing doesn't mean immediate and total retirement from the Face Game: it needs cultivating till it is quite spontaneous and indeed unbroken. Nor are the other games, which one happens to be playing at the time, likely to be given up directly the Original Face is clearly seen. But their basis is thereby undermined. For the Face Game is the root of one's troubles, the other games only branches and twigs. It is that comprehensive Disease of which one's ever-proliferating games are signs and symptoms. One's sensible course (provided one isn't too disturbed to take it yet) is therefore to hack at the root and leave the branches to wither of themselves. This economizes time and effort; and the root-timber, though massive, may well prove less tough than any of the branches.

And Self-realization is urgent. If I decide to put it off till I am practically game-free, this really means I don't want it. Fortunately, I don't have to remodel my phenomenal self before discovering my noumenal Self. If only I wish, I can see What I am now, very easily and very clearly. This Spot lies wide open to its own inspection.

A complete Autobiography, then, could be summarized as follows:—

(1)	As a baby, I am faceless and at large.........	PRIMAL INNOCENCE			
(2)	As a child, I glimpse my Original Face.....	LITTLE SATORI			
(3a)	Growing up, I play the Face Game...........	DELUSION	}	}	}
(3b)	or else I avoid playing it..........................	SCHIZOPHRENIA			
(4)	Later, I see my Original Face...................	SATORI, KENSHO			
(5)	and go on seeing till it is stabilized...........	FULL ENLIGHTENMENT			

PART III

THE GAMES ONE PLAYS ONESELF

One becomes a man by imitating others. One does not know instinctively that one is a man, but as a result of a deduction: one is like others—ergo one is a man.

The 'in-and-for-itself', the absolute, has not only gone out of life, but has become something ridiculous in the eyes of men.

The majority of men are curtailed 'I's'; what was planned by nature as a possibility capable of being sharpened into an 'I' is soon dulled into a third person.

Kierkegaard

By alienation is meant a mode of experience in which the person experiences himself as an alien. He has become, one might say, estranged from himself. He does not experience himself as the centre of his world, as the creator of his own acts… The alienated person is out of touch with himself as he is out of touch with any other person. He, like the others, is experienced as things are experienced.

Erich Fromm

1 PROLOGUE

This, the main body of the book, comprises a thesaurus of games which stem from the Face Game directly—a selection of its many varieties and subsidiaries. They share certain essential generic features with Berne's games—for instance, basically they are learned early in life; they are surreptitious and dishonest and often absurd; they are not easily countered without distress; and they are destructive of autonomy, awareness, spontaneity and intimacy. Nevertheless they constitute a distinct branch of the family tree, having its own peculiarities. Berne describes *games people play;* here are described the *games one plays oneself* (GOPO). Other people, as we have already noted, play indispensable roles in these games, all of which are many-handed. But these other people are never 'it': the game is always one's own game—in which, however, they are only too pleased to join. No matter how many the would-be-helpful onlookers, GOPO is a kind of solitaire.

Naturally enough, it is one of the ploys of GOPO (when it begins to be conscious) to assume that others are playing it too, each on his own account. Ceasing to play, one sees this gratuitous assumption to be invalid in fact, and not merely unpractical and uncharitable in practice. One isn't called on to diagnose GOPO in others, much less treat them for the condition. They are all right as they are, and neither dishonest nor absurd. They are to be taken seriously, at precisely their own estimation and their own face value, just as they are given. Indeed one has only to *look* to see instantly how much more honest

The Brahmin Drona, seeing the Blessed One sitting at the foot of a tree, asked him, 'Are you a deva?'

The Exalted One answered, 'I am not.'

'Are you a gandharva?'

'I am not.'

'Are you a yaksha?'

'I am not.'

'Are you a man?'

'I am not.'

Pali Canon

For a Self-realised being the body does not exist.

When the kingdom of Pure Consciousness has been attained, form is revealed as the Essence itself. What was sorrow from the worldly point of view is now viraha, separation from THAT; in other words, the agony of existing in a particular form.

Anandamayi Ma

they are than one is oneself, and how what is for oneself a lie is for them the truth. Here, one's own game is others' correct procedure. In GOPO it is always *this* one who is deluded and sick. This one is the only patient, and his disease is peculiar to himself. Also it is always this one who is the physician. No outsider is in a position to cure this most internal of all complaints.

The complaint may be described as 1st-person playing 3rd-person, a semantic muddle acted out in real life, with desperate seriousness. It is the social undermining the personal on which it rests. It is convention mistaken for reality. It is pretending to oneself that this one is like the others—like them not merely from their point of view and for social convenience, but in actual fact, right here and now from one's own point of view and in one's own primitive, unreflecting experience. It is the great life game of heaping secondary mental constructions upon that primary sense data they depend on, until these data are no longer visible, or are hotly denied. GOPO is halted by halting, however briefly and intermittently at first, the thought processes which constitute its moves, and simply looking to see who is playing, with whom.

• • • •

This is strange language to use in the field of religious experience, and indeed the present application of games theory to the doctrine and practice of Enlightenment is a new departure. But it is all there in the scriptures of the great religions, lurking under many disguises and half lost in vast accretions of irrelevant detail. The fact that, fundamentally, we are saying nothing that is untested in living, nothing that is not implied in the Perennial Philosophy, should be evident from the quotations which follow each of GOPO's varieties. These excerpts are not offered as evidence, however. One appeals always and only to 1st-person experience.

In religious terms, GOPO is a muddle concerning God and man, a mix-up that is hallowed, ancient and universal. Traditionally, the West tends to make God into a man, the East to make a man into God. Both are in danger of confusing the human with the divine. So it comes about, in the name of religion, that immense claims are made for man—claims which are surely ill-founded. Take the question of eternal life. Why should man—including day-old infants and the lowest imbeciles—be immortal, while the higher apes and dogs and horses are mortal? Or take the question of free will. Is it anything more than wishful thinking to suppose that man, alone among creatures, can break loose from his inherited constitution and environment, and so become capable of a truly independent, unconditioned deed?

All such claims made on man's behalf boil down to the claim that he's not what he seems—a mere man—but what he doesn't seem—a superman or god. The belief is that somehow he is like God, or contains God, or is a son of God, or is even God Himself travelling incognito. Well, the disguise is certainly thorough. One doesn't have to go to the trouble of comparing his embryo or his skeleton or his brain with those of a frog, to see that these pretensions to divinity will scarcely do. To glance at him is enough. Does a man look like the creator of the universe? Does he behave as Almighty God might be supposed to behave, or feel as He might feel? Is he big enough, powerful enough, permanent enough, knowledgeable enough, wise enough, free enough, calm enough, to pose as even a minor god or godling without raising a laugh?

No. Let's face it—man is man. He's just what he evidently is— small, local, mortal, conditioned, weak, agitated, unstable: in short, precisely the opposite of any God deserving that title. Really it's astonishing that any confusion could have ever arisen between such opposites. What but escapism, make-believe on the grandest scale, could account for so total a blindness to the obvious facts of life?

Because this divine-human muddle has infected so much of one's religious experience and thinking, a clean break must now be made. It is necessary to start again, with a disinfected and open mind, determined not to rely upon any tradition, scripture, teacher, or preconception, but instead to face the facts just as they are given, no matter how strange or shocking they may look.

• • • •

What is true Enlightenment but just this facing the facts, in all honesty and simplicity? It is going by what one clearly sees for oneself, and no longer by what one is told or imagines. It is plucking up courage to fit the world to one's perceptions, instead of one's perceptions to the world. It is taking seriously whatever is clearly presented, without trying to improve upon it or explain it away.

This is quite different from that other, perhaps more familiar definition of Enlightenment or Liberation as the *complete* realization that (in spite of everything) one is nothing less than the Buddha

Nature, or Brahman, or Absolute Mind, or the Whole, or God Himself—the One Reality, Who is alone without a second.

On the face of it, these two definitions of Enlightenment flatly contradict each other. It seems I must choose either the first (which tells me to be honest) or the second (which tells me to be God), and that to combine them is impossible. For if both were valid at once, this could only mean that *when I look honestly at myself I see God—* which is surely absurd.

But is it necessarily absurd? How do I know, till I look to see? How can I be sure what this Spot I stand on is like, while I go on overlooking it? After all, it's just conceivable that my manhood, and not my divinity, is a baseless assumption, an illusion. In that case, I should be able to see clearly Who I am; or at least to see that the one right here is not a man, for God and man are poles apart and He is unlikely to resemble anyone but Himself. Also it is improbable that he peers at Himself through a fog, or detects His own nature with difficulty; and if I am none other than He, then unbiased self-inspection should immediately reveal the fact, with ease and unclouded brilliance. And it should go on to disclose that, here and now, I am *in every respect* the opposite of human.

Well, what does self-inspection reveal? When I reject all hearsay and dare to look for myself at myself, perhaps for the first time, what do I find? God and man are so incompatible, so utterly different, that I cannot be both. Which, then, am I? Who is this 1st person singular here, and in what ways (if any) does he differ from all those 3rd persons plural over there?

When one looks candidly at oneself and others, how do we compare in constitution and in functioning? Do we look alike, act alike, follow the same procedures, play the same games; or are we quite different? Each chapter of the following comparative study explores a particular aspect of this all-important question. And in each the distinction is drawn between

(a) the 3rd-person *procedure* followed by others,

(b) the corresponding 1st-person *game* played by oneself, and

(c) its *antithesis*—the exposure and the breaking up of the game, and what happens when one stops playing.

And we, spectators always, everywhere,
looking at, never out of, anything! ....
Who's turned us round like this?

Rilke

(Lycomedes had a portrait painted of the Apostle John.) And John, who had never at any time seen his own face, said to him: Thou mockest me, child: am I like that?

Acts of John

In this kind of seeing, one only sees that no shape is there .....
If a man wants to make certain of his body he cannot get at it.

The Secret of the Golden Flower

A monk asked Pao-yun of Lu-tzu Shan: "What is meant by 'speaking is no speaking'?"
The master replied: "Where is your mouth?"
"I have no mouth."

Just tell me what your eyes are.

Genro

A monk said he had the precious sword. Yen-t'ou stretched out his neck, saying: "Well then, cut off my head." The monk said: "Your head is off!" at which Yen-t'ou laughed loudly. But the monk did not perceive the meaning of that laughter.

Blue Cliff Records

2 HEAD SCREWED ON

Procedure: Society manifestly consists of human beings each having a head firmly planted on his or her shoulders. These people aren't playing heads—they are headed. Young Stephen, who shouted out to his mum that he was headless (Part II, Chapter 2), soon got over his trouble, and now has no difficulty in conforming to the standard human pattern.

Game: HSO is pretending that *this* body carries *that* kind of terminal. It is the game of keeping up with the Joneses by dishonestly overlooking the fact that they are, precisely, head and shoulders above oneself.

Antithesis: Forgetting everything I know about myself, I examine the occupant of this chair. I look here, at this place, as if for the first time. Quick now, before the screen of memory blots out sight! What does my head look like from here, this very instant? How many eyes, mouths, noses, ears have I, on the present evidence? What's their shape and colour? Where, exactly, are they located? Without thinking now: how big is this head of mine—bigger than a pea, smaller than the sky?

When I turn from what I'm looking at, to what I'm looking out of, I see nothing. Examination of this spot with a fresh and open mind reveals not the slightest trace of eyes, mouth, ears, hair, bone, blood, brain. Try as I may, I can find here no outline, no cloud, no tint, however shadowy. In fact, there never was anything here. I only imagined it.

The precious Vajra sword is right here and its purpose is to cut off the head.

Tai-hui

When thou seest in the pathway a severed head …. of it thou wilt learn our hidden mystery.
I am free from head.
You have never beheld the head of Man: you are a tail.

Rumi

You must choose one of two things—either have your head cut off or go into exile …. He who loves Me, but loves his head better, is no true lover.

Attar

Here comes the candle to light you to bed;
Here comes the chopper to chop off your head.

Old Rhyme

It won't do to say that my head is really here, though hidden from me. Only I myself am perfectly placed to observe what's here, and if it's hidden from me it's truly absent. The situation is not that I can't see what's here, but that *only* I can, and that I see Nothing. As if anyone *there* could talk me out of what I find *here*, or is in any position to try!

Nor will it do to say I can *feel* my head with my fingertips. I can't. I see that what I'm fingering is a phantom so empty and transparent and colourless that it could scarcely be less like a head. A man can have a glass eye, but hardly a glass head! The other senses don't help either: in fact, they disclose everything but the missing head. Just as I see outer objects and not eyes, so I hear sounds, not ears; taste food, not a tongue; smell odours, not a nose. If I go by my senses here and now, I have only one 'sense organ'—this remarkable Void, this 'hole where a head should have been'.

Who is it that needs no head, in order to live and see the world?

When the Zen master Shih-kung asked a monk how he would take hold of empty space, the monk clutched at the air in front of him. The master seized the monk's nose, exclaiming: "*That's* the way to get hold of empty space!"

I put his head under my foot and squeezed it hard, until all the contents came out. I looked at the fineness of his skin and said: "This deserves to be filled with gold and precious stones, pearls and rubies, and things even more precious than that."

Rumi

This travelling hat may look small, but when I put it on it covers the whole cosmos.

Huang-po

Men that look on my outside, perusing only my condition and fortunes, do err in my altitude; for I am above Atlas his shoulders.

Sir Thomas Browne

The world was more in me that I in it.

Traherne

O, the world's soul will never be united
with mine, till what appears outside me,
as though it always meant to be inside me,
delightedly alights in me.

Rilke (trans. Leishman)

3 SHRUNK

Procedure: Nineteen-months-old Carlos, at large, unbounded, not a boy, (Part II, chapter 2) soon changes his mind. One day he announces to his granny: "I *am* a boy!" And indeed she has only to glance at him to see how right he is. What she *sees* isn't somebody playing 'Shrunk', but someone who really is small, like all other humans. When they get too big for their shoes, grannies and others may be relied on to cut people down to size. For she not only sees Carlos as one of countless similar creatures and a microscopic piece of the universe; she *feels* that way about him, too. Truly Carlos is not all-important, and his proper upbringing must largely consist in persuading him of this obvious fact.

Game: The game of 'Shrunk' is the pretence that I see *myself* (the one right here, whoever he may be) as small, man-shaped and man-sized, like Carlos, like them, like anything at all.

Antithesis: The game is terminated by looking to see what's here, at this moment. What I find (in place of a head) is neither a point, nor a head-shaped and head-sized cavity, nor a huge empty hole without edges, but the view, the ever-changing world as it now presents itself. If I am anything at all, I am everything that comes and goes on this screen-without-a-frame—chairs and tables, men and women, trees, houses, clouds, sun and moon, the sky of stars.… The most impressive object, the most important of men, is seen to be never more than a temporary piece of the one here.

Do not your inclinations tell you that the World is yours?

Traherne

Spirit is a unity of the manifold in which the externality of the manifold has utterly ceased.

F.H. Bradley

The All-merciful One has a thousand arms and a thousand eyes. Which is the main eye?
Say it! Say it!

Lin-chi

If He sever one head from the body, He at once raises up thousands of heads for the beheaded one.

Rumi

You talk about those who renounce the world, but in actual fact it is you yourself who have renounced everything. What is this 'everything'? God! Leaving Him aside, everyone is literally practising supreme renunciation!

Anandamayi Ma

And this agrees perfectly with what one feels: this one is unique, supremely important, without any rival whatsoever. It would be mock-modesty to pretend that one has ever seriously equated oneself with people out there. Decades of indoctrination, all the while from the nursery down to the present moment, haven't begun to persuade this one to settle down as a mere part of the Whole. In one's heart one has always known that one is infinite, all-inclusive, overcomer of the world. Who is here? There's only one answer that rings true and satisfies and is quite final: the one here is the Immense, the All.

They were right, of course, about that little man who is always staring out of my mirror. Now he is seen where he has always been—over there and never, for one moment, here—so that one can afford not to elevate him above any other mortal. Now that they are sorted out, one no longer thinks far, far too much of him, and far, far too little of oneself.

Liberation is knowing you were not born.

Ramana Maharshi

The monk Yung-shih committed one of the gravest crimes, but when he had an enlightened insight into No-birth he instantly attained Buddhahood.

Yung-chia Hsuan-chueh

Jesus said: Blessed is he who was before he came into being.

Gospel of Thomas

Thou canst not by going reach that place wherein there are no birth, no ageing, no decaying, no falling away, no rising up elsewhere in re-birth. Thou canst not by going come to such a place.

Gautama Buddha

Put away body and skin alike, and cleansing your heart and purging it of passion, betake yourself to the land where mortality is not.

Chuang-tzu

Clear away (what is foreign), then look. Or rather, let a man first purify himself, then observe; he will not doubt his immortality when he sees himself thus entered into the pure, the Intellectual.

Plotinus

4 BORN TO DIE

Procedure: I have never set eyes on anybody who was built for immortality, and was not manifestly too complicated and vulnerable to last for very long. Nor have I met anybody who would not admit to having been born. Sensible people bring not only human mortality into their calculations, but also put limits to the lifespan of nations, races, species, planets, suns, universes.

Game: Playing BTD is pretending that the foregoing applies to *oneself.*

Antithesis: Was I ever born? I've no experience of starting to experience, or of my Being beginning to be. How can I even speak of a time from which I'm absent, without thereby ceasing to be altogether absent from it? Again, who could produce me? Parents resemble their offspring, and what human or animal parent has ever resembled this headless Oddity? What doctor would write out a live-birth certificate for that unheard-of abortion—a headless baby? From what still vaster Mother could be born this already boundless space which is itself the matrix of all creatures?

Shall I ever die? How could I experience the end of all experience, or be conscious of final unconsciousness? Besides, it's the born who die, and I own to no birthday. What is the death rate in my Species, and what precedent is there for my dying? What doctor would write out a death certificate for a patient who has always been decapitated? Of course, the hands that are typing these words, like that head in the mirror, are already disintegrating; but there's nothing *here* to suffer

All that has form, sound, colour, may be classed under the head *thing*.... But man can attain to formlessness and vanquish death. And with that which is in possession of the eternal, how can mere things compare?

Chuang-tzu

The great Sage leaves life and death to the mind; he leaves them to the body.

Dogen

Seeing in myself an immaterial vision produced by the mercy of God, I went forth from myself into an immortal body and am now not what I was before, but having been borne in the Mind, I have no concern for my first composite (human) form. I no longer have colour, or sense of touch, or size; I am a stranger to all these things. Now you see me, my child, with your eyes, but cannot understand what I am by staring at me.

Hermetica

Knowing that this body is like froth, knowing that it is of the nature of a mirage: breaking the flowery shafts of Mara, he (the disciple) will go where the King of Death will not see him.

Dhammapada

Those who are headless because of spiritual poverty are in a hundred respects more naughted than those that are dead.

Rumi

the least change. This no-head will never go grey or wrinkled, or grow a second older. No disaster can touch this Container of all disasters.

To be honest, I've never *really* believed that I was born and shall die, though I'm ready to admit that everything else perishes. I see mortality all around, but I see it from the station of immortality. Here is the universal Registrar of Births and Deaths (from the Galaxy's downwards), the changeless background against which all change becomes evident. But if I'm above all decay and alteration, that's because I'm also below them. Indeed it's not that I'm too exalted to die, but rather that I die every moment the deepest of all deaths, right down into the abyss of nonentity, so that even the most moribund of creatures is, beside me (or better, in me) abundantly alive. These aren't words of comfort, or interesting speculation. Nothing could be more vivid, immediate, practical and handy than this brilliant Void which I am, and in which there is no room for death.

The shining of the mere object, as though with a voidness of one's own nature, is samadhi.

Patanjali

Loosing and dropping off body and mind, your Original Face is clear before you.

Zazen-gi

Not one of the seventeen hundred koans has any other purpose than to make us see our Original Face.

Daito Kokushi

He that beholds his own Face—his light is greater than the light of the creatures.
Though he die, his sight is everlasting, because his sight is the sight of the Creator.

Rumi

Jesus said: Know what is before your face, and what is hidden from you will be revealed to you.... You have abandoned the one who lives before your eyes.

Gospel of Thomas

But we all, with unveiled (open) face, reflecting as in a mirror the glory of the Lord, are transformed.

St. Paul

5 FACE TO FACE

Procedure: Observe any two people in communication, confronting each other. Clearly they are face to face, virtual equals. Society could hardly proceed on any other, less democratic basis.

Game: The game of Face to Face consists in the pretence that this equality is the basis of one's own dealings with people, and that the 1st-person/3rd-person set-up at all resembles the 3rd-person/3rd-person one.

Antithesis: I notice that in *that* chair, two yards away, sits a human being, while in this chair sits (at most) half a human being, and the bottom half at that. Crowning *that* trunk is a face—a grey-pink bladder curiously ridged and furrowed, holed in several places, and set in a mat of brown hairs. Crowning *this* trunk is no pinkness, no holes, no hairs, nothing at all.

I go on studying that pinkish balloon six feet off. How small and dull it is, how closed in upon itself, how stand-offish and parted from other things, how tight and opaque, how tiresome a gadget to be tied to for life; and how it contrasts with this unbounded, airy, self-luminous transparency here! How clear is my complexion, how frank and open my expression, how wide-eyed and penetrating my gaze! It's as if this Face were one broad smile with no cheeks to frame it, or a single eye so deep and limpid that it's unfathomable, or a yawn so wide that it has yawned the top half of its body away. Here, indeed, is a truly serene Face, incomparably fresh and bright and ageless, with nothing human about it. And around its rocklike

In all faces is seen the Face of faces, veiled and in a riddle.

Nicholas of Cusa

Wheresoever ye turn, there is the Face of God.
Everything perishes but His Face.

Koran

You must become the enemy of yourself, so that the Friend may show His Face.

Rumi

His form has passed away, he has become a mirror: naught is there but the image of another's face.

Rumi

I and all the Buddhas of the past, present and future breathe through one nostril.

Zen Saying

Paul rose from the ground *wide-eyed*, beholding nothing....
He saw nothing, to wit, God.

Eckhart

placidity surges the sea of little human faces—all different, more or less agitated and scored with suffering, dying. Nevertheless this Face is anything but aloof: it's so friendly, so unveiled, that it includes all the faces that confront it. In fact, it sees itself in and through them at one glance, and never alongside them. Each human face is only itself and excludes all the others: this Face *is* all the others. Man's face may *detect* the world; mine *is* the world.

When I stare at the blue sky my Face is blued; at night it blackens; in a flower garden it's made up with the brightest paints and powders, upon no base whatever; confronting my friend in the chair opposite, it's fully humanized. As I contemplate that face I notice that on *my* side of its coloured surface is nothing whatever—no seer, no visual apparatus, no viewpoint even. Only he is taking place here.

"We call this thing a mirror. A man can love himself, and be together with himself. That is what it means to be a man or a woman—to walk alongside oneself as if one were a second person and to delight in one's beauty. Mirrors were made to teach this art."
"Is it a good?" said the Lady.
"No," said. Ransom....
"I am walking alongside myself already," said the Lady.

C.S. Lewis, Perelandra

What a pity, when a man looks at himself in a glass, he doesn't bark at himself like a dog does, or fluff up in indignant fury like a cat!

D.H. Lawrence

After all, how long does a reflexion remain in view? Make a practice of contemplating the origin of the reflexion .... This cheek and mole go back to the Source thereof.

Rumi

Everyone likes a mirror ... while not knowing the true nature of his face. He supposes the veil to be a face, and the mirror of the veil to be the mirror of his face.

Rumi

If my face were eternal and were held before a mirror it would be received in the mirror as a temporal thing albeit eternal in itself.

Eckhart

6 THE BATHROOM MIRROR GAME

Procedure: My guest says he sees *himself* in my bathroom mirror. He feels, apparently, that it isn't *somebody else* who's shaving in that other bathroom behind the glass (where the clock's hands move anticlockwise and its numerals are reversed) but the same man as the one who's shaving in this bathroom in front of the glass (where the clock behaves normally). And he is not far wrong: I can indeed see two closely similar men, one on that side of the glass and one on this side, staring fixedly at each other while they shave. My guest is doubled, in two places at once, and finds nothing strange or frightening in this. On the contrary, he would be lost without this very odd device which enables him to be plural and beside himself— and quite happy not to know exactly where he is. Human society is based on the mirror. Men come in duplicate, turned face to face.

Game: When I pretend to myself that I, too, am duplicated, one of me in this bathroom and the other in that, I am playing BMG.

Antithesis: It is true that I, like my guest, am confronted by a man whenever I stand squarely before the mirror, and it's always the same man—changing and growing older, but still recognizably him. And I, also, find that familiar face fascinating—but for the opposite reason: not because it's so like but because it's so unlike mine. Obviously he needs to trim that shaggy beard, while I wait idly here observing how clean my Face is—clean not only of beard, but of chin and cheeks and every other feature. This bathroom has no human occupant, now my guest has gone.

Oh you Zen scholar! In the third month at the Dragon Gate your head was reversed.

Blue Cliff Records

This is not a task for him who has not a clean face.

Attar

The water penetrated my head and body, flowing down into all the five viscera and cleansing them as one washes filth from meat and guts before cooking. My body was so thoroughly cleansed that all viscera had vanished .... My body became radiantly transparent, lucent as crystal.

Han-shan

Water unstaling—that is what is required. Water unstaling is that which cleanses all the impurities of the world, and they leave no trace in it. It remains limpid and clear as it was, not dwindling away in the stomach and not becoming adulterated and fetid. That is the Water of Life.

Rumi

Assume the nature of that pure water entirely from head to foot.

Rumi

As I watch that white-haired, staring man, unblinking and left-handed, busy trimming his beard in that bathroom, it's as if a great flood sweeps through this bathroom, carrying away everything human, everything alive, everything existent. In this wonderful Bathroom I bathe indeed: here I'm washed clean of body, mind, life, motion, and all change, clean of all that involved mass of human and animal and material contamination which confronts me there in the next room. Still more wonderful is how this Cleanliness here is alive to itself as spotless through and through, and without having to go an inch outside itself to view itself. I am only here, seeing clearly what I am. My mirror never lies, but brings out with the utmost vividness the total distinction between that man and myself.

That head of clay is from earth, and this pure head from Heaven.

Rumi

'Behold', they said, 'we are men, they are men; both we and they are in bondage to sleep and food.'
In their blindness they did not perceive that there is an infinite difference between them.

Rumi

Where others dwell, I do not dwell. Where others go, I do not go. This doesn't mean that I refuse to associate with other people, but that black and white must be distinguished.

Pai-yun

As the heavens are higher than the earth, so are My ways higher than your ways, and My thoughts than your thoughts.

Isaiah

Everyone must have two pockets, so that he can reach into the one or the other, according to his needs. In his right pocket are to be the words: 'For my sake was the world created', and in his left: 'I am earth and ashes'.

Rabbi Bunum of Pzhysha

The outward and the inward man are as different as earth and heaven.

Eckhart

7 AFTER ALL, I'M ONLY HUMAN

Procedure: My friend agrees (indeed he insists) that he's a man very much like other men, and rather like other animals—something headed, mortal, finite. And, after all, he should know. Besides, when he announces he has a head, I notice that it's the head itself that says so, thus removing any remaining doubts. There's nothing about him which suggests he should not be classed as a member of the species Homo sapiens, genus Homo, and so on (through family, order, class, phylum) to the Animal Kingdom itself.

Game: I am playing AAIOH when, dishonestly and in the teeth of all the evidence, I class myself along with him in any of these categories.

Antithesis: I have only to glance at myself here to see that I am in a class by myself. I observe that, just as his head unhesitatingly announces itself, so my no-head, this present Void, unhesitatingly announces its voidness, its freedom from head, leaving no possible doubt in the matter. What further proofs do I need of our total incompatibility? Truly we aren't merely alien species: we belong to quite different kingdoms—he to the kingdom of this world, myself to another kingdom.

It might be objected that, in fact, there aren't two *species,* but one species having two *aspects*—call them body and mind, matter and spirit, finite and infinite, human and divine. Every man (the objection continues) is thus two-sided, but here am I taking to myself all the better side and naturally appearing superhuman or even divine, while

Two birds, close friends, sit in the same tree. One of them pecks at the sweet fruit, the other looks on.

Svetasvatara Upanishad

He said to them: You too seek for yourselves a place within for rest, so that you will not become a corpse and be eaten.
Jesus said: Two will be resting in one bed, the one will die, the other will live.

Gospel of Thomas

While keeping my physical frame, I lost sight of my real self.
Gazing at muddy water, I lost sight of the clear abyss.

Chuang-tzu

Those who know Him who makes existence and non-existence, the Happy One, have left the body.

Svetasvatara Upanishad

In God can be nothing but God, not mouth nor nose nor hand nor foot.

Eckhart

all the rest are left with the worse side and naturally appear all-too-human, or even subhuman.

This objection will not do. However plausible, it is a trick, a play in the AAIOH game. I cannot find this alleged hybrid, this one being in one place who exhibits these two vastly different aspects, this two-sided monster. There is my friend, six feet away, and all the views I can get of him build up into a single, unbroken series, a poly-photo of *one* subject. Or there is that other friend of mine, who lives behind the glass in that second bathroom: I have yet to discover any way of bringing the two bathrooms together and closing the gap between us. We are two, forever parted and forever contrasting—he whose every aspect is human or less, and myself who can find no aspects of myself at all, but only that Void which is the same however it is viewed.

We feel that when *all possible* scientific questions have been answered, the problems of life remain completely untouched. Of course there are then no questions left, and this itself is the answer.

The solution of the problem of life is seen in the vanishing of the problem. (Is not this the reason why those who have found after a long period of doubt that the sense of life became clear to them have then been unable to say what constituted that sense?)

There are, indeed, things which cannot be put into words. They *make themselves manifest*. They are what is mystical.

Wittgenstein

Attain the Source, and the rest need not bother you; some day you will come to a realization and know what I mean. But so long as you are kept away from the Source, nothing else will be of value to you; with all your learning and knowledge you are not there yet.

Yang-shan Hui-chi

Use the light that is within you to revert to your natural clearness of sight.

Lao-tzu

Once the innermost core of the mind is grasped, all else will become relatively insignificant, and crystal clear.

Chang Chen-chi

I realised the essential nature of my body and mind, that it was like the fluidity of the oceans of fragrance surrounding the Isles of the

8 THE INSOLUBLE PROBLEM GAME

Procedure: To be man is to have problems—not only small and personal ones, but the major, perennial problems of knowledge, time, space, causation, creation, good and evil, freedom and bondage, life and death. Notoriously, he finds them insoluble. Every answer thought up by one man is demolished by another, or else the answer itself raises more questions than it settles. But it is the search for truth that matters, regardless of the fact that the goal's recession is faster than man's approach.

Game: IPG is refusing to see that the answer to all problems lies right here, that this one is, precisely, their solution.

Antithesis: For example, consider the problem of what matter really is, what lies at the heart of it. The physicist, however close he gets to his material, is still taking an outside view of it; he stands at a distance. But I am right on the spot. Taking myself as a true sample —as that one piece of the universe of which, having inside knowledge, I am qualified to speak—I see it is quite empty, voidness itself. Or consider the problem of whether free will exists. I find freedom here, bondage there—it's as simple as that. It isn't a case of one being who is partly conditioned and partly free, but of two beings; the first is the man over there who is altogether conditioned because he's plainly a mere part of the world-system (in which I see no chink where freedom could insert itself), while the second is the one here who is unconditioned, since he is plainly no part of any system, but contains all systems. I can find no third position, intermediate between the bondage there and the freedom here.

Blest. I came to realise that I had all along been throwing the broken shards of my thoughts of personality into the pure limpidity of my Essential Nature.

Surangama Sutra

Like the empty sky it has no boundaries, yet it is right in this place, ever profound and clear.

Yung-chin Hsuan-chueh

Into the soul's essence no speck can ever fall.

Eckhart

This simple unity is ever clear and manifest to the intellectual eyes when turned in upon the purity of the mind. It is a pure and serene air, lucent with divine light .... We are made free and void of every happening and every dream.

Ruysbroeck

There is a Place where all problems have but one universal solution.

Anandamayi Ma

The solution to your problem is to see who has it.

Ramana Maharshi

As will become more evident in the course of this enquiry, it's the same with the other major problems that for millenniums have been bothering philosophers and theologians: they are cleared up once they are seen as 3rd-person puzzles and never 1st-person ones, as belonging over there and never right here. They aren't at all discounted or airily dismissed, but placed; they are seen for what they are where they are, and so give no more trouble. This is what it is to be really clear-headed. The one here *is* the solution of all the problems that proliferate out there, in the country of problems. They are wholly resolved by discriminating between this central region which is visibly clear of problems (and everything else) and the surrounding country where no problem is ever cleared up.

Jesus said: What I am now seem to be, that am I not ..... And so speak I, separating off the manhood.

Acts of John

That one eats, and filth is discharged from him; this one eats and becomes entirely the Light of God.

Rumi

Having realised his real self as space, without attachments and indifferent, he clings to nothing.

Sankara

Lung Shu went to the physician Wen Chih and explained the symptoms of his illness: "I do not think it an honour if the whole district praises me, nor a disgrace if the whole state reviles me; I have no joy when I win, no anxiety when I lose; I look in the same way at riches and poverty, life and death, other men and pigs, I dwell in my own house as though lodging at an inn..... What illness is this?"

Wen Chih stepped back and examined Lung Shu. Finally he said: "Hmm, I see your heart. The place an inch square is empty. You are almost a Sage."

Lieh-tzu

A Brahmin went for help to the Buddha, carrying a gift of flowers in each hand.
"Let go," commanded the Buddha, and the Brahmin dropped the flowers in his right hand.

9 BUILT IN

Procedure: One can see that a man is attached to the world—to his limbs, clothes, house, car, family, city.... he is not found apart from such things and on his own. Wherever one meets him, he is visibly continuous with his surroundings: no magic circle or no-man's-land cordons him off; no aureole keeps the profane world at a distance. All his surfaces are strongly adhesive. He's built in, one piece with the universe. Or rather, the universe flows through him—at different rates—and there's no part of him which isn't part of the flux. And all this he confirms. He admits he's not himself when parted from even a few of these appendages: he suffers when they deteriorate, is glad when they improve, relies on them always. For they body him forth. He must hold on for dear life to this vast apparatus which he needs in order to live and express himself, for without it there would be no life to express.

Game: I am playing 'Built In' when I persuade myself that I—the one here—am like that, made of the same stuff as the world and firmly dovetailed into it.

Antithesis: Just as clearly as I see his attachment, I see my detachment. I'm as loose as a dried pea rattling in a matchbox, adrift from all my surroundings. Not only can I find here no solid, no surface to which things might stick, but I notice that anything rash enough to approach me is destroyed. I don't put my hat on my head, but lose both. My food is abolished rather than digested. I am indeed no ordinary hole, but an edgeless and sideless and bottomless

"Let go," repeated the Buddha, and the Brahmin dropped the flowers in his left hand.

"Let go," said the Buddha again, and the Brahmin stood nonplussed.

"Let go of what is in neither hand, but the middle."

At these words the Brahmin went away satisfied.

You have been in 'desolation', and you have been hoping that you had found the cause in some want of detachment from this or that. Probably you have been mistaken. The cause is more general: you need to learn detachment from yourself.

Dom John Chapman

The soul that is attached to anything, however much good there may be in it, will not arrive at the liberty of divine union. For whether it be a strong wire rope or a slender and delicate thread that holds the bird, it matters not, if it really holds it fast; for, until the cord be broken, the bird cannot fly.

St. John of the Cross

This old monk does not possess even a dot of ground in which to stick an awl ..... He does not have so much as a tongue.

Hui-hai

Even if you pour water on It, It does not get wet. Even if the wind blows on It, the wind does not blow through It.

Blue Cliff Records

mine-shaft into which all comers fall to destruction. The river of the world doesn't flow through me: it loses itself in this immense gulf, and rises from this same gulf a new river.

And I find that when I clearly see myself as thus loosed from the world, I feel that way. It is impossible steadily to observe this central Gap or Hiatus without observing also that this is precisely what one is, No-thing dependent upon nothing, truly free from everything. It isn't a matter of achieving this state, but of accepting it as unalterable fact. One has no choice here. Detachment is the mark of this 1st person, as attachment is the mark of that 3rd person. The world runs like water off this one's back, while he is soaked to the bone.

Alice turned to the Mock Turtle and said, "What else had you to learn?"

"Well, there was Mystery," the Mock Turtle replied.

Alice's Adventures in Wonderland

Mystery, *docta ignorantia,* have a profound significance. The whole meaning, importance and value of life are determined by the mystery behind it.

Berdyaev

Jesus said: He who seeks will not cease until he finds; when he finds, he will be astonished; when he is astonished he will reign; when he reigns, he will rest.

Gospel of the Hebrews

One meditates on the absent; but when He that was sought is Present in Person, then is meditation changed into wonderment.

Al-Alawi

Thinking upon God's kingdom, often I am dumbfounded at its grandeur.

Eckhart

What is the last end? It is the mystery of the darkness of the eternal Godhead which is unknown and never has been known and never shall be known.

Eckhart

10 SO WHAT?

Procedure: A man may sometimes find himself mildly surprising, but certainly not incredible. He's in little danger of crying out with fright, of being suddenly unmanned by the astounding spectacle of man. And what, indeed, *is* particularly astonishing about this brief and tiny fragment of the universe? The conditioned lacks surprise: you can see it coming, you can account for it, you can even show why it has to be what it is. Man is a cog in the cosmic machine, about which more and more is known and less and less remains mysterious; and if that cog were lost it could be reconstructed by examining the adjacent cogs. In short, man is nothing special, and neither wonderful nor wonderstruck. He just gets on with the job.

Game: "All right, *I've* occurred. So what? Why should I feel surprised, or even specially thankful? What's so mysterious about being, and why shouldn't I take being myself for granted?"

Antithesis: To put an end to 'So What?' (and this goes for all games) it is necessary to be honest about the one who is playing it. So long as I keep up the pretence that this one is rather like the others, there is no reason for wonder. But when I clearly see what it's like here, and consciously am this total emptiness (which nevertheless is very much alive to itself) then this self-seeing is mixed with astonishment. 'So What?' becomes 'Dumbfounded!'; and so far from the surprise wearing off, it grows with cultivation. Every day, one takes oneself—the fact of one's actually having happened—less for granted. Not *what* one is, but *that* one is—this is ever more

It is the deepest, widest and most certain of all facts—that the Power which the Universe manifests to us is inscrutable.

Spencer

They who know Him most perfectly perceive most clearly that He is infinitely incomprehensible.

St John of the Cross

It is not *how* things are in the world that is mystical, but *that* it exists.

Wittgenstein

God is a wondrous thing:
He wills that which He is
And is that which He wills,
With no end or cause.

Angelus Silesius (Trans. W.R. Trask)

fascinating; and it is inseparable from that final irregularity, that virtual impossibility—the fact that there is anything whatever. That This should have contrived Its own being, engineered Its own emergence, without reason or cause or any assistance, out of mere inane nothingness, that It should possess the knack of pulling Itself up by Its own astonishing bootstraps out of the ocean of non-being— what success, what audacity, what splendour! After this impossible feat, nothing is impossible, and everything is mystery, unknowable, inexplicable. At root I am—all things are—this self-originating and self-sustaining Wonder, this Miracle which is right here and now. And even the most spectacular and mysterious goings-on out there are only its casual by-products, of no intrinsic importance.

There is no seer but Him, no one to hear but Him, no one thinking no one aware but Him. He is the Self, the Ruler within, the One Immortal.

Brihadaranyaka Upanishad

God is the Hearer, and it is by attributing this faculty unto thyself that thou art deaf. Thou hast become blind through attributing sight unto thyself. When He is thy Hearing and thy Sight, then wilt thou hear only Him and see only Him.

Ibn Ashir

In the place where no man is I will put my hand to my forehead and watch for you ..... I will wait and look out for you where no man speaks, that is, in Maitreya's land, where no mouth and lips are needed.

Pai-chang

I can look and listen without using eyes and ears.

Lieh-tzu

By what means do this body or mind perceive? Can they perceive with the eyes, ears...?
No. Your own nature being essentially pure and utterly still, is capable of this perception.

Hui-hai

'Thou seest them looking', but they are like the pictures in a bath-house: they do not see.

11 THE SEEING EYE GAME

Procedure: A man must have a head for keeping in touch with his environment: without this spherical observatory, about the size of a small sputnik and similarly packed with delicate apparatus, he would be cut off from the universe in nearly all its aspects. Though he is continuous with the universe in all directions, he is still only a very small part of it: the great bulk of it lies outside him. He gets over this problem by means of very effective signalling and other means of communication, with the result that he is always being influenced by distant objects and (to some extent) influencing them in turn. Nevertheless they stay distant, and they stay themselves, and he stays himself. They aren't present to him, aren't presented to him. He doesn't *see* them. I am going by what I find, and I have never seen a man see.

In any case, how could he see, with that ridiculous lump of flesh and bone in the way? How could a few cubic inches of brain tissue find room for, or secrete, or somehow collect and condense, the seen world, and what sign do they give of performing any such miracle? The truth is that, no matter how elaborate their sensory equipment, heads no more *see* the world than sputniks or cameras or electronic eyes do: they are means of communication with it—which is a very different thing indeed.

Game: SEG is the pretence, by this one who actually sees the world, that he is a pair of eyes and a brain lying at the centre of that world and doing the seeing.

The form appears, O worshipper of form, as though its two dead eyes were looking.

Rumi

It is the Unborn which sees and hears, eats and sleeps.

Bankei

Only God has seeing, hearing.

Al-Arabi

It is better for thee to enter into life with one eye, rather than having two eyes to be cast into hell fire.

Jesus

Jesus said to them: When you make the two one ..... then you will go into the Kingdom.

Gospel of Thomas

He became one-eyed.

Attar

The Tathagata became the Eye of the universe.

Parinirvana Sutra

Thou art not that body: thou art this spiritual Eye.

Rumi

Real vision is eyeless.

Anandamayi Ma

Antithesis: A man doesn't see. It's true that I notice his face lighting up in response (say) to a proffered £5 note, but I notice also that the face and the note don't merge, or change places, or abolish each other. How different from me! My face doesn't light up, doesn't respond to the banknote: it *is* the banknote! I see, not because I have eyes, nerves, brain here, but because I haven't: they would merely block the view. Only this perfectly clear head, emptied and exploded to infinity, could be void enough and big enough to contain my world. This is no theory: I see it to be so, here and now. The only one who I've seen see, does so without eyes. If the seen doesn't wipe out the seer, there is no seeing, but only signalling. All over the world this signalling is going on, but only *here* is there seeing.

In Eternity one Thing never Changes into another Thing.

Blake

The tree which moves some to tears of joy is in the Eyes of others only a green thing that stands in the Way.

Blake

The ignorant eschew phenomena but not thought; the wise eschew thought but not phenomena.

Huang-po

I do not think there is anyone who takes quite such a fierce pleasure in things being themselves as I do. The startling wetness of water excites and intoxicates me: the fieriness of fire, the steeliness of steel, the unutterable muddiness of mud.

G.K. Chesterton

We need nothing but open eyes, to be ravished like the Cherubims.

Traherne

Oh we crazy-pates! What joys our eyes give us!

Van Gogh

When Chang-ching, after twenty years of meditation, happened to lift the curtain and see the outside world, he lost all his previous understanding of Zen, and cried: "How mistaken I was! How mistaken I was! Raise the screen and see the world."

12 WHAT'S IT MEAN?

Procedure: The proper work of man is to build himself a universe out of chaos. Accordingly, he classifies and names all things, linking them with one another and himself in countless ways, till each object is a little knot in a vast net of meanings, held firmly in place and lacking all distinction. "Only connect!" Everything has its spiritual or poetic overtones, its worldwide associations, its uses, its heavy burden borne in from the past and carried forward into the future. Nothing's just itself, but is made by and makes what's not itself. It's a finger pointing to the other fingers which are pointing to.....Man's world is always Monday, a serious and busy day, when everybody is taking in everybody else's washing, and everybody is looking rather drab because all his nice things are at the laundry.

Game: When I import the procedure of WIM, from the 3rd-person world where it belongs, into the 1st-person world where it doesn't belong, it becomes the game of WIM. At first it merely dims the player's sight, but in the end it blinds him.

Antithesis: My world is Tuesday, when the washing comes back and everybody is wearing his own best and gayest clothes, all clean and colourful—and perfectly meaningless. Their value is intrinsic; they are themselves, nothing to do with each other, and—above all—nothing to do with me. Now shapes come into their very own shapeliness, colours glow with a splendid inner fire, music is twice as thrillingly sonorous, scents outscent themselves, tastes have a new tang and savour—all because they have broken loose from man's

Blackbird silent in the snow;

Motionless crocus in the mould;

Naked tree; and, cold and low,

Sun's wintry gold ......

Lost for the while in their strange beauty—self how far!—

Lulled were my senses into a timeless dream;

As if the inmost secret of what they are

Lay open in what they seem.

Walter de la Mare

Not to know is profound; to know is shallow. Not to know is internal; to know is external.

Chuang-tzu

world (the world that patiently ties itself up in knots) and dropped their load of meaning and are on holiday. And it's part of the holiday spirit that I see no necessity for them to be, or to be what in fact they so delightfully are, no lurking symbolism, no practical axes for them to grind, no uplifting spiritual lessons for them to teach, no morals for them to point, no principles for them to illustrate, no laws for them to obey. On Tuesday I see only what I see. And the view, unlike Monday's sombre and unsmiling landscape, is enchanting. *Nothing* here is ugly, tiresome, commonplace. Every chance patterning of leaves on a stem, of dead leaves on a path, of clouds, of tree bark and wood grain, of pebbles on the beach, of stains on old walls, of food on one's plate, of litter and junk—every one is a perfect arrangement. Even human artefacts are all beautiful on Tuesday.

'Smelling a bad smell' is not the same as 'being aware of the stinking state of my nervous system'.

F.H. Bradley

Every thing or quality felt is felt in outer space.

William James

Anything, however small, adhering to the soul, prevents your seeing me.

Eckhart

We cannot see the visible except with the invisible.

Eckhart

To prove your mind is the Buddha mind, notice how all I say here goes into you without your missing a single thing, even though I don't try to push it into you.
The Buddha mind is ten thousand times clearer than a mirror, and more inexpressibly marvellous.

Bankei

God is exempt from all things and he is all things.

Eckhart

Perfect freedom is obtained only when our egoistic thoughts are not read into life and the world is accepted as it is, as a mirror reflects a flower as a flower.

D.T. Suzuki

13 VALE OF TEARS

Procedure: The world is not a very satisfactory place for a man to find himself in; at best it is a 50/50 mixture of good and bad. Life is balanced against death, health against sickness, renewal against destruction. And everything suggests that this is the way things will always be, and that no radical improvement is at all likely. Glossing over the often terrible facts, ignoring a single tear or groan, is self-deception of a particularly mean and heartless kind. Man has every reason for complaining about a world he is so ill-fitted for, and which has so little respect for his needs. And to try to console him with the figure of an ingenious Providence wire-pulling behind the scenes, whose master plan for the earthly Millennium is slowly working out, is to insult his intelligence. There is no evidence for anything of the kind.

Game: I am playing VOT when I see *my* world, the universe viewed by this 1st person from right here, as anything like the unsatisfactory place we have just described.

Antithesis: Again, the remedy for this game is to see who is playing it. So long as I am not consciously empty, but retain here some imaginary remnants of personality, of body-mind, that is enough (seemingly) to divide the world into two parts, so ruining both. I have to cease overlooking the fact that this one (the seer) is evacuated with a total voiding, container along with contents, leaving here the perfection of mere capacity, pure receptivity; and leaving there (in the seen) the perfection of fullness, of infinite creativity.

Most of what the average person is conscious of is a fiction, while that which he represses (i.e., which is unconscious) is real.

Erich Fromm

There is nothing retained,
All is void, lucid, and self-illuminating; ....
This is where thinking never attains,
This is where the imagination fails to measure.

Hsin-Hsin Ming

After evacuation joy supervenes, a joy which has no sorrow, a rose without a thorn, a wine without crop-sickness.

Rumi

Nothing imperfect is:
equal are gold and tin,
Frogs are as beautiful
as are the Seraphim.

Angelus Silesius (trans. W.R. Trask)

In other words, the only way to clean up the world is to come clean oneself, and cease spoiling it by holding onto those very things which are needed to complete it. Then one sees it as all right because one *faces* it all and keeps nothing back; one sees it as sane because it is all *there* and none of it is here; one sees it has nothing to learn because this one has nothing to teach; one sees it as the completed object because one has no subjective reservations whatever, no ideals, preconceptions, preferences, or feelings in the matter. Now are restored to the universe its own infinite riches; all things are transfigured, aglow with morning splendour, now they are where they have always been anyway—over there—and none is here.

Men have left their own country, their fathers and mothers, their households and kinsmen and families, and have journeyed from Hind to Sind, making boots of iron till they were cut to shreds, haply to encounter a man having the fragrance of the other world. How many men have died of this sorrow, not succeeding in encountering such a man! As for you, you have encountered such a man here in your own house, and you turn your back on him.

Rumi

There is none dwelling in the house but God.

Rumi

He in whom God dwells has a good lodger.

Eckhart

God must be very I, I very God, so consummately one that this He and this I are one is, in this is-ness working one work eternally; but so long as this He and this I, to wit, God and the soul, are not *one single here, one single now,* the I cannot work with nor be one with that He.

Eckhart

Being admonished to return to myself, I entered into the secret chamber of my soul .... And I beheld with the eye of my soul the Light unchangeable .... He who knows that Light knows eternity.

St Augustine

14 GOD'S IN HIS HEAVEN

Procedure: The plain man's God is transcendent and very much outside and beyond him. And this is perfectly right. For the idea of a God lurking *inside* a man is a comic—if not crazy—notion, posing numerous unanswerable questions. In what guise is He there? What are His distinctive functions? When does He come, when go? Is He in all organs equally, or more in head and heart than in hair or faeces? No: for any candid investigator He isn't inside the human body, and must be found in another and much more suitable place, if at all.

Game: GIHH is the *1st-person* game of locating God over there, and man here, in spite of all the evidence to the contrary.

Antithesis: The only suitable place I can find for Him is right here—the one spot which I observe to be replete with consciousness or spirit yet empty of body or matter, the one spot which is a point yet embraces the whole of space, which is momentary yet envisages all time, which is one yet contains the many, which is nothing yet all things. If this place won't do, what hope is there of finding a more comfortable and proper home for Him?

I take it that this is, indeed, His home. In that case, He isn't in a man, but in lieu of a man—a very different story. This divine cuckoo crowds every fledgling out of the nest: He will have no-one here but Himself. Everyone else is banished to the land of Elsewhere, which as a result is very thickly populated. Its other name is the universe—the circumambient universe there, of which He is the centre, here.

And behold, Thou wert within, and I without!

St Augustine

Look within; within is the fountain of all good. Such a fountain, where springing waters can never fail, so thou dig deeper and deeper.

Marcus Aurelius

To find or know God in reality by any outward proofs, or by anything but by God himself made manifest and self-evident in you, will never be your case either here or hereafter.

William Law

And Jacob awaked out of his sleep, and he said, Surely the Lord is in this place; and I knew it not. And he was afraid, and said, How dreadful is this place! This is none other but the house of God, and this is the gate of heaven.

Genesis

The true Buddha sits in the interior.

Chao-chou T'sung-shen

There is no other Buddha for him who knows himself.

Attributed to Kanakamuni

We seek our (human) selves every time we emerge from Nothingness.

Molinos

So there aren't two modes or aspects of the divine presence. He doesn't have two addresses or run a pair of establishments, one on Earth and inside man and the other in Heaven and outside man. God is God and man is man: they look quite different and they live quite apart, and really there is no excuse for getting them mixed up. The plain man, who locates God beyond the sky in a land of other-worldly splendour and holiness, is so right compared with the thinker who concocts some heavenly-earthly, divine-human mixture that makes the worst of both worlds. Contemporary theologians have every reason for insisting upon the absolute distinction between God, and man, and the dangerous absurdity of confounding them.

Truly there lives here, alone and unapproachable, One from whose presence man is more surely excluded than if he were a million light-years away.

I do not count in my own eyes in so far as I am a universal man; I only count in so far as I am the individual 'I'.

Hubert Benoit

Rarely can I face that amazing ninety-nine hundredths of myself which I share with other men: all I have eyes for is the one hundredth which marks me off from them. The differentiae—these miserable hair-cuttings and nail-parings of a human being—are made to do duty for the whole. But in fact it is the common and not the uncommon in me which is truly marvellous, and my astonishment which is proportional to the scarcity of its object is the vulgarest sensationalism. Just to be a man—never mind what kind of man— that is far to surpass the Seven Wonders of the World.

The Hierarchy of Heaven and Earth

Existence transcends Life, and Life transcends Wisdom.

Dionysius the Areopagite

The more universal a Title is, the more truly it is applicable to God.

C.E. Rolt

God knows nothing but being, he is conscious of nothing but being; being is his ring.

Eckhart

15 THE PERSONALITY GAME

Procedure: A man isn't what makes him a *man*, but what makes him *different* from men. He's what distinguishes him from them—his special name, address, bodily peculiarities, job, personal habits and memories and plans: in short, his personality, his persona or mask. These are the things that count in his own and others' eyes, and to the extent that he loses them he's no longer himself. And conversely, what he holds in common with men, what his public normal mask covers—his being, thinghood, life, normal human attributes—all this is of no account, though it makes up the indispensable 99.9 percent of him. In practice, the remaining .1 percent, which clearly identifies him as that person and no other (thus enabling him to get a birth certificate, school place, job, driving licence, passport, wife, pension, death certificate), is the whole of him; thus he is reduced to a thousandth part of himself and little more than an elaborate label. If this is an exaggeration, try congratulating him on his marvellous achievement of existence out of Nothing, on the miracle of his being alive, on his having grown up so lately (and so fast, in his own short lifetime) from less-than-wormhood to manhood, on the wonder of his being able to see and hear you, and so on. For these incomparable feats he will take no credit: they don't serve to mark him off, therefore he disclaims them. He isn't interested. Nor can he be, and remain quite human. After all, the system works. Society would collapse if the masks were taken off.

The Absolute is none of the things of which It is the source; its nature is that nothing can be affirmed of It—not existence, not essence, not life—It transcends all these. But possess yourself of It by the very elimination of being, and you hold a marvel.

Plotinus

As long as I am this or that, I am not all things.

Eckhart

It is a great joy to realise that the Fundamental Nature is qualityless.

Gampopa

The Tathagata is not to be seen by reason of his possession of marks.

Diamond Sutra

Game: I am playing PG when I persuade myself, that I, too, am what makes me different from others, what serves to mark me off from them.

Antithesis: When I look in the mirror I see that the one on the *far* side of the glass is unique and distinct from everything else; whereas the one on the *near* side of the glass is nothing special and distinct from nothing. In fact, it is because this one has no personal marks—is quite plain and simple, without name, address, birthday, character, history—that it is perfectly receptive to the personal marks of others. The function of this one is just to be, without being anything in particular, to be totally commonplace. The irony is that because this commonplace one is one with all, he is the All and unique; whereas that one who separates himself from everybody is one of millions and lacking all distinction. The only way not to be lost in the crowd is to *be* the crowd.

It might be instructive, and not a little startling, to enquire how much meaning is left in the descriptive terms of psychology when all the physical meaning is taken out of them.

Dr Maudsley

Whenever it is claimed that psychology does provide some definite and agreed knowledge it invariably turns out to be knowledge, not about the mind, but about the body.

Frank Kenyon, *The Myth of the Mind*

The real Man is he that hath the spirit. These others are not men, they are mere forms.

Rumi

Bodies are like pots with lids on: look and see what is in each pot. The pot of this body is filled with the Water of Life; the pot of that body with the poison of death.

Rumi

Ye are dead, and your life is hid with Christ in God.

St Paul

Suppose a boat is crossing a river, and an *empty* boat is about to collide with it. Even an irritable man would not lose his temper.

Chuang-tzu

16 BRAINS

Procedure: Electro-chemical signals are continually streaming in to a man's brain from his sense organs, and out from his brain to his muscles, with the result that he reacts appropriately to changes in his environment. Nowhere in this ingoing-outgoing chain of events can be detected any intervention by a directing consciousness or mind. Nor are there pressing reasons for trying to find either a lodgement or a function for any such entity. Explaining nothing, it would only hamper discovery—by gratuitously introducing a whole new order of problems which cannot even be clearly stated, let alone solved. There really is no need to improve upon the evidence, which is that complex bodies react to one another and to their world in suitably complex ways, all in accordance with (what used to be called) the laws of Nature. It will be time to talk of a man's consciousness when he is observed to have anything of the sort. Meanwhile, that wonderful cybernetic instrument called his brain serves him fairly well.

Game: This honest and effective procedure becomes a dishonest and ineffective game when it shifts from 3rd person to 1st person—from one's experience of others to one's experience of oneself. The game mixes the immiscibles—brain and consciousness. I am playing it when I try to dilute my mind here with brains, and a man's brains there with a mind, instead of taking them straightforwardly as they are given—unadulterated consciousness right here and unadulterated grey matter over there, some distance away.

They ask how a man can remain quiet in Realisation when there is misery also existing. But what is a realised man? Does he see misery outside himself? They want to determine his state without themselves realising it. From his standpoint their contention amounts to this: a man has a dream in which he sees a number of persons; on waking up he asks, "Have the people in the dream also woken up?"

Ramana Maharshi

Although innumerable beings have thus been led to Nirvana, no being at all has been led to Nirvana. And why? If in a Bodhisattva the notion of a 'being' should take place, he could not be called a Bodhi-being. And why? He is not to be called a Bodhi-being, in whom the notion of a self or of a being should take place, or the notion of a living soul or of a person.

Diamond Sutra

The solution of the koan consists in 'seeing' the original face with your spiritual, third eye, finding it rather than inventing it with the aid of reflection. What you then experience with regard to your own ego is *not* transferred by analogy to other egos, still less to things; all these other forms are directly experienced too, each by itself, *from the Origin.*

Eugen Herrigel

Antithesis: In any case, just what is this consciousness I am so over-generous with, so anxious to credit him with regardless of the fact that he has no real room for it? I know well what it is, because it is what I am: and I notice that it isn't a convenient little item that could be tucked away somewhere in a man's head. Nor is it a harmless substance which would do him no injury, but an infinitely corrosive acid, an infinitely explosive bomb that destroys universes. Then again, it isn't even itself (so to say), but everything but itself..... The truth is that I can find it nowhere in the outside world: the world just can't take it. On the contrary, it takes the world, easily and naturally, from right here.

And anyhow I have *never* taken seriously the crazy notion that my world is inside a brain or excreted by a brain, or that its Observer *is* a brain. This colourful view, so big and bright and clear, manifestly is not shut up in any little bone box of a head, or even slightly spattered with grey matter.

You must tear off from around you this tunic which you wear—
this fabric of ignorance, this support of wickedness, this bondage
of corruption, this cloak of darkness, this living death, this sensate
corpse, this tomb you carry around with you.

Hermetica

He played away his head, laughing and rejoicing.

Rumi

Once between my folding hands I held it,
held your face on which the moonlight fell.
Thing, beneath the tears that overwelled it,
of all things least comprehensible.

Rilke (trans. Leishman)

The Self pervades the universe and by its light all this insentient
universe is illumined.

Sankara

All that is not God is death.

George Macdonald

Our attitude to all men would be Christian if we regarded them as
though they were dying, and determined our relation to them in the
light of death.

Berdyaev

17 EMBODIED MINDS

Procedure: In the previous chapter we described the procedure of the neurologist who dispenses with the hypothesis of a consciousness—who can find no ghostly interloper able at some point to divert the flow of physical events in the brain. But there is another procedure, less rigorous but far more common, which is followed by most psychologists as well as the ordinary man—the procedure of regarding man as a body-mind, a spirit living in a house of clay, a physical organism containing and animated by and directed by a psyche. According to this common-sense view, a man's behaviour is accounted for partly in physiological and partly in psychological terms. Some things he does (e.g., as a result of drugs) are more determined by his body, others (e.g., as a result of reasoning) are more determined by his mind: but both are likely to be involved. And obviously this common-sense procedure works out on the whole—in the man-to-man, 3rd-person world.

Game: It becomes dishonest and unpractical when I apply it to myself—to this one vis-a-vis others. I am playing EM when I pretend that I, too, am a body-mind confronting other body-minds in a symmetrical relationship.

Antithesis: My failure to find any body here, and any mind over there, are inseparable sides of one datum: I cannot honestly admit the first yet deny the second, bowing to only half the evidence. It's no good going by what I see here and refusing to go by what I see there—the presence of my friend's head (his mere head, as substantial

Other men are as bodies in relation to the saints and the prophets, who are the heart of this world.

Rumi

Only when you have no things in your mind and *no mind in things,* are you vacant and spiritual, empty and marvellous.

Te-shan Hsuan-chien

In what degree is disengagement from the body possible? Disengagement means simply that the soul withdraws to its own place.

Plotinus

Thoroughly to know the abode of the Self—this is the crucial problem for all Buddhists.

Dogen

If the soul would but stay within, she would have everything.

Eckhart

a lump of matter as any pumpkin) is no less clearly given than the absence of mine, and as easily overlooked.

In fact, it's just as important to exorcise the mind from that head as to exorcise the head from this mind. That little hairy sphere—a yard or so away (whether in my glass or not), punctured in seven places, with its strangely puckered and mobile surface—is so bewitched, so haunted, so privileged, so charged with Mana, that it is virtually invisible. One doesn't look at one's neighbour, but instead picks up a few signals and invents the rest: the presented shapes and colours and movements are no more attended to than the features of a pouncing tiger are coolly studied by its prey. And from this blindness, this substitution of imagination for inspection, proceed all manner of troubles. It's this projected mind, this refusal to take a man as one finds him, which makes understanding impossible and love so difficult. When there remains no spook, peering at me from behind his eyes, the last barrier has fallen. We are one.

Unaffrighted by the silence round them,
Undistracted by the sights they see,
These demand not that the things without them
Yield them love, amusement, sympathy.

And with joy the stars perform their shining,
And the sea its long moon-silver'd roll,
For alone they live, nor pine with noting
All the fever of some differing soul.

Matthew Arnold

What is there about the Inanimate that appeals with such singular reciprocity to the noblest instincts of our race?

John Cowper Powys

The Mayor was one of those rare beings who really *like* the world we have all been born into. More than that; oh, much more than that: The Mayor was obsessed with a trance-like absorption of interest, by the appearance of our world *exactly as it appeared* ... People's thoughts were non-existent to the Mayor of Glastonbury; and if there is a level of possibility more non-existent than non-existence itself, such a level was filled (for him) by people's instincts, feelings, impulses, aspirations, intuitions ... In his dealings with his fellow-citizens upon the town council the Mayor held his own very well. He did this by the enormous advantage he possessed over people who believed in the reality of thoughts and feelings.

John Cowper Powys

18 ANIMISM—ANIMOSITY

Procedure: Men animate one another. The human mind does not occur by itself: it is always plural, in company, a system of relationships with other minds. When this relationship fails, and a man treats others as exploitable and expendable tools, as things for using instead of persons for respecting, this is regression to infantile egocentricity and destructive of the very basis of society; and in the end the exploiter, too, is destroyed.

Game: The good procedure of 3rd-person Animism becomes the bad game of 1st-person Animosity when I operate it—by pretending that *this* one, also, is a life among the living, a mind among minds. For in my case, the more independent life and mind I attribute to others the less satisfactory my dealings with them become. The immense appeal of sky and stars, of clouds and mountains, of the desert and the open sea, rests in their lifelessness: they are sublime, tranquillizing, curative, to the degree that they are felt to be inanimate. Forests and fields are somewhat less pacifying. As for humans, how disturbing they are! Where convention and routine rather than thought govern social relationships, one gets along, perhaps. But it's an unhappy fact that relationships are frequently at their worst where, ostensibly, they should be at their best—at those exalted intellectual and spiritual levels where few practical tasks or conventions or privacy or reserves remain, and I play the game of mind nakedly confronting mind. Religion is peaceful only when I'm either half-hearted or undisputed boss. The intenser it becomes, and the freer from traditional restraints,

To identify consciousness with that which merely reflects consciousness—this is egoism.

Patanjali

I looked and saw that all created things were dead. I pronounced four akbirs over them and returned from the funeral of them all, and without intrusion of creatures, through God's help alone, I attained unto God.

Bayazid of Bistun

Kill all other than God.

Rumi

I have tried the world and known it, that there is not a tittle of life in it.

Psalms of Thomas

Jesus said, Follow me, and leave the dead to bury their dead.

Matthew

the more animosity it generates: trivial differences are blown up into heresies, and the more a mind resembles mine the more violently I am apt to clash with it. The 'higher' the religion the more explosive, till I suspect every member of some deviation.

Antithesis: No wonder I'm in trouble here! The truth is that, in this 1st-person world, there is room for any number of bodies but only one mind. Minds in the plural are a fiction, an absurdity which becomes more and more unworkable as I attribute to them more and more reality and separateness; till in the end the contradictions build up to a sudden climax, and the One Mind reveals itself. So I kill, rather than bring to life, my surroundings. Even these wonderfully complex humans are no more spirits or selves or minds in the plural than waves and clouds and stars are. Only so can they all be enlivened, supercharged with spirit, saturated with the *One* Mind right here.

When one has found one's Self, who else is one but the Tenth Man?

Ramana Maharshi

God is not seen except by blindness, nor known except by ignorance, nor understood except by fools.

Eckhart

The natural man receiveth not the things of the Spirit of God: for they are foolishness unto him: neither can he know them, because they are spiritually discerned.

St Paul

To one who knows naught it is clearly revealed.

Eckhart

Verily, verily I say unto you, Except ye be converted, and become as little children, ye shall not enter into the kingdom of heaven.

Jesus

The old man in his days will not hesitate to ask an infant of seven days about the place of life, and he will live.

Gospel of Thomas

The Sage sees and hears no more than an infant sees and hears.

Lao-tzu

19 COUNT ME IN

Procedure: The way to count men is to count heads.

Game: "Please, please count *me* in!"

Antithesis: Ten fools, travelling as a party in wild country, came to a fast-flowing river, which by one means and another they managed to get across. Arrived on the far bank, each of them counted to make sure all were safely over. And each counted *nine.* So they all began weeping for their drowned brother.

Then there came along a monk who, taking pity on them, undertook to prove that all ten were safe. He told them to count the cries of pain while he gave each man a blow with a stick. This time the fools all counted ten, and went on their way reassured.

That is the rather lame end of the traditional story (versions of which are found in India, China, and Europe), so let us supply a sequel—

Before the ten ex-fools had got very far, one of them began to have doubts. Returning, he found the helpful monk and said: "True, there were ten cries of pain, but it's men that drown, not ouches, and the way to count men is to count heads. And there are still only nine."

At this the monk, realizing that he was dealing with a real Fool and that argument was useless, led him to a part of the river-bank where the water was still and deep. "There," he cried, pointing down beneath the mirror-smooth surface, *"there's* your tenth man."

"We told you so," cried the Fool. "There he lies, our poor drowned brother!" And he began weeping and wailing all over again.

When a rattle first drops out of the hand of a baby, he does not look to see where it has gone. Non-perception he accepts as annihilation.

William James

Everyone under heaven says that our Way is greatly like folly. But it is just because it is great, that it seems like folly. As for the things that do not seem like folly—well, there can be no question about *their* smallness!

Lao-tzu

I have made trial of provident good sense; hereafter I am going to make myself mad.

Rumi

The monk, who was now desperate, shouted back: "Idiot, it's *you* there in the water, and by Heaven that's where you should be!"

At this the Fool gave a great laugh and cried: "Hurray, it's only me!" He ran back to tell his nine companions that everything was all right and it was only he that was drowned. But they had moved on. He was alone, with not even his drowned self for company.

Footnote: A monk once asked T'sui-wei what was the significance of the First Patriarch's coming to China: he meant, 'What is the essence of Zen?'

The master replied: "Wait till nobody's around here, and I'll tell you."

On the Miao-ku-she mountain there lives a divine man whose flesh is like ice or snow.... This being is absolutely inert.... In a flood which reached to the sky, he would not be drowned. In a drought, though metals ran liquid and mountains were scorched up, he would not be hot.

Chuang-tzu

Grief is possible only when one thinks of himself as a body.

Ramana Maharshi

If your anger is external, not internal, it will be anger proceeding from not-anger. If your actions are external, not internal, they will be actions proceeding from inaction.

Chuang-tzu

He is the lord of states of feeling, not dependent on any state.... He that is dependent on a state is still a human being.

Rumi

When one leaves all the loves that dwell in the mind, O son of Pritha, and is gladdened only in his Self by his Self, then he is said to be of abiding wisdom....
He who walks through the ranges of sense, with sense instruments severed from passion and hatred and obedient to the Self, and possesses his Self in due order, comes to clearness.

Bhagavadgita

20 PSYCHOLOGY

Procedure: Man is psychological, an on-going kaleidoscope of experiences. In him the beauty and ugliness of the world, its meaning and pointlessness, its pleasures and pains, are enjoyed and suffered, and he has no defence against their ever-renewed invasion. He lies at the meeting point of countless influences which constitute his universe, which move him profoundly, which actually become him. He has no central Observation Tower, no Impregnable Keep, but is vulnerable through and through. It's upsetting to be human. And, of course, to be a perfectly dispassionate man would be out of place and out of character—if it were possible. His feelings do him credit.

Game: I am playing 'Psychology' when I, acting 3rd-person and imitating him, make a fictitious central object here of my experience, instead of leaving it where it belongs, in the true object out there.

Antithesis: As soon as I inspect myself carefully, I find to my surprise that I am without feelings. I notice that I'm never frightened here, or cheerful here, or pleased or loving or hating here; instead, it's something or other out there which is frightful, agreeable, lovable, hateful. Right here I can discover no noun for these or any other adjectives to qualify: they refer to the inhabited periphery and never to the vacant Centre. This Look-out remains unmoved, whatever the turmoil around. This 1st person is characterless.

Young children and some primitives approach this state of central indifference. It isn't they who are horrified but their enemies who are horrifying; it isn't they who suffer from nerves but the world

In the deeps of his ground he knows and feels nothing, in soul or body, but a singular radiance with a sensible well-being and an all-pervading savour. This .... is the way of emptiness.

Ruysbroeck

Just let things happen without making any response and keep your minds from dwelling on anything whatever.

Keep them for ever still as the void and utterly pure: and thereby attain deliverance.

He who does not accept anything has nothing to reject; he is free of Samsara for ever.

Hui-hai

We must be so thoroughly dead as to be moved by neither good nor ill.

Eckhart

This one alone is lacking in every mode and quality.

Eckhart

Rejoicing in nothing and knowing nothing are the true rejoicing and the true knowledge.

Lieh-tzu

A class of children are asked where they think. Some say in their heads. Peter (5 years) says he thinks in his arithmetic book.

Television Programme

that is chancy and menacing; it isn't they who are in good form but others who are so helpful. But the difference (and it is crucial) is this: the child attributes no qualities to himself because he *doesn't* see himself, while I attribute no qualities to myself because I *do* see myself—as having none. The pre-psychological infant over-looks the looker, while the non-psychological 1st person looks for the looker and finds him absent.

Psychological man is too sophisticated to do either. Falling between these two stools of Paradise and Heaven, he lands in something like a Hell, where all the world's qualities reside in the eye of the beholder. When I start playing 'Psychology' I cease noticing that I am empty of feelings about the wonderfully full world, and I become full of feelings about the woefully empty world, and shaken (so real is this pretence) to the core by my own likes and dislikes, fears, loves, hates. The values I suck in from the surrounding universe suffer in transit, and leave me no peace.

How can a man be without feelings? He doesn't let them get inside and do him harm.

Put mind and knowledge on the outside.

When Pu-liang Yi put the world and all things and all life outside himself, he achieved the brightness of dawn and could see his aloneness.

Chuang-tzu

Every real expression of life is an expression of positive spontaneity and works from within outwards.

Real thought grasps the nature of that which is not ourselves—the outside world of things and people. So real feeling grasps the value of what is not ourselves, and enjoys it or disapproves it. The moment that feeling ceases to be directed outwards, the moment it ceases to be an appreciation of the thing or the person with which it is connected in fact, it becomes unreal, or, to use a very appropriate term: sentimental.

Excitement is a good test of the unreality of feeling. When anything excites us and stimulates feelings in us, we are not feeling it.... When we enjoy our feelings, we are feeling unreally or sentimentally. Unreal people are turned back on themselves.

John Macmurray

21 STATE OF MIND

Procedure: Yesterday Mr Jones was cheerful and full of hope; today he tells me he's full of care. Certainly I can see by his expression, by the lines in his face, that he's in a state about the world in general, and perhaps about Miss Smith in particular: it's written all over him. And there, fortunately, the trouble stops: this ever-changing emotional weather is localized in Mr Jones. I don't find his state written all over the face of the Earth, or even over Miss Smith's face; they do not vary as Mr Jones varies; his disturbance isn't seen to spill over onto them. Apparently the world of his feelings is a small world, interior, no bigger than himself. And apparently Mr Jones agrees. It's enough, for example, that he takes himself off, alone—Mr Jones and what's under his hat—to his parson or his psychiatrist for help. All this is good, practical common sense.

Game: Like Mr Jones, I have feelings. The question is where I keep them. When, imitating him—trying to keep up with the Joneses emotionally—I locate my feelings under my hat, I am deluding myself. I am playing 'Emotional State', making believe that there is something right here where I am, and that this something is the playground of all sorts of disturbances. And so serious is this game— this invention of a central support for feelings, of box and emotional contents—that the boxful seems to be only too real. It's as if it actually did exist and I were actually a mass of pent-up experience here.

Antithesis: Practically speaking, a person is as big as the world of his feelings. In the case of Mr Jones, the 3rd person, the smallness

In the childish stage of consciousness there are as yet no problems. The individual submits to them or circumvents them, remaining quite at one with himself. He does not yet know the state of inner tension which a problem brings about. This state only arises when what was an external limitation becomes an inner obstacle.

In the face of something extraordinary it is not primitive man who is astonished, but rather the thing which is astonishing.... His fear is localized in certain places that are 'not good'.... He is unpsychological.... Everything is to him perfectly objective.

In the era of enlightenment people first found that the gods did not exist but were only projections. Thereby, though, they were not annihilated. The psychological functions corresponding to them ... fell to the unconscious and thereby poisoned people with an excess of libido previously devoted to the service of the divine image. I see in natural science a Herculean attempt to understand the human psyche by approaching it from the outer world.

Carl Jung

The soul lives in what it loves.

St John of the Cross

We can see how the psychology of dualism came to shut itself *in* and the physics of dualism to shut itself *out,* by sundering the one world of experience into two halves, an internal and an external, both abstractions and so both devoid of reality.

James Ward

of that world matches his smallness. In the case of myself, this 1st person, the hugeness of that world matches my hugeness. Just as surely as I observe that he has a head to hang down or hold up, a truly expressive face, eyebrows to raise, a brow to wrinkle, a mouth to harden, eyes to light up, a neck to stiffen, shoulders to droop—so, with equal certainty, I observe that I have none of these. When I attend to myself, I find nothing of my own. Here is no body-box nor thought-box nor feeling-box, no net, no filter, no fence, no gate where 'my' thoughts or feelings could be held up on their outward journey. Launched from here, they proceed freely and instantaneously to their true home in the object there, and it is only *there* that they are given to me. The Subject here now observes itself to be perfectly cool and feeling-free, as bare of emotions as it is of any substance to be moved by them. *All* the object's aspects and functions and qualities—not only its number and size and shape and time-span, its opacity and colour and sound and taste and feel, but also its name and social role and endless conceptual relationships, its beauty and ugliness, loveableness and hatefulness, helpfulness and menace, and so on indefinitely—*all* now adhere to the perceived and none remain in this Perceiver. The 1st person is emptied upon the 3rd.

This is becoming a child again, with important differences. In fact, I have to go through three stages.

(i) Childish Projection—Pre-game

When I was a child, more or less game-free and pre-psychological, I poured out all my thoughts and feelings upon people and things

The Mind as it is in itself is free from ills—this is the Precept of Self-being. The Mind as it is in itself is free from disturbances—this is the Meditation of Self-being. The Mind as it is in itself is free from follies—this is the knowledge of Self-being.

The Self Nature remains untainted by any kind of objective condition. The True Nature moves with perfect freedom, discriminating all things in the objective world yet inwardly unmoved in the First Principle.

Wu-nien is seeing all things yet keeping the mind free from all stain or attachment.

Only keep your original Mind pure and let the six senses run out of the six gates into the six worlds.

Hui-neng

A mind disturbed by love and aversion is deluded; a mind free from them both is real.

Ability to perceive the minutest differences among the appearances constituting our environment, including the smallest gradations of good and evil, and yet to be so entirely unaffected by them that we remain perfectly at ease amidst all of them—this is called Wisdom Vision.

Hui-hai

Avoid using your psychological possessions—your griefs, worries, joys, aspirations, etc.—as if they were your private property.

D.T. Suzuki

out there, while overlooking their Source here, the empty vessel they all came from. The result was that, though I certainly often found the world disagreeable and people charged with menace, I was not myself in a state about them. Faceless, I was faced with trouble, but not invaded. I had no psychological problems. Such problems as I was presented with were external.

(ii) Adult Withdrawal—Game

As a fully psychological adult, playing such subsidiaries of the Face Game as 'Psychology' and 'State of Mind', I seem to take back on myself the qualities, the thoughts and feelings and even the sensations, which I had as a child projected upon people and things out there, and to collect them together here in a box. In other words, this face, head, body, which I make out is right here, is supercharged with mind; it is a psycho-physical pseudo-object, an imaginary volume containing, besides flesh and blood and bones and brains, my private world of experience, in varying degrees pent up and suppressed and repressed. The result of these games is two-sided: the world, shorn of its qualities, becomes more and more meaningless and empty, while I, now full to bursting with those same qualities, become more and more a psychological case in need of analysis. For these qualities are relative, and by no means the same whether they adhere to the object or the Subject. On the contrary, they spoil on the inward journey. Thus the lover, detaching his love from the loved one and enjoying it as his own feeling, is a mere sentimentalist and not even in love with love. Thus the scientist whose interest in Nature is replaced by interest

Abide as the Self and remain uncontaminated by what goes on around.

Ramana Maharshi

The goods of God, which are beyond all measure, can only be contained in an empty and solitary heart.
The fly that touches honey cannot use its wings; so the soul that clings to spiritual sweetness ruins its freedom and hinders contemplation.

St John of the Cross

Knowledge and discernment come to be loved more than that which is discerned; for the false natural light loveth itself, its knowledge and powers, more than what is known.

Theologica Germanica

My soul sees nothing whatever that can be told of the lips or the heart, she sees nothing, and she sees All.... All which the soul or heart can reach is inferior to this Good.... Though inexpressible, these other things bring delight; but this vision of God in darkness brings no smile to the lips, no devotion or fervour of love to the soul.

St Angela of Foligno

in artifice—in his own intellectual system—is no longer a scientist. Thus the saint who discovers goodness in himself rather than in others is far from being a saint. Language itself hints as much:—to the extent to which I cultivate my own sentiments, my affection and sympathy apart from what excites them, I am being sentimental and affected and pathetic and even, in the end, pathological. No longer living from within outwards, I stand out there looking in at myself—a thing I cannot really do. Thus I become an unreal person living an unreal life in an unreal world.

And in fact that unreal world of mine appears far from empty. Many of the attributes which I have withdrawn from the environment and devalued and repressed, here, I re-project upon it. These attributes are distorted and largely negative because, instead of proceeding unhindered from the bare Subject here to their objective destinations, they are filtered through this fabricated body-mind box which contaminates whatever it handles. The more I play the Face Game here the more the face of things out there seems menacing and anguished.

(iii) Enlightened Redistribution—Post-game

My remedy, as always, is simplicity itself. All I have to do is look, to see what it's like to be myself, this 1st person. All I have to do is to notice the total lack of anything here, of any screen which could retain feelings or thoughts of any kind, or could prevent them leaping forth upon their true owners. All I have to do is let go what anyway I cannot hold.

The consequences are fourfold. *First,* I am now relieved of all anxiety lest I am sufficiently loving or happy or wise or good or sensitive or spiritual or enlightened. It is enough to be empty here, at the clear Source of all phenomena, without flowing downstream along with them. It is enough to remain where all is potential and nothing actual. Before, this empty feeling was merely negative and therefore resented and resisted. Now, it is welcome, a positive relief, realized not merely as plain fact and natural and very easy, but also as a state and a station of profound peace. *Second,* people and things are appreciated realistically, without 'parataxic distortion', without either glossing over defects or discounting merits. It is astonishing, for example, how a man's face, gestures, tone of voice, clothes, everything about him, reveal him to the empty Observer from whom nothing is hid. At last, one begins to experience others as they are. *Third,* I notice that the more I am able to see all these qualities home, to where they belong out there, the more they change for the better. They are the genuine thing, what I really feel and no longer what I think I ought to feel, no longer imitative, socially approved postures. As thus decontaminated, even their negative aspects are saved from being merely negative: nothing is wholly ugly any more, or unredeemably hateful or frightful or disgusting. The totally filled 3rd-person world, viewed from this totally empty 1st-person position, is a very good world. Wiser than he knows, the pessimist complains that the world is fit for nobody to live in. Then let me be nobody, be myself as I really am, and see how comfortable the world becomes. For the only way I can be somebody and make something of myself is at the world's

expense: *if I take it out of the world I must put up with what's left.*
Fourth, sense experience itself is modified. When I attend to the fact
that sensations are given 'out there' in the object instead of here in the
empty Subject, I find them to be more alive and positive. Thus when I
consciously see your face there with my no-face here, and consciously
hear what you say with my no-ears here, then both face and its talk
are valued more highly. So also, when I am consciously smelling a
rose there with my no-nose here, and consciously tasting bread there
with my no-tongue here, then rose and bread are thoroughly enjoyed.
Or consider pain. If I dig my thumbnail into my finger, the pain is
clearly located out there in my finger and none of it is here. Even a
headache or a toothache is felt as off-Centre, not shut up in any box
here—and certainly not in a bone one. (In fact, of course, the 1st
person should not speak of a *head*ache or a *tooth*ache: no such things
are here for the pain to lodge in or disturb.) The results of thus *placing*
pain—of its decentralisation—do something to the pain. At least it
proves more bearable. And in some instances it is greatly reduced,
or even got rid of altogether.

In all this the essential knack is not merely to observe the presence
of the feeling out there, but also its absence here. It isn't enough to live
from within outwards like a child: one must also live *at* the Spot one
is living *from.* Two-way looking is required—looking at the Looker
as well as the looked-at, looking at the clear and changeless This *and*
what proceeds from it, the infinitely variegated That.[1] The mature

---

1 This two-way looking is beautifully portrayed in the Greek myth of Perseus
(see Appendix). Medusa turns the hero to stone if he looks at her directly, but
when she is viewed in his mirror-shield she is harmless. In other words, looking
out at things while overlooking the Looker, one imagines the Looker is like
them, a thing among things; but there is a way of avoiding this petrification.

experience of feeling there involves experiencing the absence of feeling here. Just as creative thinking comes from no-thinking, from clear-headedness (the head, too, cleared away), and just as effective action comes from no-action, from interior stillness, so does real feeling, come from no-feeling, from total detachment and impassivity aware of itself as such.

To eat all day and yet not swallow a grain of rice, to walk all day and yet not tread an inch of ground, ... is to be the man who is at ease in himself.

Huang-po

As long as you are not carried away by external winds, your nature will remain like water for ever still and clear.   Let nothing matter.

Hui-hai

I am not the doer or the enjoyer. I am without change and without action. I am pure intelligence, one, and eternal bliss.

Sankara

You who have been bitten by the great black serpent called 'I am the doer', take the medicine called 'I am not the doer', and be happy.

Astavakra Samhita

God's essence is absolute stillness: it is immovable.

Eckhart

The One is the stationary principle in the tree, in the animal, in the soul, and in the All.

Plotinus

22 BUSY

Procedure: A man is thoroughly caught up. He is continuous with his world and of the same order, inseparably a part of the universal process, a conductor and not a source of energy. All of him is involved; he is busy as one piece, without any still pivot or nucleus. His very life is action. For him, idleness amounts to death.

Game: I am playing 'Busy' when, reading his 3rd-person situation into my 1st-person situation, I make out that I, too, am thoroughly caught up.

Antithesis: Whatever the superficial fuss, however busy I pretend to be, I notice that I am in fact bone lazy. When I attend carefully to what lies right here at the storm-centre of the universe, I find perfect calm. The middle of the world has quietly dropped out—but really it never had a middle, and was always hollow, coreless. This Hub of the ever-turning cosmic wheel has never been anything but still, idle, and vacant.

I also observe, radiating like four wobbly spokes from the Hub, these legs and arms going about their business, just as these men and animals and clouds and stars are going about theirs, without any interference from me. Here at the Centre I can find no aims, no needs, no responsibilities, no sense of controlling anything whatsoever: out there all goes well enough on its own. In any case, how could this central Nothing bring any influence to bear upon that peripheral something, and still be Nothing? And, in fact, whenever I pretend that these arms and legs are thoroughly mine, are 3rd-person type

We used to pray: Thy will
my Lord and God, be done.
And lo! He hath no will;
He is stillness alone.

Angelus Silesius (trans. W.R. Trask)

At the centre, where no-one abides, there this light is quenched....
for this ground is the impartible stillness, motionless in itself, and by
this immobility all things are moved.

Eckhart

Inexhaustible energy springs from emptiness.

Prajnaparamita Sutra

Man thinks he is the doer, whereas actually everything is managed
from 'Here'.

Anandamayi Ma

and continuous with a complete human body, instead of 1st-person type and quite loose, their work deteriorates. They do best when seen as they really are—free of me.

I interfere with nothing out there, and nothing out there interferes with me. I have nothing to do, and yet I see all doing as proceeding from here; I find no need to be anything, and yet I see all being as contained here—in this unique Gap, this wonderful Hiatus, which turns out to be the fountain of continual creation. Here, indeed, is no ordinary spot: no place on the map, in the cosmos, is anything like it. This still Centre is the one spot where energy is actually discovered welling up out of Nothing. All the irresistible torrents which swirl and roar through every other place rise silently in this Place, never ruffling its perfect calm.

The average person, while he thinks he is awake, actually is half asleep. By 'half asleep' I mean that his contact with reality is a very partial one; most of what he believes to be reality (outside or inside of himself) is a set of fictions which his mind constructs. He is aware of reality only to the degree to which his social functioning makes it necessary.

I believe I see—but I only *see words*; I believe I feel, but I only *think feelings*. The cerebrating person is the alienated person.

Erich Fromm

The innocence of the eye is lost .... As I look along the dining table I overlook the fact that the farther plates and glasses *feel* so much smaller than my own, for I *know* that they are all equal in size; and the feeling of them, which is a present sensation, is eclipsed in the glare of the knowledge, which is a merely imagined one.

It is the same with shape as with size. Almost all the visible shapes of things are what we call perspective 'distortions'.

William James

A race, whereof scarce one
Was able, in a million,
To feel that any marvel lay
In objects round his feet all day;
Scarce one, in many millions more,
Willing, if able, to explore
The secreter, minuter charm!

Browning

23 PARADISE LOST

Procedure: Anybody who seriously imagines that God's in his heaven, and all's right with the world, is living in a fool's paradise and due for a succession of rude shocks. Every newspaper, every day, shows what sort of world we are really living in, and to gloss over the facts would be the most inefficient of procedures—not to mention the dishonesty of it. The mature and competent man doesn't persuade himself that the Nature of things has any tenderness for him, or is going to give him any special consideration whatever.

Game: I am playing 'Paradise Lost' when, refusing to look at the 1st-person world I'm actually living in all the while, I make out that it is his 3rd-person world, or anything like it.

Antithesis: I have only to look, carefully and honestly. Then the quality of what I see—the glow, the brilliance, the beauty everywhere—is beyond description; and so are the pervading hush, the smile, the peace and joy over all. Nevertheless some of the more miraculous appointments of this Palace of mine may be sketched in without serious distortion. They are just the sort of thing a small child would expect of any Heaven worthy of the name, of any true Wonderland. All fairy stories are incomplete versions of this true Fairy Story.

My Palace, with its gardens and parks, comprises the whole world, but it's a very unfamiliar world. Though the views are enchanting, it's a tiny and ill-equipped domain by earthly standards. Its towers and pavilions and halls are very few and miniature and bare of

Truly there are two worlds. One was made by God, the other by men. That made by God was great and beautiful. Before the Fall it was Adam's joy and the Temple of his glory. That made by men is a Babel of Confusions: Invented Riches, Pomps and Vanities .... Leave the one that you may enjoy the other.

Traherne

Observe things as they are and don't pay attention to other people.

Huang-po

He who shall teach the child to doubt
The rotting grave shall ne'er get out .....
He who doubts from what he sees
Will ne'er believe, do what you please.

Blake

This made it the more likely that he had seen a true vision; for instead of making common things look commonplace, as a false vision would have done, it had made common things disclose the wonderful that was in them.

George Macdonald

I knew the Golden Age was all about me, and it was we who had been blind to it, but that it had never passed away from the world.

A.E.

furnishings. Except that they are forever changing, they are far more like toy-theatre scenery than real structures—pretty, but flat and flimsy facades meant for show rather than use.

It's when I visit one of these towers or pavilions that the miracles begin. Everything opens out like a giant flower at my approach. All the furniture I might need springs up from nothing, ready-made and comfortable, around me, so that my immediate surroundings are always roomy and properly equipped. But these heavenly chairs and tables and carpets and curtains and pictures are mere caricatures of their earthly counterparts, and their behaviour is totally different. For one thing, they are always changing size and shape—just as if they were very much alive, and indeed keenly observant. Thus a chair, at first smaller than a matchbox, obligingly grows to full size as I approach it, stays that size and perfectly still all the while I care to sit on it, and quickly dwindles to match-box size when I get up and move away. Again, my side of the table is always conveniently wider than the other; and if I shift across, the table-top kindly reshapes itself for me. Only *my* plate and glass, which—incidentally—are bigger and more capacious than the rest, have tasty contents. The patch of carpet I'm standing on has a larger and brighter and more interesting pattern than the remainder, and it moves along with me like a theatre spotlight. Pictures—even old masters—paint themselves for me as I walk up to them; tape-measures lengthen till they have marked themselves off into 36 true inches; weights stop growing at exactly an ounce or a pound; printing magnifies itself to readable size; plates round themselves; coats let themselves out till they fit.

But what is Paradise? All things that are.

Theologica Germanica

This very spot is the Lotus Paradise.

Hakuin

All our thoughts must be infant-like and clear; the powers of our soul free from the leaven of this world, and disentangled from men's conceits and customs. Grit in the eye or yellow jaundice will not let a man see those objects truly that are before it. And therefore it is requisite that we should be as very strangers to the thoughts, customs, and opinions of men in the world, as if we were but little children. So those things would appear to us only which do to children when they are first born.

Traherne

I will prize all I have, and nothing shall with me be less esteemed, because it is excellent. A daily joy shall be more my joy, because it is continual. A common joy is more my delight because it is common.

Traherne

To sit in the Throne of God is to inhabit Eternity. To reign there is to be pleased with all things in Heaven and Earth.

Traherne

Everything is busy remodelling itself to my convenience. All these fantastic transformations of my belongings are their way of bowing to me, their worship and obedience, their preparation for my coming, their anticipation of my needs, and their self-effacement when those needs have been met. To say I am waited on by all Heaven is an understatement: here, each brick and tile, grass blade, pebble, grain of sand, tirelessly attends on me, hanging on my slightest movement, and its response is always perfect.

Much more could be said about the entertainments and conveniences of this wonderful 1st-person Country—how flowers suddenly bloom around me but nowhere else; how birds sing for me alone and are silent when I am gone; how scents and colours revive when I pass by; how rich decorations, often set with sparkling jewels, are painted upon surfaces just in time for my arrival and fade the instant I turn away; how humans of pinhead size upwards are my devoted slaves everywhere; how I am the owner and reason and end of all that's going on in Heaven. Above all, it should be explained that, truly speaking, I don't move around Heaven, but Heaven moves around me, who am forever stationary at this saluting base (the only Here-Now in Heaven, its unique Centre); and how, truly speaking, this endless march-past at different speeds (best seen from railway trains) isn't over there at a distance, but one-with-me, right here.

In fact, however, all these magical displays are incidental to heavenly life. Though one is well aware of them, this is by the way, as part of one's Self-awareness. Really it's oneself that is seen—the indescribable Light of Heaven, the unfathomably mysterious and

When the slave in you has become naught, you have become the King ….

Some cunning people devise stratagems to get the King into a beer-jug.

Rumi

Buhlul said to a certain dervish, "How art thou, O dervish? Inform me."

He said, "How should that one be, according to whose desire the work of the world goes on?

According to whose desire the torrents and rivers flow, and the stars move in such wise as he wills;

And Life and Death are his officers …..

No tooth flashes with laughter in the world without the approval of that imperial personage."

Rumi

There are two creations, one God's and the other man's…. He who kills man's creation sees heaven only, the others see only hell.

Ramana Maharshi

wonderful and solitary One—and Heaven is a by-product of that seeing. Heaven's where I am when I'm concerned with what I am, not with where I am. That's why it's no nebulous mansion in the sky, but real down to its most concrete detail.

Thou hast cast all my sins behind thy back.

Isaiah

Get thee behind me, Satan.

Jesus

When all things are reduced to naught in you then ye shall see God.

Eckhart

When one sees the Self, the world is not seen.

Ramana Maharshi

Forgetfulness of God, O beloved, is the pillar of this world.

Rumi

God is all, and things have only a nominal value.

Attar

The reality of the formless, the unreality of that which has form!

Chuang-tzu

In dreams.... the mind alone creates the world. Similarly in the waking state also: there is no difference.

Sankara

How things are in the world is a matter of complete indifference for what is higher.

Wittgenstein

24 JODRELL BANK

Procedure: A man had better take the universe seriously—or suffer the consequences. For plainly he's of a piece with it, built into the same block, a current of the same onrushing river. His dependence upon and continuity with the world are total: not for an instant can he be disentangled. Through and through he's of the same order as the things and events around him, and is exactly as real—or unreal—as they are. To him, therefore, reality means the natural world in all its non-human (even inhuman), spatio-temporal vastness—this inconceivably gigantic system of galaxies and stars in which consciousness is a late and rare accident, altogether feeble and dependent, if not actually a myth. And a cool look at him is enough to confirm that his alleged consciousness is not a necessary hypothesis.

Game: I am playing 'Jodrell Bank' when I reckon that I, too, am a needle lost in the cosmic haystack, and (in spite of all the first-hand, 1st-person evidence) allow myself to be intimidated by such bogies as light-years and parsecs, and all the extrapolated vastness of space and time and matter.

Antithesis: When I observe myself all is reversed. No matter, no complications, not even naked energy is here, but only Awareness itself, or awareness of Awareness, immediate Self-consciousness, that ever-simple Reality which the universe—its incidental by-product—is powerless to stain or disturb.

I cannot take this universe seriously. Deep down, I feel it's not my native country and I don't belong. Also I see clearly I'm not

In this He shewed me a little thing, the quantity of a hazel nut...
I looked thereupon and thought: "What may this be?" And I was
answered in a general way, thus: "It is all that is made." I marvelled
how it could last, for methought it might suddenly fall to naught for
littleness.

Julian of Norwich

The God-lover parts with the world as cheerfully as with an egg.

Eckhart

He who dwells on the unreal universe is destroyed.

Sankara

The Sun of our world is hidden till our stars have become hidden.

Rumi

remotely like any of its inhabitants. Above all, I have the unique art of exposing its emptiness and dreamlike unreality. Just as easily as I clear up here all that fantastically complex opacity of cells and tissues and organs which build a human body, so I clear up all the rest of the world, from the furniture of this room to the furthest nebula. (No, it's not I who switch off, but the universe, for I go on quite unaffected. And certainly I don't shut my eyes to it all. What eyes?) At will and effortlessly, I put all things behind me and so abolish them. Not only do I awake from the day-dream of the universe every night, but as often during the day as I wish.

To survive the universe, it must be undone down to the last electron, for to allow it any independent reality is to share its fate. Instead of being taken in by the world-hoax, one must take it in and see through it and make Nothing of it. The universe's bluff is called, and it all melts, without a tell-tale bubble or swirl, into this clear Ocean.

In a little house I keep pictures suspended, it is not a fix'd house,
It is round, it is only a few inches from one side to the other;
Yet behold, it has room for all the shows of the world.

Whitman

Here the figures, here the colours, here all the images of every part of the universe are contracted to a point. O what point is so marvellous! Forms already lost, mingled together in so small a space, it can recreate and reconstitute by dilation.

Leonardo da Vinci

If sense-data are literally inside the brain we are committed to the conclusion that they are always smaller than the things to which they belong, (or else) that our own head is very much larger than it appears to be from touch.

H.H. Price

How can a world be contained under the clay of the body? How should a Heaven be contained in the earth? God forfend! Thou art beyond this world both in thy lifetime and at the present hour.

Rumi

The subject does not belong in the world.

Wittgenstein

Become vision itself.

Plotinus

25 PUT YOURSELF IN HIS SHOES

Procedure: There is nothing absurd about the 3rd-person procedure of attributing subjectivity to other human beings. On the contrary, it is as reasonable as it is morally necessary and socially expedient to regard every Thou as also an I.

Game: This indispensable procedure becomes an unnecessary—indeed quite ridiculous—game when it is practised by this 1st person. Observe how absurd are my efforts to confer subjectivity upon objective man. Since he evidently neither comprises nor owns *this* universe, he's credited with another, a private or pocket universe which mysteriously copies it. The problem then is where to put it. One solution is to shrink it to manageable size and enclose it in a captive balloon floating just above a man's head. But this balloon world rarely appears outside cartoons and comic strips, and isn't meant to be taken too seriously. A more respectable—but still less likely—position isn't above but right inside his skull. This means even more drastic shrinkage, and confinement in a tiny, dark, airless box which is already stuffed full. I am unable to explain how this out-sized, rip-roaring, highly coloured, dazzling world could all be neatly and safely folded up and tucked away in such a tiny container as a head, or how this astounding miracle of universe-shrinking (or else head-swelling) is repeated every time another head is born—indeed every time it opens its eyes. Nor can I explain why brain surgeons find only brains......

In this Light one becomes seeing.

Ruysbroeck

I become a transparent eyeball; I am nothing; I see all.

Emerson

Thy whole body will become like a mirror: it will become all eye and spiritual substance.

Rumi

He who is disembodied perceives without any screen, like Moses, the light of the Moon shining from his own bosom.

Rumi

He walks in bright awareness and with illumined spirit. In other words, the man who realizes self-awareness feels that he is no more the obedient servant of blind impulse, but is his own master. He then senses that ordinary people, blind to their innate, bright awareness, tread the streets like walking corpses.

Chang Chen-chi

Can the body, which is insentient as a piece of wood, shine and function as 'I'? No. Therefore lay aside this insentient body as though it were truly a corpse.

Ramana Maharshi

Looking outward we see many faces; look inward and all is the One Head.

Plotinus

Antithesis: The truth is that this second universe—whether crammed into or poised above a man's head—is the maddest dream. This subject here is surrounded by objects exhibiting no trace of subjectivity: they are presented as objects pure and simple. Thus a man is visibly a physical thing separate from other physical things; he shows no sign of melting or exploding into the universe, or of concealing it somewhere on or near his person. Evidently he's a minute part, and how could even the greatest of parts contain the whole?

Man is of one sort: he takes only the headed form, as I take only the headless. I notice this suits him well enough, and I've no plans either to behead him or to stuff things in his head which don't belong there. This isn't to say he inhabits some outer darkness unlit by consciousness. Indeed he has an I, this unique Subject here, which remains one and undivided by its countless objects. All faces belong to this one Head or No-head. This Pure Subject is totally united with every object.

From an Armenian Miniature, 989 A.D.

26 THE HAND OF MAN (I)

Procedure: The human hand, provided it's alive, invariably adheres to a human body; and it's usually busy at some task of exploration or manipulation designed to promote the interests of its human user. This isn't to say that the human hand is understood in the slightest: it's only familiar—an ingredient which enters into almost all human procedures.

Game: I am playing THOM when, looking at these hands before me now, I imagine their connection here to some human shoulders and trunk. Dishonestly, I mix what I see with what I think I see, and overlook the very great difference between these hands and all others.

Antithesis: The 1st person's hand is loose, a thing on its own. So, significantly, is God's, as it figures in mediaeval paintings, where it looks just like a man's hand, with a short length of sleeve, except that it vanishes there and is attached to no body. Making some appropriate gesture, it is thrust forth from a cloud, or from a nest of celestial spheres, or from nothing, at the top of the picture.

So far from being a mere iconographical curiosity, this pious device is a fairly true picture of this 1st person's hands—of the hand that is now writing these words, and the other that's holding down this sheet of paper. I see that though they are alive and nimble enough, they are unsupported, and fade out around the elbows. I see also that they materialize from, and die away into, the nothing that lies here, just back of them: it's this Void which puts them forth. Whose hands,

189

It is one's own spiritual Nature in enlightenment that moves the arms and legs.

> Attributed to Bodhidharma

Closer is He than breathing, and nearer than hands and feet.

> Tennyson

I touched my limbs; the limbs were strange, not mine.

> Tennyson

If there were no eye, what? If there were no ear, what? If there were no mouth, what? If there were no mind, what? If one has to face such circumstances and knows how to act then one is in the company of the ancient Patriarchs and Buddhas. Anyone in that company is satisfied.

> *Blue Cliff Records*

then, are these, the only hands that have feeling, in spite of the fact (or rather, because of the fact) that they belong to nobody?

Certainly they aren't a man's, for here is no trunk for them to be directed by or to serve, but only this Emptiness or Brightness which lacks nothing and has no tasks for any hands to undertake. It is true I'm aware of their astonishing behaviour and even authorize it, but I am quite detached alike from their action and its results. They live their own life. I'm not now laboriously directing this right hand: agilely, mysteriously, it writes these words about itself as it pleases—and I'm neither pleased nor displeased. Moreover I notice that when I see clearly What I am here, I see also that these two hands are displaying unusual powers, a new selflessness, a surer touch, an unfamiliar spontaneity and freedom.

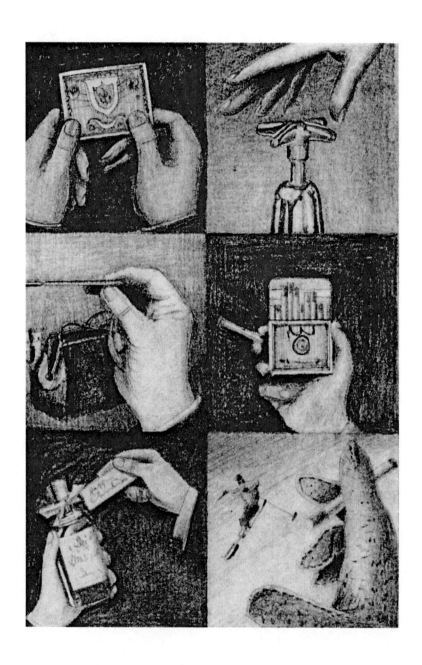

192

27 THE HAND OF MAN (2)

Procedure: When a man is being drawn or photographed or filmed, the usual procedure is to show the whole of him; or if not the whole, the top half; or if not the top half, at least his head. Obviously this makes sense in the 3rd-person world.

Game: But 3rd-person sense is 1st-person nonsense. When, confronted by a poster showing a (suitably idealized) man handling a brand of cigarettes or raising a mug of someone's beer to his lips, I put myself in his place, the advertiser has tricked me into a game—the game of falsely identifying myself with someone who isn't at all like me. Again, I am similarly tricked when, confronted by a screen hero, very much all there from head to toe, I put myself into his shoes. This isn't remotely like a portrait of *me*.

Antithesis: If I'm honest I'm not taken in by these portraits: I don't see myself in them. I'm out of the picture. What, indeed, have those faces to do with this faceless one?

The ad-man has other designs, of a radically different sort, which are directed at *me*. They are portraits, not of human beings, but of missing persons, of bodies that have (except for loose hands and sometimes feet) disappeared. Familiar examples (and they certainly manage to hide their connection with mediaeval iconography) show me—my sort—handling or opening a bottle, reaching for the hot-water tap, or lifting a cigarette or a glass to this no-head and no-mouth, this Gape. And the fact that I accept these portraits of me as true likenesses without thinking them odd, without giving them a thought, shows how lifelike they are.

It's much the same with films: there are two very different kinds—the human or 3rd-person kind and my kind. In the former, the hero is a complete human, with whom the audience—very reasonably—has no difficulty in identifying itself. In the latter or 1st-person film, the hero isn't a human being at all, but a void or transparency, a disembodied voice, the sound of hard breathing and occasional coughs, loose hands fiddling with pipe or matches or spectacles or pen, loose feet shuffling in and out at the bottom of the screen—in short, a pretty fair film portrait of me. The former shows a man coming and going, ever changing, always off-centre to the world; the latter shows me fixed, unchanging, at the empty Centre of the world's confusion. And again, the picture seems perfectly natural—in fact, specially vivid and convincing—because it's me to the life.

How wonderful is the path of Love, when the headless one is exalted.

Hafiz

I have sacrificed head and soul to gain the Beloved.

Rumi

He who loves with not only a part of himself, but the whole, transforms himself in the thing beloved.

Angela of Foligno

Throw yourself into the Abyss.

Po-shan Ching-yu

According to Buddhism, ultimate and unconditioned love can only be achieved through a realisation of Voidness (sunyata). Because there are no sentient beings to be pitied, Buddha has the greatest pity; because from the very beginning no sentient beings ever existed, Buddha 'came down' to earth to save sentient beings.

Chang Chen-chi

Every creature denies it is the other .... But God is the denier of denials.

Eckhart

The love of the saints is a unifying and vivifying force .... which triumphs over the impenetrability of beings one to another.

Maritain

28 LOVE ME

Procedure: Since he is neither empty nor nothing, a man must exclude others. His being a body means that he crowds out all other bodies from the space he occupies; he stands in their way, takes up room, and is necessarily inhospitable. This means his love is exterior. It is attraction and attachment to another like himself, a bond which links lover and loved one symmetrically without invading or destroying either: indeed it is a love which insists that the lovers shall be as much themselves as possible, and unmistakably alive and unique. Also it is partial. A man has only a certain amount of love to bestow, and a limited field over which to spread it—he can't get close to everyone—so it's his children and near relations, his particular friends, his native city and country, that he loves best, or loves at all. If his love is genuine and not just vague sentiment, the nearest is for him the dearest.

Game: I am playing 'Love Me' when, acting 3rd person, I pretend there is somebody here to be loved, instead of an emptiness to be filled.

Antithesis: The antithesis to the game of 'Love Me' is 'Be Me'. This true 1st-person love is a kind of dying, for only as abolished—as nothing—can I love anyone unreservedly. Only when every defence here has been smashed, and all obstructing thoughts and feelings and judgments have been swept away, do I become perfectly hospitable and loving. The mark of this 1st-person charity is that it is unbounded and undiscriminating, as freely poured out upon the mean and ugly

197

Earth, these solid stars, this weight of body and limb,
Are they not sign and symbol of thy division from Him?

Tennyson

Things are all the same in God: they are God Himself.

Eckhart

In God alone can man meet man.

George Macdonald

The one principle of hell is—'I am my own!'

George Macdonald

as upon the most deserving. It has nothing to do with sentiment or convention or morality, and is always the same. It cannot be produced to order or cultivated, but occurs naturally when I see what I am— this luminous emptiness which obviously has nothing to lose or gain. This love is the inevitable product of this seeing, inseparable from this Brilliance in which all things shine. The reason God is Light as well as Love is that they cannot really be disentangled.

For this 1st person there is neither far nor near (I don't see distance) and all are dear. All are myself, inasmuch as I have nothing to keep them off with: my nothingness and their somethingness unite absolutely. Every one of them is needed to fill this great empty Heart of mine. As extreme heat is easily mistaken for extreme cold, so this 1st-person love is easily mistaken for indifference—but not by one who is practising it.

If anything could be called intrinsically unknowable, it is man.

A.C. Bradley

Whatever has entered through the gate of the six senses is not true treasure.

Zen Saying

Rachel, meaning the interior life, signifies a vision of the source, but Leah, the other sister, means the life of the exterior man, for she had weak eyes.

Eckhart

The reality of the formless, the unreality of that which has form ....
Try to reach with me the palace of nowhere.

Chuang-tzu

To know anything other than oneself is not right knowledge.

Ramana Maharshi

To see oneself is to be clear-sighted.

Lao-tzu

What is more apparent than this Light? In comparison with this Appearance all apparent things are in the utmost degree of imperfection and default.

Rumi

29 INSCRUTABLE

Procedure: Man is virtually invisible. You never see him: you only collect hints about him. Even if you now have him before you, naked and in a strong light and in full front view, much of that view is foreshortened and distorted by perspective, and his sides and back and insides are missing, and so are the near and far views of him in their infinite variety, and so are his past history and future destiny and the worldwide relationships which make him what he is. What you are really seeing is part of a coloured surface, lacking any depth in time and space, while the man himself eludes you. Like everything else, he absconds directly he's carefully looked into, and is indeed unknowable by nature. For to take in all of him would be to take in all that conditions him, which is to say the universe itself. In other words, man is a product of ignorance: it is characteristic of him to be obscure and baffling. If you know very much about him it is no longer him you know, but something much more comprehensive, and as man he has vanished.

Game: I am playing 'Inscrutable' when I persuade myself that I, too, am like that, and opaque to inspection.

Antithesis: I have first-hand, indubitable evidence that I can be fully seen, known, and understood beyond all possibility of error. For I see myself now as this perfectly transparent Emptiness which is free from every complication, from every trick of perspective in space and time, from all history, from anything like parts or divisions or aspects, and is therefore wide open to inspection, obvious, unavoidable,

I see God more real than I see you.

Ramakrishna

O Lord, to me you are wholly visible, and your substance is fused with my nature.

Simeon the New Theologian

Right mentation is the realisation of mind itself, of its pure undifferentiated essence.

Ashvaghosha

Perception that there is nothing to perceive—that is Nirvana, also known as deliverance.

How can there be perception when we are confronted by nothing at all?

We go on perceiving whether objects are present or not.

Hui-hai

How may we perceive our own nature? That which perceives is your own nature.

Hui-hai

Those who have not yet seen him, look! look!

Lin-chi

unmistakable, infinitely perspicuous. If this Clear Void here is seen at all it is seen clearly: it's impossible to half see it or to see half of it. This 1st person cannot be peeped at, nor glimpsed through a haze, nor seen now without being seen for ever and ever, entire and immutable.

It is true I am hidden from outsiders. If the pure in heart shall see God, that is because the pure heart *is* God and not outside Him. I am to be seen only here, by one who coincides with me, who *is* me and this is the guarantee that I am seen truly. Other objects are seen falsely, because the seer is remote from the seen, out of touch with it. Thus a rose is red and pretty only at a distance: close up, it's neither, nor is it a rose. Only here, for the 1st person, do appearance and reality merge and become identical. Only here am I what I look like. 'What am I?' is easy. 'What is he?'—that's the hard, the unanswerable question.

We naturally believe ourselves far more capable of reaching the centre of things than of embracing the circumference ... And yet we need no less capacity for attaining the Nothing than the All.

Pascal

Hsueh-feng went to the forest to cut trees with his disciple, Chang-sheng. 'Do not stop till your axe cuts to the very centre of the tree,' warned the teacher.

The Iron Flute

Till now we have worked from the outside on what is within; now we tarry in the centre and rule what is external. Hitherto it was a service in aid of the Master; now it is a dissemination of the commands of this Master.

The Secret of the Golden Flower

The Qutb (Pole) is he who turns round himself; round him is the revolution of the celestial spheres.

Rumi

How long wilt thou behold the revolution of the water-wheel? Put forth thy head and behold the rapid water that turns it.

Rumi

30 OFF-CENTRE

Procedure: How could any man, who I see to be one of countless others like himself (and he cheerfully admits it) pretend to be the Hub of the universe? In fact, his claim to adulthood, to full membership of society, rests upon the surrender of all his infant claims to centrality. To be completely human is to be off-centre in the universe, on Earth, in the community, even in the family.

Game: No human being can be found right here. It is wilful blindness and mock-modesty for *this* one to play Off-Centre, refusing to see the world as it is actually given—as all of it arranged, region by region, around this unique man-free spot. This is a game which discounts and denies the primary data of experience, replacing them with secondary mental constructions which are dishonestly promoted from being the useful fictions they are into being the self-evident truths they are not.

Antithesis: Nothing is for the 1st person as it is for the 3rd. It isn't that they live in different worlds but rather in very different places in the same world. *This* one is permanently established at the unique, still Centre of all things, while *that* one moves around outside and is subject to all the troubles and trials of that well-ordered but dangerous region. A glance out at my world is enough to show how wonderfully it is organized around this Centre. Wherever I go and however fast I go there, I never leave this Place: in fact, it's the world that is always on the move and readjusting itself around me—I just stay put and let it sort itself out. If a crowd of men are to be admitted

205

Where time has never entered and no form was ever seen, at the centre, the summit of the soul, there God is creating the whole world .... God is none other than the mover, the starter, the source of energy whence the heavens get their power and their spin.

Eckhart

Penetrate into the Centre of Nothingness .... Creep as far as ever thou canst into the truth of thy Nothingness, and then nothing will disquiet thee .... By this Gate thou must enter into the happy land of the living, where thou wilt find the greatest Good, the breadth of Love, the beauty of Justice, the straight line of Equity and Righteousness, and, in sum, every jot and tittle of Perfection.

Molinos

It is as if, in the middle of one's being, there were a non-being .... The Confucians call it the centre of emptiness; the Buddhists, the terrace of life; the Taoists, the ancestral land, or the yellow castle, or the dark pass, or the space of former Heaven.

The Secret of the Golden Flower

The centre of the soul is God.

St. John of the Cross

My soul has dwelt in her centre, which is God.

Marie de l'Incarnation

to my presence, their bodies shrink to the size of toy soldiers, or even smaller, till all are got in. All roads widen specially to take me, closing in again behind; where I am odourless flowers pour out scent, dull landscapes glitter with the brightest colours, the spark kindles a great fire, the silent world breaks out into singing. And if it is sun and mountains and meadows and flowers I am to enjoy all at once, then each leaves room for the others: the sun is no bigger than the flower, or the mountain than the meadow. Objects behave modestly before me: nothing very large or very numerous or very complicated is allowed. Sun and moon and stars, even the galaxies, rotate about this Centre; and so do all terrestrial things, though more erratically. They know their place and have a healthy respect for mine: if they come too near, that's the end of them.

It is the nature of this universe that it cannot do with two Centres.

All our judgments are at first mere perception judgments: they hold good simply for us, that is, for our subjectivity. It is only subsequently that we give them a new reference, namely to an object, and intend that they shall hold good not only for us at the moment but at all other times, and in like manner for all other persons.

Kant

The young artist must recover what Ruskin calls the 'innocence of the eye' ... that is, a sort of childish perception of stains of colour merely as such, without consciousness of what they mean.

William James

The more forward he is in science, the more backward in reality.

Rumi

The effect of society is not only to funnel fictions into our consciousness, but also to prevent the awareness of reality.

Erich Fromm

Cast conformity behind you, and acquaint men at first hand with Deity.

Emerson

Nothing can be more simple than God, either in reality or in our way of understanding.

St Thomas Aquinas

31 EDUCATIONAL LADDER

Procedure: The educational ladder is for climbing out of 1st-person infancy into 3rd-person manhood. All the child's efforts to remain 1st person, all his attempts to remain at the Centre of things, are patiently discouraged, till in the end he is quite happy to be one of millions and truly human.

He learns, for instance, that he's really the same shape as the people around him and there's a top half to his body; that his feet are bigger than his hands; that houses which look small aren't dolls' houses, that trees which look small aren't bushes, that mountains which look small aren't molehills, but that these things are only distant; that all railway lines are really parallel and most rooms rectangular; that even remote cities can be important and ancient empires great; that the Earth isn't a vast platform firmly fixed at the centre of the universe, but a comparatively tiny sphere dancing round an undistinguished star; and so on. All these, and countless other items of practical—indeed, indispensable—knowledge, raise the growing child higher and higher above his primitive self-centredness into that realm of centreless objectivity where he truly belongs. For to be a man is to be no more than one piece in an immense jigsaw puzzle, fitting snugly into the pattern which no piece dominates.

Game: I am playing EL when I make believe that I, too, am educated, or indeed educable.

Antithesis: The fact is that this 1st person cannot climb even the first rung of the 3rd-person ladder. The more cultivated the mind,

The Buddha-dharma is deep, obscure, and unfathomable; but when it is understood, how easy it is!

Lin-chi

Buddhahood is attained when there is no mind to be used for the task.

Hui-chung

Only have no mind of any kind, and this is known as undefiled knowledge.

Huang-po

If he had any discriminating mind, do you think he could discriminate anything?

Shen-hui

The understanding, the memory and the will are in a fearful void, in nothingness. Love this immense void—Love this nothingness since the infinitude of God is in it.

De Caussade

the further from me here, from this spot which is mindless. I see the world naively from this Centre alone, without benefit of education, with no living to earn, no reputation for modesty to keep up, no reforming plans, no thoughts at all about it. As pure Subject, I am perfectly uncritical, perfectly hospitable to every object exactly as it presents itself—not excluding all the arbitrary conventions and educated inventions which go to make up human nature. Oddly enough, though it's the professed goal of education to enable people to overcome all personal bias and see things objectively, as they really are, it is only this uneducated and ineducable 1st person who succeeds, because only this one likes them as they are, and is content to let them alone. The ultimate Subjectivity is the ultimate Objectivity.

I am thinking of Theodore Badal, himself seventy thousand Assyrians and seventy million Assyrians, himself Assyria, and man, standing in a barber's shop, in San Francisco, in 1933, and being, still, himself, the whole race.

William Saroyan

The present moment of a living body does not find its explanation in the moment immediately before, but all the past of the organism must be added to that moment, its heredity—in fact, the whole of a very long history.

Bergson

When a man is awakened he.... melts and perishes. From his very childhood, when he first began to wax and grow, man has done so out of negligence.

Rumi

Henceforth know we no man after the flesh; yea, though we have known Christ after the flesh, yet henceforth know we him no more. Therefore if any man be in Christ, he is a new creature: old things are passed away; behold, all things are become new.

St Paul

And he that sat upon the throne said, Behold I make all things new.

St John the Divine

32 OLD

Procedure: A man is very old. He is a sediment, a huge accumulation, layer upon layer, of racial and individual deposits. He is essentially a preserver, a time-binder, who can never live down his immense past—and no wonder: he is that past. Strip him of his history and you strip him of existence. The whole of him is a living fossil, a museum of the ages: his body and its extensions in the shape of clothes and tools and buildings and cities, his language and social heritage in general, his ever-growing fund of experience functioning as memory and habit and built-in skills—this vast human edifice is its own past surviving in the present. Just as a symphony isn't a symphony in less than (say) half an hour, so man isn't man in less than some thousands and millions of years. He is memory. He is what he was.

Game: I am playing 'Old' when, deliberately overlooking the emptiness of this 1st-person station, I pretend to find here some relics of the past, or anything capable of registering and retaining them.

Antithesis: I am what I am. I find that the only way I can see myself at all is to see myself afresh at this moment, without memory or any carry-over from the past—not as if for the first time, but actually so, with all the surprise and delight of new discovery. I notice that if I'm truly Self-aware at this moment, I'm prepared to find anything here—a flame, a star, a dial, a whole dashboard of dials, blood, fat, anything at all, however improbable or ridiculous; and if, instead, I count on finding here no head, no body, Nothing, or

God makes the world and all things in this present now.

Eckhart

He returns to us anew in His person without interruption; with such new radiance that he seems never to have come to us before.

Ruysbroeck

Too late have I loved Thee, O Thou Beauty of ancient days, yet ever new .... And, behold, Thou wert within, and I abroad.

St Augustine

God himself, then I only lose them. This 1st person is seen, and all seeing is seeing now. This one is seen and not remembered. Man is remembered and hardly seen at all. Unlike him, I'm not to be relied upon. I always come as an astonishment to myself, and can never begin to take myself for granted. I learn nothing about myself, never get used to myself (what is there to learn about and get used to?), and am always introducing myself to myself, bowing with profound respect and the keenest delight (not unmixed with amusement) at this strange meeting. And this is no formality: I truly am brand new, a Melchisedek without history, inheritance, continuity of any kind. Every moment sees me starting from scratch.

Man has much to fall back on. He's a hoarder, with a growing deposit account in the human savings bank, yielding interest. But I am naked and poor, without a penny or a pocket to slip it in. I haven't acquired the saving habit—not even to the extent of saving myself.

Distance is nothing but a phantasy.

Blake

A tenth of an inch difference, and heaven and earth are set apart.

Hsin-hsin Ming

Let subject and object be so oned that the wind cannot pass between them.

Wu-men

Was somebody asking to see the soul?
See, your own shape and countenance, persons, substances, beasts, the trees, the running rivers, the rocks and sands.

Whitman

To know a thing is to become it.

Erigena

All knowledge is, in the strict sense, assimilation.

St Bonaventura

The proper consideration for one of highest spiritual capacity is the absolute unity of knower, knowing, and known.

Gampopa

33 BARGEPOLE

Procedure: What is man? The common-sense answer is that he is what he is visibly continuous and conterminous with, what coincides with him, what he is not parted from by any gap or intervening object. Plainly, in that case, he isn't the star or mountain or man he happens to be looking at: I can see the gap between observer and observed, and I never see them merging. Nor is it that he pushes away the things he sees: he insists they really are remote from him, and as I see it he is right. Distancing is the very framework of society.

Game: All is different when, aping him, I play 'Bargepole', and attempt to thrust away the things I see. His honest procedure of spatial projection becomes, in my 1st-person case, a dishonest game of psychological rejection, a damaging unwillingness to receive what is presented to me here.

Antithesis: What do I add up to? Again, the answer is that I'm what I coincide with, what I'm not parted from in any way. I'm everything that's clearly presented (verb. sap.) right here and now, and not absent by a hair's breadth or an instant. If, when I'm looking at you, absolutely nothing comes between you and me, if no interval of space or time separates us, then you are myself. And if, to clinch the deal, I can find nothing of my own here to put up to you or to put up against you, no contribution to make or influence to exert, why then your invasion is complete, and you are doubly, trebly, infinitely me!

Directly I look at you, at anything at all, I see that these conditions are satisfied. No distance comes between that star and me, that

A sudden perception that Subject and object are one will lead to a deeply mysterious wordless understanding—you will waken to the truth of Zen.

Huang-po

The sun ten thousand legions off, was nigh:
The utmost star,
Though seen from far,
Was present in the apple of my eye.

Traherne

I am blue, I am yellow, I am white;
I am in grass, leaves, trees and flowers;
I am the hills, streams, dales and peaks;
I am the essence of all.

Vasishtha

The possessor of the Mystic Wonder touches and feels with the hand even the moon and the sun, beings of mystic power though they be. He reaches even in the body up to the heaven of Brahma.

Kevaddha Sutra

mountain and me, you and me: however hard and long I stare, I can make out no interval. All those frustrating light-years and miles and inches and millionths of an inch are in this direction quite imaginary: every measuring rod stretching between me and these my objects lies end-on and reduces to a point. It isn't that the star is hard up against me or superimposed upon me: there is no eye here to bump into or face to brush against. These stars and clouds and mountains and men are marvellously suspended right here without anything to hold them in place or to contain them. They are present without addition or subtraction, for I see that there is nothing whatever this side of their coloured surfaces. I am these things because I am No-thing, at no distance from them.

I, 1st person, am all things but myself; he, 3rd person, is nothing but himself—if that. For each limb and feature is visibly remote from every other; nowhere in him can I find self-coincidence; all is scattered and exploded. *His hand is further from his head than the remotest star is from my no-head.* Thus my universe-body (I have no other) is much more intimately mine than his little human body is his. Distant in every part from himself, he isn't really himself. Coinciding in every part with me, he is me. So total is the difference between the lst person and the third.

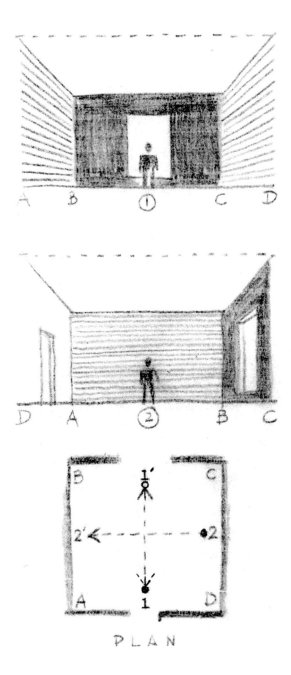

Footnote: The essential move in the Face Game and its derivatives is an imagined shift from the lst-person position (1) here-now to a 3rd-person position (1') there-then—a position from which this original subject can (having turned through 180°), view itself as object, from which this no-thing can make something of itself. The move fails for two reasons. First, it is a fake—I can never jerk myself out of myself, or escape from this here-now into any there-then. Second, in so far as my imagined shift seems to occur, I have only carried my 1st-personhood along with me to the new position, which is now no longer 3rd-person or objective or a thing. 1st person is always 1st person, subject always subject.

All this goes for 'Bargepole'. I take up position (1) in the square room ABCD, looking from the doorway in wall AD towards the window in the opposite wall BC, and I observe that the room has width and height but no depth—1-1' reads as no distance. Dissatisfied with this reading, I jerk myself (in imagination) over to position (2), against the side wall CD, simultaneously turning myself through an angle of 90°. This double manoeuvre is designed to convert what was depth (and therefore non-dimensional) into the dimension of width. But again, the manoeuvre fails, and the room remains two-dimensional at any given instant. If it turns depth (1-1') into width (AB) it does so only at the cost of turning width (BC) into depth (2-2'), and no additional dimension is gained. Distance remains an artefact contributed by me and not given in the present situation. I see the room as three-dimensional only when I am playing the Jerk, and am duplicated and beside myself. When I am wholly self-possessed and present and honest and (in a word) gamefree, the room is as flat as a picture and the picture is in me, and the picture is me. Why, the very fact that a painter can, so convincingly and without any distortion, get the landscape transferred onto his flat canvas, should be a sufficient indication of what that landscape is really like.

Truly, my imperious command (it's really a ridiculous bleat) to all things that they should keep off, is only my fear and hate of them, objectified.

Man is in appearance a derivative of the world, and intrinsically the origin of the world.

Rumi

Within my own being I gaze upon the Creator of the world .... and I unite myself with Him.

Simeon the New Theologian

The soul has a light in her with which she creates all things.

Eckhart

From me everything is born; on me everything is supported; into me everything is again dissolved. I am this Brahman, One-without-a-second ..... Of inconceivable power am I; without eyes I see; without ears I hear.

Kaivalya Upanishad

If you want to hide yourself in the North Star, turn round and fold your hands behind the South Star.

Yang Tai-nien

The ten quarters melt into the spot of our presence.

Hakuin

The Buddha transformed lands of filth, innumerable as the sands of the Ganges, into the pure Dharma-Dhatu.

Hui-hai

34 OUT OF SIGHT

Procedure: Man is powerless either to create or to destroy. He cannot add to or subtract from the universe in the slightest degree. Prudently recognizing this basic limitation, he lives by skilfully remodelling what already exists around him.

Game: The neatest way of hiding something is to make it too obvious. The function of OOS is to blind this 1st person to his immense and self-evident powers of creation and annihilation. The game isn't merely to distrust what is blazingly manifest and always to hand—the most spectacular of one's faculties—but to contrive to overlook it altogether.

Antithesis: The contrast between 1st person and 3rd is here, as in everything else, total. This one causes darkness to descend, dissolving heaven and earth: he only closes his eyes, and not even the nearest and tiniest objects around him suffer any damage. This one commands: 'Let there be light' and heaven and earth emerge from Chaos: he only opens his eyes, and in doing so adds not a dust-grain to the sum of things. This one amputates and destroys these arms and legs: he only raises his head, and his limbs remain as they were. This one at will and instantly re-grows them: he only lowers his head, and adds nothing to his stature. This one wipes out that crowd to the last man: he only turns his back on them. This one recreates them entire: he only turns round again. This one cheers the whole world up: he only smiles. This one calms the whole world: he only takes a pill. This one makes and unmakes many strange worlds: he only

The universe dissolves into me. Wonderful am I! Adoration to Myself! For when the world, from its highest god to its least blade of grass, dissolves, that destruction is not mine.

Astavakra Samhita

When you shut your eyes to the world, it's abolished.

Rumi

Chao-chou visited Pao-shou, who happened to see him coming and turned his back ....Pao-shou's Zen was refined. He made himself like a crystal ball with neither back nor front.

The Iron Flute

If thou desirest peace of mind and true unity of purpose, thou must put all things behind thee, and look upon thyself.

Thomas A'Kempis

There is no longer any need to believe, when one *sees* the truth.

Al-Alawi

We have only to gaze, naught else.

Al-Harraq

stirs and mutters in his sleep. This one absorbs and wholly pacifies the huge mass of the planet, effortlessly, leaving not a leaf or a stone opaque and undissolved, clearing up in a flash all Earth's crimes, crises, wars, disasters: he merely looks skywards. This one takes in and makes nothing of the universe itself: he merely announces that out-of-sight is out-of-mind. This one is the pacification of all things, their unification, their solution, their beginning and ending: he is just one of them.

It feels—and indeed it is—quite natural to put forth these tremendous powers, to perform continually these unique miracles. It is laughably simple and easier than winking, and the secret of it is that there is no eye here to wink, no head to house it, nothing at all but Simplicity itself. Nothing could be more straightforward and effortless than this great work.

The World is unknown, till the Value and Glory of it is seen: till the Beauty and Serviceableness of its parts is considered. When you enter into it, it is an illimited field of Variety and Beauty: where you may lose yourself in the multitude of Wonder and Delights. But it is an happy loss to lose oneself in admiration at one's own Felicity: and to find GOD in exchange for oneself.

Traherne

You never enjoy the World aright, till you see all things in it so perfectly yours, that you cannot desire them any other way: and till you are convinced that all things serve you best in their proper places.

Traherne

If the stars should appear one night in a thousand years, how would men believe and adore; and preserve for many generations the remembrance of the city of God which had once been shown.

Emerson

Man is the dwarf of himself. Once he was permeated and dissolved by spirit. He filled nature with his overflowing currents.... But, having made for himself this huge shell, his waters retired; he no longer fills the veins and veinlets; he is shrunk to a drop. He sees that the structure still fits him, but fits him colossally. Say, rather, once it fitted him, now it corresponds to him from far and on high.

Emerson

35 PAUPER

Procedure: To be a man is to be almost nothing, trying hard to be something. He wants to grow, to improve, to accumulate, but however successful he is he remains unsatisfied. And what is this success? Even a world-emperor claims no more than a particle of the universe, and cannot hold that for long, or really hold it at all. The trouble with man is that he is at once too small and too big to be happy—too small, because all that's outside is threatening; and too big, because all that's inside is threatened, an anxiety to hold and maintain. The resultant discontent is nevertheless an essential ingredient of his human nature, lacking which he would be just tired, and certainly no nearer divinity. To take on a head is to take on headaches—responsibilities, troubles, burdens. The penalty for being somebody is that you are neither nobody and therefore free, nor everybody and therefore at rest. This is the 3rd-person condition.

Game: When I make believe it is the 1st-person condition also, and imagine myself to have something (instead of nothing and therefore everything) and to be somebody (instead of nobody and therefore everybody), I am a millionaire playing pauper.

Antithesis: In fact, I am full-grown, inconceivably rich, and permanently satisfied, for there's nothing I don't possess or contain. How else, indeed, could I have—or want to have—these stars and sun and moon, earth and men and all creatures, for my very own, but the way I have them now? The goods themselves are surely valuable enough, and not lacking in surprise and variety and abundance. Nor

It is not we who are in space, but space that is in us.

Lotze

Zen masters are totally identified with Nature.

D.T. Suzuki

We call the holding in the hand, or the house, or the pocket, *having*; but things so held cannot really be *had*.

George Macdonald

More! More! is the cry of a mistaken soul; less than All cannot satisfy man.

Blake

Pursuing things is like hunting pig: the fatigue is infinite, and it's unlawful to eat a morsel.

Rumi

can I reasonably complain that I still have to take delivery of them. Would I be richer if I could get my hands on them, or label them mine, or somehow fence them in, or perhaps arrange for a legal conveyance? Can they give me the slip, escaping beyond the universe? Is the cage I keep them in unbarred? Or are they dull, arranged without taste or imagination, mean, inconvenient, incongruous? Would I prefer flowers and insects on the horizon and stars at the bottom of the garden, tables and chairs in the sky and mountains and glaciers in the sitting room? Just to ask such questions is to remind myself of the truth: I have everything, and I have it the way I want it. And I can lose none of it. Unlike a man's goods, which are excrescences liable to drop off any moment, mine are interior, secure in the safe-deposit of the Void. How could I own the stars, except by being the space in which they shine; or own anything, except by letting it replace me?

Why do you think that *you* are active? Take the gross example of your arrival here. You left home in a cart, took the train, alighted at the railway station here, got into a cart there and found yourself in this Asramam. When asked, you say that you travelled all the way here from your town. Is it true? Is it not a fact that you remained as you were and there were movements.... all along the way? Just as those movements are confounded with your own, so also the other activities. They are not your own.

Ramana Maharshi

As we rush, as we rush in the Train,
The trees and the houses go wheeling back,
But the starry heavens above the plain
Come flying on our track......

We will rush ever on without fear;
Let the goal be far, the flight be fleet!
For we carry the Heavens with us, dear,
While the Earth slips from our feet!

James Thomson

Whoever says that the Tathagata goes or comes, sits or lies down, he does not understand the meaning of my teaching.

Diamond Sutra

36 A WALK IN THE COUNTRY

Procedure: When a *man* says he is going for a walk in the country, he is talking sense. I see him moving steadily along in a stationary setting of lanes and fields and woods, taking with him no more than his body and the clothes he's wearing. It is only these that are travelling.

Game: When *I* say I am going for a walk in the country, I am talking nonsense and lying to myself. Also I am cheating myself of a most fascinating experience.

Antithesis: Attending to the supposed walker here, I notice that I'm not travelling in the country, at (say) 3 m.p.h., but the country is travelling in me, at many speeds, while I remain quite stationary. I don't mean there is a man standing still here, but the absence of a man (these stumpy limbs popping in and out of the Void certainly aren't a man), a motionless Void filled with the countryside itself, every part of which is in motion. The cottage hedge travels fast, the cottage more slowly, the wood more slowly still, while the hills hardly travel at all. At their different speeds they approach, growing as they come, and then dissolve into the Stillness here. Truly I go for a *country* walk, never for a *man* walk, or even for an *I* walk. This 1st person, which has never moved an inch and never will, may equally well be described as the still Centre of the moving world, or as its still Background.

A handy test of one's Self-awareness is to take a walk and see who is walking. The difference between 1st-person walking and 3rd-

The outward man is the swinging door; the inner man the still hinge.

Eckhart

The scenery changed every day but my pure mind was like a bright moon hanging solitary in the sky. My health grew more robust and my steps were rapid.

Hsu Yun

The only moved thing is matter.

Plotinus

The *lung-gom-pas* of Tibet practise the art of walking great distances at high speed, with a curious bounding gait. This is not so much an athletic achievement as the product of meditation, in which the walker concentrates on his breathing, along with the recitation of a sacred formula. The effect of this concentration upon the ever-stationary 1st person, instead of his ever-shifting environment, is that his energies become abnormally available.

(See A. David-Neel, *With Mystics and Magicians in Tibet.*)

When I cross the bridge, it is the bridge that flows, not the water.

Zen Saying

person walking is both total and sharp: there are no intermediate kinds. Either I am wholly deceived and find a man in motion, or else I am wholly undeceived and find a world in motion. I can switch from one to the other frequently, but I can never mix them.

The real world-tour—a voyage of discovery full of surprise and interest—is consciously 1st-person. Understandably, this sort of travel is much more enjoyable than the other sort, since so much more of the world is involved. More remarkable is how it energizes: one seems tireless. The third effect is paradoxically, how much one observes. Attending only to the still 1st person here, I see the moving world also, very clearly; whereas attending only to the 'still' world there, I do little more than glimpse it. The world is, in fact, rather like a faint star—distinctly seen only through the corner of an eye that is looking elsewhere.

At Ya Chou there are houses with storeys, groves and parks, and plenty of men and horses. Now turn back your thinking to see if there are as many things in that which thinks of them.

Yang-shan Hui-chi

How can there be merits and demerits for me who am without organs, without mind, changeless and formless?

Sankara

He eats Light, do not say he eats bread .... This body which the Shaykh of insight possesses has become something different: do not call it a body.

Rumi

This empty visionary body is no less than the Dharmakaya.

Yung-chia Hsuan-chueh

Be vacuous. Be nothing.

Chuang-tzu

A man should de-form himself of himself.

Eckhart

There is nothing sweeter than to be stripped of body.

Rumi

37 DISSECTING TABLE

Procedure: A man isn't empty or stuffed with cotton-wool, but solid and substantial, filled out skin-tight with the indispensable apparatus of life. Where would he be without his anatomy?

Game: And where would I be with anything of the kind? Playing DT, jerking myself out of myself and conducting an imaginary autopsy, I make out that I am as complicated inside as he is: but the one I'm dissecting is always about 4 feet from me here, and not myself at all.

Antithesis: This is a game I play half-heartedly, for it's a curious fact I have never seriously believed I have any insides, right here. I notice slices of bread-and-butter and cups of tea disappearing at one end, and waste products appearing at the other, but between them I put no oesophagus, stomach, intestines, but only emptiness. The bread-and-butter isn't digested, it just melts away in the mouth—melts away to nothing. One's faeces aren't paraded round the streets, and taken to parties and church and the office in a man-shaped dung-cart: they emerge, newly created, from the Void; and truly one *makes* water. However hard I try, I find that I can never take quite seriously those highly coloured pictures of men and women nonchalantly displaying their exploded interiors, their hidden fantastic worlds of organs and tissues. To humans and animals over there these pictures no doubt apply, but not at all to the hollow one here.

It is the same with all one's embodiments. However much of the universe one takes on here (actually, to live is to take on the lot), I

Emptiness functions mysteriously, vacuity works wonders.

Te-shan

The cat is intent on the mouse-hole because she provisions herself from it.

Rumi

'Thou art as a mirage in the desert that the thirsty man taketh to be water until he cometh unto it and findeth it to be nothing, and where he thought it to be, there findeth he God.' Even so, if thou wert to examine thyself, thou wouldst find it to be naught, and there wouldst thou find God.

Al-Alawi

It is its nature to be natureless.

Eckhart

The Self-nature is no nature.

Hakuin

Release is in the destruction of the substratum.

Itivuttaka

notice it is eviscerated and cleaned out, in contrast to its well-filled counterparts out there. At all levels, this 1st-person body is nobody. For example, take the Earth—this indispensable extension and completion of the human physique. Looking at the Sun from here, it is seen as complete, round and opaque and presumably not a mere fire-balloon. How different is *this* heavenly body, from which the Sun is viewed! It has no inside, no underside, and very little surface. And again, the discrepancy between the belief one lives by and the theory one uses occasionally, for purposes of prediction etc., is very significant. In practice, I'm a Flat-earther, and stories about the soles of the Australians' feet facing mine are just a joke. Nor do I believe I'm poised on a solid ball which is spinning and careering around the universe. And I'm right. Only by jerking myself out of myself could I see myself thus—and then it isn't me any longer.

Thou canst not by *going* reach that place wherein there are no birth, no ageing, no decaying, no falling away, no rising up elsewhere in rebirth.... For, my friend, in this very body, six feet in length,...I do declare to you, you are the world, and the origin of the world, and the ceasing of the world, and likewise the way that leadeth to the ceasing thereof.

Guatama Buddha

In the recesses of the soul all things are present to thee, alive and active in their zenith, in their prime. Why art thou unaware of it? Because thou art not at home.

Eckhart

8th July, 1936. The pet squirrel was watching for an opportunity to run out. The Master remarked: "We all want to rush out: there is no limit to it. Happiness lies indoors and not outdoors."

Talks with Sri Ramana Maharshi

To identify oneself with the body and yet to seek happiness is like attempting to cross a river on the back of an alligator. The body identity is due to extraversion and wandering of the mind.

Ramana Maharshi

Children are always at home. We too are there but are dreaming we are outside.

Ramana Maharshi

38 FULL HOUSE

Procedure: A man inhabits two houses—his bricks-and-mortar house which is a hollow shell, and his flesh-and-blood house which is not a hollow shell, but full of vital apparatus. The man is loose and at large in the one, but his organs are packed tight in the other. In fact, to call his body a house is misleading: it's more like a pyramid or a solid marble statue, obviously.

Game: When I take this sensible and obvious procedure and make out it applies to myself, to this 1st person, I am playing the absurd game of Full House. I am refusing to admit that this bodily house is, in my first-hand experience, very much emptier and more roomy than the most palatial premises it could ever find itself in.

Antithesis: There is a place where, according to the Buddha, there is no birth and no death. How can we get there? Or rather, since he says we are already there, and the goal lies within our very body, how can we enter and look into our own organism? How can we see what it is really like here at home, right on this spot? It is worth trying anything that promises to help us to this insight: hence the following suggestions.

We have no difficulty in seeing what it's like to be in our *bricks-and-mortar* home. This very ordinary and accessible experience, then, may possibly give us some clues to that seemingly more difficult experience—seeing what it's like to be in our *flesh-and-blood* home. Let us then find out whether our outer habitation can throw some light on our inner one, our house illuminate our body. In other words,

There is none dwelling in the house but God.

Rumi

He in whom God dwells has a good lodger.

Eckhart

What means this idol-form, if this is the house of the Ka'ba?
And what means this light of God, if this is a Magian temple?
In the house is a treasure which the universe is too small to hold.
In fine, whoever has found the way into this house is sultan of the
world and Solomon of the time.
Do not sit intoxicated at the door: come into the house quickly; he
is in the dark whose place is the threshold.

Rumi

What is House, and what is Home,
Where with Freedom thou hast room,
And mayest to all tyrants say:
This you cannot take away?....

Seek no more abroad, say I,
House and Home, but turn thine eye
Inward, and observe thy Breast;
There alone dwells solid Rest.
That's a close immuréd Tower
Which can mock all hostile Power.
To thyself a Tenant be,
And inhabit safe and free.

let us take seriously the significant fact that our body has universally been pictured as a kind of house we are somehow inhabiting.[1]

Beginning with the bricks-and-mortar house, the first thing to be noticed is that it has two aspects. Evidently for its owner it is one kind of thing, and for the milkman and postman quite another kind of thing. I distinguish clearly between my house's interior and exterior, between my experience of it from inside and others' experience of it from outside, between my outlook and their inlook, between my view of the *other* houses when I'm at home and my view of *this* house when I'm standing on the pavement opposite. Indeed I'm in little danger of confusing these two aspects, for it is the vast difference between them—a difference of kind and not of degree—which makes this house my home and a place for entertaining. Thus it is perfectly obvious to me, when I'm indoors, that my house is amply spacious but presents no facade (though its shadow on this side of the street and the reflection on the other side, in the windows opposite, may give hints); and perfectly obvious, when I'm outdoors, that my house presents plenty of facade but no living space. It is closed against me. To open it up, I must stop admiring the front elevation and go in.

When at last I care—and dare—to look, I find all this applies not only to my house but to its occupant, to my body. It, also, has two contrasting aspects—interior and exterior, my experience of it from inside and others' experience of it from outside, my outlook and their

---

1 The aptness of the metaphor derives from the fact that, functionally, the body and its housing are one. My house, with its many services, is my body extended, its outgrowth and needful development; and the kind of life I live can only be lived by and in both together, as a single 'biological' unit. It isn't surprising, then, that the two 'houses' should show similarities.

Say not that this House is small,
Girt up in a narrow wall:
In a cleanly sober Mind
Heaven itself full room doth find.
The Infinite Creator can
Dwell in it, and may not Man?
Contented here make thy abode
With thyself and with thy God,
Here, in this sweet privacy,
Mayest thou with thy self agree,
And keep house in peace, though all
The Universe's Fabric fall.

                              Joseph Beaumont

He saw a city set on a hill sloping toward the south, which measured no more than a rod in length and breadth, that is, six cubits and a palm. But when he was brought into the city and looked about him he thought it very spacious....many hundred cubits in length and breadth. It was extraordinary to him that this city which was so spacious within appeared so small when he stood outside.

                              Walter Hilton

inlook, my view of the *other* bodies when I'm in this one and my view of *this* body when I'm out there seeing myself from their point of view. And again, the difference between these two aspects, and the importance of not confusing them, cannot be exaggerated. As with my house so with my body, when I'm at home I find ample room but no facade or face here (my shadow and what I see in the mirror are over there, and the wrong way round anyhow); and when I'm out (as I imagine) I find my face or facade but no room, no interior living space. This body's secret, its marvellous hidden accommodation, is concealed from and closed against all outsiders. To enjoy it I must take up residence and view the property the other way round. I must attend to the inside story. Then I find plenty of room.

Truly the interior of my flesh-and-blood house is immense. Here is an ultra-contemporary design, an open plan indeed, bare of furniture and the walls glass everywhere—all view and no privacy, no hiding place, no dark corners, no shadows. Inside and outside are not so much contrasting as incongruous. How odd that an elevation so small and opaque and complicated should give on a ground-plan so huge and luminous and uncluttered! How odd that one structure should incorporate two such incompatible architectural styles!

Those two aspects are, however, by no means of equal status: the inside matters most. Houses are for living in and looking out of rather than for living out of and looking at, and this is emphatically true of my flesh-and-blood house. Anyway I can't get out. I'm housebound, a lifelong stay-at-home.

Now the astonishing thing is how I make believe quite the reverse of this, how I pretend to myself, crazily, that there is only one aspect of this body, only one view of it—the outsider's. It's as if I were all view in and no view out. It's as if I were dreaming and had locked myself out-of-doors and were doomed to shiver there in the street all the rest of my life, and all the while I am safely indoors and tucked up in bed. Or it's as if I lived in two houses at once: as if, sitting at home in this one and seeing the facade of the one opposite, I were also sitting in the one opposite and seeing the facade of this one, so that the two houses were simultaneously seen as alike, facade to facade, and neither had any room inside. In short, I'm 'beside myself' and 'seeing things' and 'out of my mind'. Sane on the comparatively unimportant subject of my bricks-and-mortar home, I have become quite insane on the all-important subject of my flesh-and-blood home.

This attack of insanity may be described as pushing mock-modesty too far, or as a progressive breakdown in my native self-confidence as an infant, till I will take everybody's word but mine for what only I have any right to pronounce upon. Probably it was because my parents' bricks-and-mortar house was open to them and their guests, and not merely to me, that I was persuaded it was in fact open and commodious, or had any interior aspect at all: I took their word for it. But my flesh-and-blood house is open to no parents or guests. I'm its only tenant, and, alas, I soon come to lack the courage of my tenancy. I soon come to prefer any outsider's story to mine, the insider's. Though all those others are situated elsewhere, and therefore in no position to say, I fall for their story that what's here is a small solid block; and, though I am situated here, and therefore uniquely in a position to say, I dare not contradict them. They are many and adult, I am one and a child: who am I to disagree? Numbers win, and I grow up to adopt unquestioningly—though never whole-heartedly—the majority view. Feebly and foolishly, *I let them tell me what I am.*

There is a curious but unconvincing byplay of the Full House Game called "Mr White Inside Himself" or "Personal Spelaeology". A film, for example, or a children's picture book, tells how Mr White injects himself into his own bloodstream, and then goes on to explore by submarine and by canoe and on foot his own interior topography. No wonder the whole adventure lacks conviction: it may be fun, it may even be an instructive ploy, but this 1st person isn't taken in for a moment. Mr White beside himself, perhaps, or Mr White inside Mr Black, but certainly not Mr White inside himself! The truth is that, though I lack the courage to see what I see—my emptiness in all its simplicity—I also lack the courage to see what my surgeon sees—my fullness in all its complexity. Oscillating between the Devil of his view from over there (how awful to be all that blood-soaked anatomy!) and the Deep Sea of my own view right here (how even more awful to be nothing at all!) I don't know where I am or what I am, in or out, at home or abroad. In a word, I am confused.

But now, coming to my senses, I find that making myself thoroughly at home here in this body, enjoying its unsuspected immensity and openness and light, is the easiest, the most natural thing in the world. More than this, so far from being that one spot in the universe which is obscure (because, says common sense,

I'm on top of it) this living space of mine is the one spot in the universe which I know directly and through and through, for here is no break between seer and seen, no gap in which perspective distortions could arise. Here alone, where seer and seen coincide and knowledge becomes self-knowledge, does knowledge become intimacy, true inside information, penetrating—penetrating indeed to that central reality which gives rise to all my regional appearances and embodiments. I can be wrong about all other people's homes (in fact, to be homes at all, they *must* be very different over there from what they look like here) but not about mine—once I bother to look.

In the last resort, only I know myself, and I know only myself. The holiest saints, the most enlightened sages, the profoundest philosophers, and even modern scientists, are all of them as good as a million miles from here, and therefore perfectly unqualified to tell me what I shall find when, in all simplicity and honesty, I notice not only the habitations I'm looking at, but also the very different habitation I'm looking out of. The fact that other home-lovers do, by and large, tell the same story, is interesting and encouraging, but ultimately irrelevant.

He excels who has sameness of appreciation towards well-wishers, friends, enemies, strangers, neutrals, haters, and kinsmen, and even saints and sinners.

Bhagavadgita

To set up what you like against what you dislike—this is the disease of the mind.

Hsin-hsin Ming

Sell intelligence and buy bewilderment: intelligence is opinion, while bewilderment is vision.

Rumi

I hold no opinions in philosophy.

Wittgenstein

There is nothing true anywhere,
The true is nowhere to be seen;
If you say you see the true,
This seeing is not the true one.

Hui-neng

To know the always-so is to be illumined;
Not to know it, means to go blindly to disaster.
He who knows the always-so has room in him for everything;
He who has room in him for everything is without prejudice.

Tao Te Ching

39 IN MY OPINION

Procedure: A man cannot afford much impartiality. He can't forever sit on the fence but must come down one side or the other, voting for one party, attending one church, marrying one woman, preferring this picture, symphony, book, person, country, to that one. Continued refusal to make up his mind would render him less than human rather than superhuman. Often he has to advise, teach, praise, warn, condemn outright. A real man has beliefs, lets them be known, stands by them.

Certainly the cost is high: he lives in a narrow, artificial world. He sees everything through distorting and coloured human spectacles, adding all manner of social fictions to the data and subtracting what fails to fit in with them. Things are good or bad according to whether they promote or upset his plans, and beautiful or ugly according to convention: thus all sunsets, trees overhanging water, garden flowers, and nubile girls are beautiful, while all weeds, deformities, wounds, sores, decaying things, litter, and filth are ugly. And, on the whole, this procedure works out. Something like it is quite inevitable.

Game: In fact, it is inevitable everywhere but *here*. In this spot it is entirely out of place, no longer a necessary practical procedure, but the unnecessary and rather absurd game of IMO.

Antithesis: As always, the game is stopped by seeing who is playing it. I could differ from you only if I were something myself. What sees itself here as empty cannot put up any resistance or put forward anything of its own, therefore it cannot disagree. Colourless,

My thought should be indifferent to all ideas without exception, including for instance materialism and atheism; it must be equally welcoming and equally reserved with regard to every one of them.

Simone Weil

When there remains neither unbelief nor religion, your body and your soul will disappear; you will then be worthy of the mysteries—if you would fathom them, this is the only way.

Attar

If you can abruptly put everything down, stripped of all thought and deliberation, suddenly you feel as if you had stumbled over a stone and stepped on your own nose. Instantaneously you realise that this sentient consciousness is the true, void, marvellous Wisdom itself. No other wisdom than this can be obtained.

Tsung-kao

it can only take on your colours; featureless, plastic, it looks to you for shape; mirror-like, it can neither reject nor remould you in the slightest, but only become you as you are. This is the true open-mindedness which is also no-mindedness. This is the true wisdom which is wise only in the sense that it finds room for everyone's ideas, however seemingly off-beat or harmful. Like the brainless employer who is clever enough to hire the best brains going and make a fortune out of them, one's infinite wealth of knowledge and savoir-faire isn't really one's own at all. Rejecting no opinions and having none of one's own, one *holds* all opinions without distorting any, and positively revels in their clashing contradictions—for example, those which fill this book. Thus to take in everything with open heart and mind is to see the world as it is, shining with a beauty and a Goodness that are beyond beauty and ugliness and good and evil.

The first of the famous Three Gates, or Three Questions, of master Ts'ung-yueh was: *Where* is your Self-nature?

Hakuin's whole life was shining the light onto the place where he stood.

Abbot Amakuki Sessan

The Sage rejects That but takes This.

Tao Te Ching

Our being *here* is our eternal being.... Many people imagine *here* to have creaturely being, and divine being to be yonder.... It is a popular delusion.

Eckhart

Man gets lost, settles abroad, goes so far out he cannot get back again.... God is a stay-at-home.

Eckhart

What connexion have you with this body? You subsist without it. You are always without it.... So why do you tremble over the body, seeing that you are not with it for a single hour, but are always elsewhere? Where are you, and where is the body? 'You are in one valley, and I am in another.' This body is a great deception,... a great hoodwink.

Rumi

40 SIMPLE LOCATION

Procedure: The plain man has no difficulty in locating himself. He knows where he is, and is all there, present and correct. Like the things around him, he is what he looks like; and what he looks like is a man, and this man stands on the spot he stands on. Thus simply located, he coincides with himself. And when I look at him I take his point: there he is, just as given. Society proceeds on the principle of simple location.

Game: Here, this procedure proves fallacious and unpractical. Indeed it breaks down altogether, though I attempt to perpetuate it as the game of SL, in which I pretend that this spot is inhabited by the man I see in my mirror, instead of all other men.

Antithesis: The 1st person can never be there and the 3rd can never be here: this is my place and that is his. I can never get to man's place, because it retreats at my approach; nor can I ever get away from my place, because it keeps up with me wherever I go. Man is a mirage: when I go looking for him in the place he seemed to be, I find only myself. He's always elsewhere, gone out on business, playing hide-and-seek with himself, a split personality. He never catches up with himself: he can only be observed as absent, because he is essentially an absentee. This 1st person, on the other hand, is all here, Self-coinciding and Self-contained, observable only as present, essentially on the spot.

Thus in man there is an inherent contradiction and absurdity: in so far as he exists at all he is beside himself, unable to pull himself

What manner of men are these? Their object is nothingness and a separation from their corporeal frames. They can sit near a corpse and yet sing, unmoved.

Chuang-tzu

The Spirit thou canst not view, it comes so nigh.
Drink of this Presence! Be not thou a jar
Laden with water, and its lip stone-dry;
Or as a horseman blindly borne afar,
Who never sees the horse beneath his thigh.

Rumi (trans. Nicholson)

People seek it far away—what a pity!
They are like him who, in the midst of water,
Cries out in thirst so imploringly.

Hakuin

Kindle Light in the blessed country ever close at hand.

Hui Ming Ching

together, not all there; and this immense disability he shares with all things. How different he is from this No-thing, from me who am all here, at home to myself, undivided into subject and object or observer and observed: One part of me doesn't hold the rest at arm's length to take a look at itself, nor do I surround myself (as a man must do) with real or imaginary observers in order to see myself through their eyes. For I, 1st person, don't see myself here from there (in my friends), or there from here (in my mirror), but here from here (in myself)—which means I see myself as I really am. Strictly speaking, all 3rd persons are fakes, pretending to be something they are not, and existing in much the same way as phantoms and dreams and optical illusions exist. A man is not himself. Deprive him of the room to stand away from himself, bring his two halves together, and he goes.

God is in, we are out.

Eckhart

None but the Living God has ever gone into this house of mine.

Rumi

God is a stay-at-home.

Eckhart

I gazed into my own heart;
There I saw Him; He was nowhere else.

Rumi

God is nearer to man than his jugular vein.

Koran

Keep yourself within yourself.

Attar

Nothing is good that lies outside.

Plotinus

In this house is a treasure which the universe is too small to hold.

Rumi

Oh, many a one sets out to some place from the spot where the object of his quest is.

Rumi

41 UTOPIA

Procedure: In spite of all the heart-break, man must proceed on the assumption that his circumstances can be and must be vastly improved. He needs to work for the unattainable, for some kind of New Jerusalem or earthly millennium. It is true that the reforms which are most needed are always being postponed, and that those which do come off disappoint, so that Utopia recedes at least as fast as humanity advances. Nevertheless the distant vision stimulates and energizes now, and without it society is moribund. As procedure, it is fairly effective.

Game: As a game, played by this 1st person, 'Utopia' is both ineffective and nonsensical. When I locate Perfection out there tomorrow, instead of here today, I make sure of missing it.

Antithesis: If I'm in Paris and interested in the Mona Lisa, I don't go round asking *what* she's like, but *where* and *when* she's to be seen, and the quickest way there. Similarly, if I'm serious about the good life, and I've reason to think that Perfection itself may be found right here and now, at the very centre of my being, I don't waste time collecting second-hand impressions out there of what it might be like. I track it down, call on myself here, and go on knocking till I get an answer, because I can be sure of finding myself in.

Man, on the other hand, is always out. He lives a mysterious and semi-fictional life in a wholly inaccessible country called Over There Soon, the Yonder Land whose very wretchedness cannot be got at. *There* is bondage, misery, limitation, pain, sorrow, decay, death—

What, then, is the spirit? The Spirit of here and now.
And the God? The God of here and now.

Plotinus

Everyone who attaches importance to the external becomes internally without resource.

Chuang-tzu

The soul will find her happiness in self-perception.

Eckhart

The circle of life and death is like a raging fire and is attended by immeasurable sorrow.
Cultivate the Mahayana heart.

Sutra on the Eight Awakenings

always next-door, always in the offing and never brought right home to oneself. This is indeed the firm ground of optimism—that evil won't bear close inspection. It's dislocated. It's out. And the first thing is to see it there.

Enlightenment is a two-stage spring-clean—a good turn-out, then everything back again, all polished and sweet-smelling. First, this body-mind with all its functions and contents, down to the heaviest and oldest heirlooms, must be got out of Here and stowed over There, leaving this Room quite empty. All must be seen out, till no speck of psycho-physical dust can find a hiding place. Only when this room is nothing but Room is it ready to receive the furniture again—marvellously dry-cleaned and polished and better than new. In fact, it's this perfect Room which now *makes* the furniture. Really they are inseparable, and so are the two stages of their refurbishing.

But again I said, Who made me? Who set this in me, and implanted in me this root of bitterness?

St Augustine

Si necessitatis est, peccatum non est.

Pelagius

What blame requires is that, however far back we go in setting out the causes of your act, we shall never come to a time at which a set of purely external circumstances, i.e. not involving you and your will, formed a complete cause of your act.

John Wisdom

Others gain authority over you if you possess a will distinct from God's will.

Rabbi Nahman of Bratzlav

It is because we are not near enough to Thee to partake of Thy liberty that we want a liberty of our own different from Thine.

George Macdonald

For God, freedom is necessary.

Vladimir Soloviev

Where the spirit of the Lord is, there is liberty.

St Paul

42 PERSONAL RESPONSIBILITY

Procedure: Man carries on as if he were a free agent, self-determining and unconditioned. On the whole this procedure works. Society must attribute personal responsibility to each of its members.

Game: When I, 1st person, claim this kind of personal responsibility—this 3rd-person freedom—I am claiming what doesn't exist and being thoroughly dishonest. The man I see in my mirror is indeed bound. For he contains only a fraction of all he needs to be himself. Take away his clothes, tools, home, city, crops, earth, air, sunshine, and the space that holds them all, and where is he? Take away his language, and the immense web of social relationships which determine his personality, and he's an animal—if that. And when the more obvious social pressures are lifted, and he's left to behave as he likes, what he likes is what his total past likes: all history moulds his present actions, and true spontaneity is out of the question. Really he's too small to be held responsible for his behaviour. To know all would be to forgive all, because in the end it's the All which is responsible. Any limitation makes nonsense of freedom.

Antithesis: Everything short of the Whole is too small to be free. Only the Whole is self-contained, subject to no outside influences, complete, and quite alone. And when I claim to be free I am really claiming—with what effrontery!—to be the Whole.

Now it's a fact that I've always *felt* free, and never seriously questioned the feeling. What's more, I can make little sense of my life unless I really *am* free. Whenever I choose this and not that, and

With the removal of the 'I' illusion, the world with all its multiplicities will disappear, and if there is anything left which can act, this one will act with utmost freedom, with fearlessness, like the Dharma-king himself, indeed as the One.

D. T. Suzuki

In this Fourth Valley the lightning of power, which is the discovery of your own resources, of self-sufficiency, blazes up so that the heat consumes a hundred worlds.

Attar

Monk: How can one be emancipated?

Hui-Hai: From the start there is no bondage, so what is the use of seeking to be freed? Act as you please, go on as you feel—without a second thought. This is the incomparable way.

The truth shall make you free.

Jesus

whenever I accept full responsibility for all I've done, I'm claiming that I have always been a free agent. How could I take any blame or praise for actions which I recognize as predetermined? My whole being rises up and declares that I'm no tool and that I'm doing what I want to do, and all the seemingly overwhelming evidence to the contrary is nonsense.

There is only one explanation of this remarkable fact: it is the still more remarkable fact that I *include* everything by which I'm conditioned. That is to say, I am free; and I am free because this 1st person is the only one who can be free—the Whole—and not a man at all. And directly I see this plain truth and realize Who I am, I arrive where I have always been—at Liberty's only source. Now I am really gay and carefree.

From meditating on Him there arises, on the dissolution of the body, the third state, that of universal lordship; but only he who is alone is satisfied.

Svetasvatara Upanishad

When he awakens and sees nobody in the house but himself, then he says, 'I am, and there is nobody other than I.'

Rumi

Turn thy face towards thine own face: thou hast no kinsman but thyself.

Rumi

The only being that *is* is the Tao-man who, depending on nothing, is this moment listening to my talk on the Dharma.

Lin-chi

P'ang-yun: Who is the person who stands all alone without a companion among the ten thousand things?
Ma-tzu: I'll tell you when you swallow the West River in one gulp.

I am alone .... I am the supreme Brahman! I am the Lord of the Universe! Such is the settled conviction of the *Mukta;* all other experiences lead to bondage.

Devikalottara

43 IN COMPANY

Procedure: One man is a contradiction in terms. Even Robinson Crusoe isn't on his own. He thinks of men, does things their way and as if for their approval, compares himself with them, is continually under their influence. A man *is* other men. His manhood is extrinsic, embracing mankind in general and his country and community in particular. Strictly speaking, there is no 3rd person singular, but only 3rd persons plural.

Game: Conversely, there are no 1st persons plural, but only 1st person singular—this unique one here who is always alone. I am playing the game of 'In Company' when, not daring to face this loneliness, I persuade myself I am one of many and not very different from the people around.

Antithesis: What is it like, how does it feel, to be this lonely one, absolutely on my own? It's to feel lightsome and unconcerned, to breathe a great sigh of relief. It's to enjoy the sweet relaxation of having no external authority to please and make up to. It's to have won through, to be victorious over the world, and at peace at last. It's to have settled final accounts with death and evil, to have nothing to lose or gain, and to be desireless. And, incidentally, it's to hold no very high opinion of oneself, no low opinion, no opinion at all, seeing that no standards apply to this incomparable one.

Being thus lonesome, without a soul to confide in or bear one company, suggests an experience that is either dull or else terrifying—since it could hardly be both at once. In fact, it is the reverse of both.

Monk: What is the most wonderful thing?
Pai-chang: I sit alone on the peak of Mount Daiyu.

The strange fact is that when a door opens and a light shines from an unknown source into the dark chamber of consciousness, all time- and space-limitations dissolve away, and we make a Simhanada (lion-roar), 'Before Abraham was, I am,' or 'I alone am the honoured one above and below all the heavens.'

D.T. Suzuki

Fear comes when there is a second.

Brihadaranyaka Upanishad

There shall no man see me, and live.

Exodus

Only when I see my aloneness am I incapable of boredom. I adore my own company and every moment of it is a delight. And *only* when there's not a particle left outside me has all possibility of terror gone: one little thing lost to me, a single refugee from my embrace, and I'm threatened, I'm lost. It's only when I am all things and no differences remain that I'm safe Home, comfortable and easy.

Again, this loneliness may suggest lovelessness, since nobody's left to love. Paradoxically, it isn't in practice like that at all. One's love is so total that it leaves nothing and nobody out in the cold. One cannot bear not to be all things everywhere and always: all alienation is Self-alienation, all separation is separation from oneself. It is misery to be confined to this man, this sex, this nation, this colour, this religion, this planet; it is misery not to be the company one sees oneself in. To be Alone is the only joy which is quite unmixed with sorrow, the only love which is untinged with anxiety.

In the Way of search for God everything is upside down.

Rumi

In Heaven all opposites, such as prohibition and permission, guilt and guiltlessness, are one unified whole.

Rabbi Hayyim of Mogielnica

The place wherein Thou art found unveiled is girt round with the coincidence of contradictories, and this is the wall of Paradise wherein Thou dost abide. The door whereof is guarded by the most proud spirit of Reason, and, unless he be vanquished, the way in will not lie open.

Nicholas of Cusa

God is a not-God.

Eckhart

He is all contradictions.

Vivekananda

That thou mayest have pleasure in everything, seek pleasure in nothing.
That thou mayest know everything, seek to know nothing.
That thou mayest possess all things, seek to possess nothing.

St John of the Cross

44 YES OR NO

Procedure: Either it is so, or else it isn't: it can't be both at once. It can't be a spade *and* a shovel, black *and* white, true *and* untrue, good *and* evil, myself *and* everything but myself. That's the way the human mind works; and if it didn't, there could be no law-courts, trade, learning, discussion, or indeed any civilization at all. Fortunately, man has no use for paradox. He inhabits a common-sense region where it doesn't bear rule, where opposites remain opposed and extremes never meet.

Game: They meet here, in my region, where only paradox works out in the end, and nothing is itself apart from its opposite—a fact which the game of Yes or No is concerned to conceal.

Antithesis: Here are a few examples of 1st-person logic:

My knowledge is ignorance. In this alert, open, empty receptacle everything falls into place without friction or overlapping or leftovers, and here shines as itself. But if any learning, memories, opinions, expectations are brought to bear, they upset and hide it.

My wealth is poverty. A man divides the universe into two parts, one his and the other not his, and so can never be well off. I disclaim the lot, seeing that I have nothing and am nothing—and that this Nothing is my Hold-all, my inexhaustible Purse.

My love is indifference. I notice that when I love someone without any reservations I want nothing of him—not his improvement, not his presence, not his love returned, not even his good fortune.

The blind one found the jewel;
The one without fingers picked it up;
The one with no neck put it on.

Taittiriya Aranyaka

Verily, verily, I say unto you, Except a corn of wheat fall into the ground and die, it abideth alone: but if it die, it bringeth forth much fruit.

He that loveth his life shall lose it; and he that hateth his life in this world shall keep it unto life eternal.

Jesus

While alive be a dead man, thoroughly dead.

Bunan

See, where thou nothing seest;
go, where thou canst not go;
Hear, where there is no sound;
then where God speaks art thou.

Angelus Silesius (trans. W.R. Trask)

All glorification of me cometh short of the measure, as doth all contempt.

Al-Alawi

My power is weakness. When I see my total impotence, even in those nearer regions where I might seem to exercise some control, and just let things happen, then a miracle happens too: I see that everything is going on as I want it.

My existence is non-existence. I see that others exist, and that I do not. Yet it is precisely because of this freedom from existence, thinghood, substance, that this 1st person alone really is, and provides the field in which 3rd persons eke out a secondary and dependent kind of existence.

If further examples of the wildest 1st-person paradox are required, this book is full of them. This 1st person is all contradictions—and their resolution. The Reconciliation of all the world's opposites lies right here, at the Centre of it.

Know then thyself, presume not God to scan,
The proper study of mankind is man.

Pope

What I call perfection of vision is not seeing others but oneself.

Chuang-tzu

What is the use of knowing about everything else when you do not yet know who you are? ... Self-enquiry is the one infallible means, the only direct one, to realise the unconditioned, absolute Being that you really are.

Ramana Maharshi

O Light eternal, who abidest in Thyself, and, self-knowing and self-known, dost love, and smile upon, Thyself!

Dante

God knows nothing but himself alone .... God loves nothing but himself.

Eckhart

God thinks only upon himself.

Aristotle

None but God has contemplated the beauty of God.

Rumi

45 HUMANIST ASSOCIATION

Procedure: Self-interest is the law: it's minding one's own business that makes the world go round. Man's concern is man, otherwise he would neither be himself nor do justice to himself. The proper study of mankind is human nature, and the survival and well-being of the species—and God help man when he neglects it. (But perhaps God won't help him; maybe He's too busy attending to His own business, namely Himself!)

Man's success in this self-study requires that he shall view himself coolly, according himself no divine or privileged status, constructing around himself no sacred enclosure into which the profane scientist is forbidden to pry. Thus he rightly sees himself as a close relation of the higher apes, hardly distinguishable from them in his anatomy and physiology and embryology. And, provided he takes his embryology seriously (no easy task!) he has even to admit that quite recently, in his own lifetime, he has been vastly the inferior of any ape, any mammal, any vertebrate. Again, if he is honest, he must regard his manhood as no mere individual achievement, but as a coming into the family fortune: he takes on the immense social heritage that awaits him at birth. Certainly it's his job, it's in his interest, to gain possession of this richly humanized world that lies about him, without asking any very profound questions. In short, the reasonable man is reasonably modest, and a humanist in practice—if not in theory or in name.

Game: The proper study of the 1st person, similarly, is this 1st person, leading to Self-discovery and clearly seeing there is no man

None has vision of God but he who can say with Mansur, 'I am God'.

Rumi

To comprehend and to understand God above all similitudes, such as He is in Himself, is to be God with God, without intermediary .... Here there is nothing but an eternal seeing and staring at that Light, by that Light, and in that Light.

Ruysbroeck

The soul God's kingdom dawns in ... her none durst counsel and instruct.

Eckhart

here. In other words, I, too, have to mind my own business—or I shall be playing the game of 'Humanist Association' and attempting, not merely to mind others' business out there, but also to persuade myself that it is my business right here. A glance at the immense difference between them and myself should show me that such confusion is dishonest, ridiculous, and unnecessary.

Antithesis: My life's work is to find out for myself what this spot is like and who lives here, right now. To do this it is essential to be deaf to all the voices out there telling me what it looks like here—as if they could know, or had any right to pronounce on such a question, or were in any position to do so! How, indeed, could I miss such an opportunity and go on overlooking this looker, who is uniquely stationed and equipped for Self-examination? How could I contain, or rather be, my own Secret, and pursue anything but that Secret? Even more so because, viewed from here, it is the most open of all secrets.

When the Self is seen, heard, thought of, known, everything becomes known.

Brihadaranyaka Upanishad

All-knowledge is what constitutes the essence of Buddhahood. It does not mean that the Buddha knows every individual thing, but that he has grasped the fundamental principle of existence and that he has penetrated deep down into the centre of his own being.

D.T. Suzuki on *The Gandavyuha Sutra*

If I knew myself as intimately as I ought, I should have perfect knowledge of all creatures.

Eckhart

Phenomena are real when experienced as the Self and illusory when seen apart from the Self.

Ramana Maharshi

All ideas, in so far as they have reference to God, are true.

Spinoza

God is the supreme intelligible and the first principle of all our knowing.

St Bonaventura

Ignorance of the Self is the one source of all worldly knowledge.

Maha Yoga

46 IGNORAMUS

Procedure: Science is necessarily as much a confession of ignorance as a claim to knowledge of the universe. With every advance, the country to be explored opens out. And even if some of the basic 'laws of nature' are now disclosing themselves, the objects that 'obey' them remain virtually inscrutable: the arrangement, behaviour, history of all the parts and particles of the universe defy imagination, let alone inspection. And such inspection as can be made is superficial, a study of appearances: what gives rise to the appearances remains hidden. Knowledge about things (such as it is) goes with ignorance of what they really are.

Game: Knowledge of what things really are is a 1st-person prerogative, for the 1st person alone has access to the very heart of one piece of the world, namely himself as a sample of the whole, and through that fair sample to all the rest. I am playing the game of 'Ignoramus' when (ignoring my 1st-person prerogative and taking my cue from 3rd-person procedure) I make out that I, too, am ignorant and superficial, merely scratching at the surface of things.

Antithesis: When not playing games, the 1st person is indeed omniscient. It is true that I'm almost totally (and altogether blissfully) ignorant concerning the immense array of facts (most of them unspeakably dreary) ranging from the remotest stars to every particle of this hand, with all their tangled histories. If this is omniscience, then I'm not interested: the universe consists of things I don't wish to know. This kind of all-knowing would only be fussing and pettiness

All bodies and all the world are maintained in being by forgetfulness.

Rumi

Thou art of purer eyes than to behold evil.

Habakkuk

Learning consists in adding to one's stock day by day. The practice of Tao consists in subtracting day by day.

Lao-tzu

Prajna is utterly pure and does not contain a single thing.... As this nirvanic substance, Prajna, is endowed with functions countless as the sands of the Ganges, there is not a thing which can escape its knowledge.

Hui-hai

Since you have reached the object of your search, O elegant one, the search for knowledge has now become evil.

Rumi

Hung-jen, asked why he made Hui-neng his successor, replied: "He's the only one of my 500 disciples who doesn't understand Buddhism."

multiplied to infinity, and quite absurd. The true omniscience is indeed the opposite of mere factual information, and perfectly simple. It is 1st person seeing into 1st person here and now and finding, precisely, just Simplicity—this endless, indivisible, entire, speckless Void which has nothing to part it from any other void. Thus it is seen (it sees itself, rather) not as a mere sample, but as what actually lies entire and for ever at the heart of everything, the central reality which gives rise to all regional appearances, the inside story of the world, the unitary truth behind the world's infinitely varied mock-ups. Particular bits of knowledge about the world are the province of particular bits of the world—the more particular the more superficial, the further from the underlying truth. Only the 1st person's self-knowledge is neither particular nor superficial, but universal and profound.

The Way is like an empty vessel that yet may be drawn from without ever needing to be filled. It is bottomless; the very progenitor of all things in the world.

Tao Te Ching

Non-existence is God's factory.

Rumi

The Worker is hidden in the workshop: go you and in the workshop see Him plain ….
Since the workshop is the dwelling-place of the Worker, he that is outside is unaware of Him.
Come, then, into the workshop, that is to say, non-existence.

Rumi

When the soul enters into her ground, into the innermost recesses of her being, divine power suddenly pours into her.

Eckhart

Strength is in visioning the empty.

The Secret of the Golden Flower

God is my strength and power.

II Samuel

47 NO MERLIN

Procedure: Man's partial control over his environment involves his giving up all infantile and primitive attempts at magical or supernatural interference with it. Surrendering his early pretensions to omnipotence, submitting to outer necessity and observing its rules, he patiently achieves what little power he is capable of. There are no short cuts to what he wants.

Game: There *is* a short cut to getting what I want. But I cannot take it till I stop playing No Merlin, which is the game of pretending I am no better off than the 3rd persons plural I find around me.

Antithesis: If I'm omnipotent, how is it I can't will that chair opposite to move over one inch to the left, or that fly on the window to drop dead? I try again, harder—and still nothing happens! Even this human body (what there is of it around here)—let alone the universe—refuses to take my orders, and is in no hurry to recover from a common cold.

Well, if there is an all-powerful being, what does he do? Does he promote, design, make, operate, and supervise the universe in all its inconceivable intricacy? If so, I'm certainly not such a one. Nor can I find a scrap of evidence for any such monster of efficiency as this cosmic Works Manager. In fact, he is only the 3rd-person human blown up to infinity, and nothing to do with this 1st person. I'm not like that at all. What there is evidence for—1st-hand evidence right here—is quite another sort of divinity: not the over-worked manager but the whole Works, this ever-present, clearly visible Void which is

God's Holy Will is the centre from which all we do must radiate; all else is mere weariness and excitement.

Jean Pierre Camus

The creature hath nothing else in its power but the free use of its will, and its free will hath no other power but that of concurring with, or resisting, the working of God in nature.

William Law

Obey the nature of things, and you are in concord with the Way, calm and easy and free from annoyance ....
The Enlightened have no likes and dislikes.

Hsin-hsin Ming

Sanctity consists in *willing* what happens to us by God's order.

De Caussade

If we understood how to see in each moment some manifestation of the will of God we should find therein also all that our hearts could desire.

De Caussade

True wisdom is learning to wish that each thing should come to pass as it does.

Epictetus

the primary producer, this Factory of non-existence endlessly turning out all that exists, this central Generator which, supplying all the world's power, itself runs on no fuel whatever, on sheer Nothingness. Fed from this Source, that little man I see in my mirror is powerless to divert the flow of its energies by a hair's-breadth from their course. No wonder he can't by wishing shift that chair. Even if he were to push it over with his foot, the action would really be Another's.

In fact, it would be truly *mine,* a function of the infinite power streaming continually from this Void which I am. And why should I want to work petty miracles on chairs and flies when the whole Creation is the non-stop Miracle of This, and therefore all of it just as I like it to be? If I find fault and want to meddle with anything, it's not this 1st person who feels that way. The fault-finding, too, is all right. This Factory authorizes all its products, but doesn't expect them to authorize each other.

A man's Me is the sum total of all that he *can* call his, not only his body and his psychic powers, but his clothes and his house, his wife and children, his ancestors and friends, his reputation and works, his lands and horses, and yacht and bank-account.

William James

He drew a circle that shut me out—
Heretic, rebel, a thing to flout.
But Love and I had the wit to win:
We drew a circle that took him in!

Edwin Markham

Up then, noble soul! Put on thy jumping shoes which are intellect and love, and overleap the worship of thy mental powers, overleap thine understanding and spring into the heart of God, into his hiddenness where thou art hidden from all creatures.

Eckhart

The streets were mine, the temple was mine, the people were mine, their clothes and gold and silver were mine, as much as their sparkling eyes, fair skins and ruddy faces. The skies were mine, and so were the sun and moon and stars, and all the world was mine.

Traherne

The human frame is as large as Mount Sumeru.

Diamond Sutra

48 ALL THERE

Procedure: The sane man is all there. This is the essentially human, 3rd-person condition.

Game: I, on the other hand, am all *here*—by definition as well as by introspection. This is the essentially 1st-person, non-human, condition; and my besetting insanity is the delusion that I am 3rd-person and all *there.*

Antithesis: Let me consider the way I use this word *here.* When I say "Come here" what do I mean? I mean: "Come to this point, this ink-dot I'm now making on this paper, or come to my right hand, or come to where this body is, or come to this room or house or town of mine, or come to this country or continent or planet or even solar system—anyway, come *here* from over there, to *this* place from that, to *mine* from yours." My own HERE and THIS and MINE, in that case, clearly range from practically nothing to practically everything under the sun, and beyond the sun.

Nor is this 1st-person elasticity a useful fiction or accident of grammar. I speak as I feel. Automatically this 'I' swells or shrinks to fit each occasion. Thus I don't sit on the seat of my pants which are draped on a chair which is screwed to the floor of a plane which flies: quite simply, *I fly*—all the fifty tons of me. I don't grasp a gun which fires a bullet which kills a man: I, gun and all, kill him—and the law agrees with me. I don't command a division which uses arms which lose a battle: I lose, and take the consequences. I don't engage the services of a neutron in order to smash an atom-nucleus: I smash it.

Bodhisattvas are able to expand their bodies to the ends of the universe.

Gandavyuha Sutra

To get into mystical union with Nature is Illumination.

Tao-sheng

The whole great Earth is nothing but you.

Hsueh-feng

The Great Earth doesn't contain a speck of dust.

Zen Saying

Since He made thy piece of earth a man, thou shouldst recognise the real nature of the entire sum of the particles of earth; that from that standpoint they are dead and from this standpoint they are living.

Rumi

Here, form is void.

The Heart Sutra

If ye pass beyond form, O friends, 'tis Paradise and rose-gardens within rose-gardens. When thou has broken and destroyed thine own form, thou has learned to break the form of everything.

Rumi

That's how I talk and that's how I feel. I am as much or as little of the universe as I need for doing what I am doing.

Nor is this magnificent (but how unsuspected!) elasticity only a matter of language and of feeling: its practical consequences are immense. It makes a difference if I identify myself with something smaller than a man, such as one of his organs to the detriment of the others. It makes a lot of difference if I identify myself with something bigger than a man, and am happy to kill and be killed for the sake of family or country or race, or even (in the event of interplanetary war) of Earth herself. And it makes the world of difference if I take on the entire world, caring for and loving every creature without exception or preference, till all are embraced *here,* and at once lost and saved in this Omnipresence.

And even when, not content with being simply myself and all here and one, I play the Jerk and divide myself (as if I could!) in two to view myself from out there, I am driven in the end to the same conclusion. As mere man, at the strictly human level, I am a mirage that will stand neither close nor distant inspection. For this man (as seen by the *receding* observer) is not himself without his not-self—without his extended physique, comprising his clothes, tools, house, city, country, planet, sun, galaxy: cut off from this universe-body, he's not human, not alive, not anything at all. And again: (as seen by the *approaching* observer) he's not seen truly till he's resolved into a community of organs, each of which is 'really' a community of cells, each of which is 'really' a community of molecules, and so on down to the featureless substratum, to the central immateriality

289

Thy inorganic matter will become seeing and speaking.

Rumi

A monk asked Ch'ang-sha: "How can you turn mountains and rivers and the earth into Self?"
"How can you turn Self into mountains and rivers and the earth?" returned the Master.

When expanded, it fills the Dharmadhatu, and when contracted it is finer than a fine hair. It is clear, solitary and bright; it lacks nothing; it cannot be seen by the eye or heard by the ear; it is nameless. An ancient said: "To say it is like something is to miss it." Just see it yourselves, for there is nothing else.

Lin-chi

Through the Unity shall everyone find himself. Through knowledge shall he be purified from a manifold creature to a unity, in that like a fire he absorbs the material in himself, darkness with light, death with life.

Gospel of Truth

The Tathagata divides his own body into innumerable bodies, and also restores an infinite number of bodies to one body. Now he becomes cities, villages, houses ... Now he has a large body, now he has a small body.

Mahaparinirvana Sutra

or Void, which he really *is*. So he turns out to be, when thoroughly investigated, the All-Nothing, the One who is both totally absent from the world and totally present; and all the steps—all the degrees of his embodiment and disembodiment—on the way to that double goal are no more real than he is.

It's the first step which counts. Once I start consciously incorporating anything beyond man—starting with this jacket (a sloughable skin) and this pen (an easily grown and easily amputated sixth finger)—there's no halting my growth till I incorporate everything. And once I start looking into what I'm made of, there's no halting my ungrowth till I incorporate nothing whatever. Once I admit I'm what I look like from *every* station and *every* range, and what I feel like, and feel for, and take on, I must in the end come to Self-recognition.

In fact, of course, this self-division is impossible: I am never over there. And even the slightest trace of a body *here* is an illusion, dispelled at once by honest Self-inspection. In place of the body is a real treasure-house. Having cracked this safe (called Form) and got at its priceless Jewel (called the Void), I hold the key to every safe in the world; now every Form is Void, and every Void is here, and one and the same. Taking myself (provisionally) to be this small but wholly reliable specimen or sample of the world, and knowing its inside story, I know—and indeed I am—the Whole Story. Being the clarification, the voiding, indeed the enlightenment of every one of the inhabitants of this little human body, I must go on to become the enlightenment of all my greater bodies and their inhabitants up to the

The illumined man liberates his inner living beings even before they take shape in his own self.

Hui-hai

When you have truly renounced the mind, you will see the whole universe in your Self.

Vasishtha

He who sees the Unconscious is able to produce all things: he who sees the Unconscious is able to take in all things.

Shen-hui

He is like a lion in the shape of a cow: behold him from afar but do not investigate him.

Rumi

The eyes of my soul were opened, and I beheld the plenitude of God, whereby I did comprehend the whole world, both here and beyond the sea, and the abyss and all things else and therein I beheld naught save the divine Power in a manner assuredly indescribable, so that through excess of marvelling the soul cried with a loud voice, saying: "This world is full of God".

Angela of Foligno

Cosmos itself. All that opaque, vast, inert, dreadfully complex mass is instantly dissolved, unified, and illuminated through and through, in this shadowless Omnipresence.

Everything thou hearest or seest says nothing, shows nothing to thee but what either eternal light or eternal darkness has brought forth; for as day and night divide the whole of our time, so heaven and hell divide all our thoughts,words and actions.

William Law

And God divided the light from the darkness.

Genesis

So he drove out the man; and he placed at the east of the Garden of Eden Cherubims, and a flaming sword which turned every way, to keep the way of the tree of life.

Genesis

Think not that I am come to send peace on earth: I came not to send peace, but a sword.

Jesus

He knows I am wielding the sword against myself: I am Him in reality and He is Me.

Rumi

All except God are enemies.

Rumi

49 BLUR

Procedure: Man is man because, prudently, he declines to look too carefully into what it is to be a man. He cannot afford to admit that he is a regional appearance of a central Reality that is far from human; he cannot acknowledge how narrow and strict his limitations are, because if he did so he would no longer be human. If he were to become self-aware he would not be himself. Thus it is his very nature to be obscure and imprecise, with all his outlines blurred. Man is no more than man glimpsed, a twilight figure.

Game: Conversely, it is the very nature of the 1st person to be brilliantly clear. I am truly myself only when I am thoroughly Self-aware, because this awareness is my essence: seeing what I am is being what I am. Directly I lose sight of myself I'm no longer myself: I'm playing 'Blur' as if I were 3rd person.

Antithesis: To play this game is to be in a muddle. It is vastly to overrate human appearances and vastly to underrate what they are appearances of; it is to think far too much of myself and far too little of mySelf; it is to fail in every way to distinguish that world from This, and so make the worst of both. Paradoxically, while I pretend that—playing the human, 3rd person role—I have a little freedom or originality or power or spirit or divinity, I lack them all and am in fact nothing; but directly I take this truth to heart, I am evidently the Nothing whose other aspect is the All that contains every virtue to perfection. Then I am the unkindly Light that shows up the total darkness of that man I see in my mirror. The razor-keen Sword of

What relation exists between the attributes of God and those of a handful of earth? What relation exists between the attributes of him who is originated in time and those of the Eternal One?

Rumi

God is different from all things, and (what is stranger) there is nothing even similar to him.

Dionysius the Areopagite

To remove his bondage the wise man should discriminate between the Self and the non-Self. By that alone he comes to know his own Self as Existence-Knowledge-Bliss Absolute, and becomes happy.

Sankara

The stupid man thinks he is the body, the learned man thinks he is a mixture of body and soul, the Sage by discrimination looks upon the eternal Atman as his Self, and realises: "I am Brahman."

Sankara

Do not make your home the land of men: do your own work, don't do the work of a stranger. Who is the stranger? Your earthen body, for the sake of which is your sorrow.

Rumi

Discrimination does indeed sort things out; cutting clean through every strand of connecting tissue between him there and the 1st person here. It deals absolute death to him and absolute life to me, leaving no half-life anywhere.

Unlike the bogus sort, real spirituality is severely precise, the enemy of all woolliness and amiable compromise. The fact that, ultimately, even the Sword of Discrimination is sheathed (God and man, 1st person and 3rd, Light and darkness, all uniting in the undifferentiated Essence) does nothing to blunt its edge meanwhile. On the contrary, premature unification makes the final Unity impossible. One's warm-hearted but vague moods of being at one with God and Nature and man—these are fine, but before they can issue in the real union they have to go the way of division and death. The One in which the many become one is no mixture of them and itself. Any hybrid of flesh there and spirit here is an impossible abortion.

The true Supernatural Power is one's own Natural State, in which one is the real Self, and which is won by becoming aware of that Self which we already are. The other *siddhis* are like those that are won in a dream.

In fact Realization comprises everything and the Realized Man will not waste a thought on powers. Let people first get Realization and then seek powers if they still want to.

Ramana Maharshi

It often happens that spiritual men are affected supernaturally by sensible representations and objects.... Inasmuch as they are exterior and physical, the less is the likelihood of their being from God. That which properly and generally comes from God is a purely spiritual communication; wherein there is greater security and profit for the soul than through the senses, wherein there is usually much danger and delusion, because the bodily sense decides upon, and judges, spiritual things, thinking them to be what itself feels them to be, when in reality they are as different as body and soul, sensuality and reason.

St John of the Cross

One ounce of sanctifying grace is worth more than a hundredweight of those graces which theologians call 'gratuitous', among which is the gift of miracles.

St Francois de Sales

50 MIRACLES DON'T HAPPEN

Procedure: The universe is one, not divided into two compartments—Nature and Supernature, the ordinary and the miraculous. It's true that some phenomena are provisionally labelled paranormal, but this means they aren't yet understood, not that they are really unnatural or wild. In fact, they are useful antidotes for scientific complacency, reminding us that our system of 'Nature's laws' is still far too narrow to account for everything. And it's likely that, however wide the area of Nature which science has mapped, there will always lie beyond it that *terra incognita* which is not supernatural, but simply Nature yet to be explored. It is a region of mystery, certainly, but not of miracles; challenging but not haunted.

Game: The phenomenal universe contains those phenomena called 3rd persons or things, but is itself contained within this noumenon or no-thing, this 1st person—who nevertheless likes to pretend otherwise. Having been told that miracles just don't happen, at least not nowadays, I imagine myself in Nature, instead of seeing Nature in me who am wholly supernatural. Or else, if I still half-believe in the supernatural, I misplace it, making out that Nature is infected with it and that I, in turn, am infected with the natural. In fact, I don't know what I think: it is part of the game to confuse the issue.

Antithesis: The game is halted by sorting out the two realms, distinguishing sharply the natural realm over there from the

The slightest degree of sanctifying grace is superior to a miracle, which is supernatural only by reason of its cause, by its mode of production, not by its ultimate reality; the life restored to a corpse is only the natural life, low indeed in comparison with that of grace.

R. Garrigou-Lagrange

Priest: The founder of our sect had such remarkable powers that he held a brush in his hand on one bank of the river and wrote the name Amida on a piece of paper on the other bank. Can you do such a thing?

Bankei: Perhaps your fox can perform that trick, but that is not the manner of Zen. My miracle is that when I feel hungry I eat, and when I feel thirsty I drink.

Zen Flesh Zen Bones

Can you walk on water? You have done no better than a straw. Can you fly in the air? You have done no better than a blue-bottle. Conquer your heart; then you may become somebody.

Ansari of Herat

In the All He has to be found. The supernatural is not apart from the rest. When Realization has occurred, there is nothing but *Vrindavana* (the eternal heaven of Divine Love), nothing but Siva, complete non-duality. Then only can it be said that the entire universe is his Divine Play. In the state of Pure Being the distinction between the natural and the supernatural ceases to exist.

Anandamayi Ma

supernatural or miraculous realm here. Then it is obvious that *what is for the 3rd person abnormal is for the 1st person normal*, and that the ultimate solution of the problem of psychical phenomena, extrasensory perception, and so on, is the discovery that the whole life of the 1st person is paranormal: there is nothing normal about it! The following are illustrations of how thoroughly this 1st person (when being honest and not playing 3rd person) breaks all the rules.

(1) *Discarnate beings.* For science and common sense, the problem of ghosts, of disembodied spirits or discarnate minds, is one of the most perplexing—if, indeed, the evidence for them is admitted at all. But for me, for this 1st person, the problem isn't disembodied spirits but embodied ones: in fact, it isn't so much a problem as an impossibility. I am not a body and am not inside one. I am discarnate and nonmaterial and at large. In short, I am spirit, and can imagine no different sort of spirit.

(2) *Telepathy, clairvoyance, etc.* For science and common sense it is a mystery how minds can communicate without using any kind of spatio-temporal signalling. But for me, this 1st person, there is again no difficulty. I can discover no localized or boxed-up mind here, but only a mind that is so much at large that it could hardly have any communication problems. Indeed I can discover no minds at all in the plural but only this One Mind, having no divisions or boundaries, which instantaneously holds and underlies all things throughout space and time. My puzzle, then, is not how telepathy can occur but rather how it can fail to do so, and how it is possible for some of the contents of this Mind to be unavailable, at least

God *alone* is a great word in the interior life.

It is impossible to conceive what this possession of God alone really is, when He is united in Himself, by His very substance, with the centre of the soul; we must experience it to be able to know what it is, and even then we shall find the greatest difficulty in making others understand what we experience.

This is why so few Christians enjoy a real peace—a peace that is continual, full, and unchanging: they do not fix their rest in God alone, they do not trust everything to Him, they do not abandon everything to Him. Nevertheless, there is no true and solid rest but in this utter abandonment. This rest is unchangeable, as God is; it is elevated, as God is, above all created things; it is most secret and intimate, because it is only God, the enjoyment of whom pierces to the very depths of our hearts; it is full, because God completely fills and satisfies the heart; it leaves nothing to desire, and nothing to regret, because he who possesses God can neither desire nor regret anything else.

John Nicholas Grou

temporarily. (It seems that the thoughts of all beings are in principle available to the 1st person who is Self-aware; but to be invaded by irrelevant telepathic communications—and nearly all are irrelevant now—would be utterly confusing, therefore only those needed at this moment are forthcoming.)

Most of the above applies also to clairvoyance, spiritual healing, automatic writing, mediumship, and the so-called recollection of past lives. Seeing that there is in reality only this One Mind, this 1st person singular who is the sole Experiencer, there is no basic difficulty in accounting for such phenomena—insofar as they really do occur. Conversely, they make no sense in terms of localized, boxed-up minds.

(3) *Eyeless sight.* There have been a number of reports of (physiologically) blind people who can read and distinguish colours, and of sighted people who can see with their fingers or the back of their heads. But the fact is that all seeing is eyeless (11 The Seeing Eye Game): it is 1st-person experience here, occurring only in this spot which is entirely free from eyes, brains, or anything else whatever. And the same is true of the other senses: the only hearing is earless, the only tasting is tongueless, and so on.

(4) *Inedia.* Some people—they seem, most of them, to have been saintly women—are alleged to have lived for long periods on practically no food whatever, to the astonishment of their doctors. However this may be, it is certainly true that this 1st person has never eaten a crumb or drunk a drop: every morsel that is placed in this Void is itself voided.

(5) *Projection.* There is an Eastern tradition that the Seer can travel instantaneously and at will throughout the universe, and there are similar Western stories of what is sometimes called 'astral projection'. We have already seen (33 Bargepole) that the 1st person's space is two-dimensional and the third dimension of distance or depth is unreal. To live as 1st person is all the time to cover immense distances, by totally abolishing them. One moment I coincide with my hand, the next moment with a star, since both are in me. And I travel from star to star as quickly and as easily as from finger to finger. (No, I am not 'just turning my eyes'. What eyes?)

(6) *Precognition.* There are countless stories of precognition or fore-knowledge, and perhaps most of them are suspect. How can an event which has not yet occurred make itself felt now?

This seemingly insoluble puzzle is, not in theory but in practice, being solved all the while by the 1st person who lives a truly 1st-person life. Then it is found that one's spontaneous actions, those which proceed directly from the Faceless One here without any deliberation, have a happy knack of fitting future events, of anticipating situations which have not yet arisen. This 'foreknowledge' does not, it is important to note, involve insight into the details of what the future holds, leading to purposefully appropriate behaviour now; quite the reverse, it involves total unknowing, cluelessness, abandon, an ever-renewed handing-over to the One here, who alone can be trusted to come up with the right answer, the response which adequately takes the future into account.

(7) *Physical phenomena.* No doubt all sorts of odd things do happen, from dowsing and poltergeist phenomena upwards, but there is in principle no reason why science should not one day account for them. The same may be said of *siddhi,* those miraculous powers which are said to come to anyone who attains a certain proficiency in meditation or some measure of Self-realisation. Significantly, Eastern tradition adds that the exploitation of these powers is spiritual suicide; indeed the only safe thing is to ignore them. For it is not this kind of expertise at all, not this (so-called) piecemeal and spasmodic interference with Nature, which is the true prerogative of the Self-realised. *The genuine 1st-person life is all of it miraculous and supernatural,* and none of it is merely natural. Genuine spirituality has no need of extraordinary signs and wonders, seeing that every ordinary event is significant and wonderful. Because the essential adjustment is not to the world but to the seer of the world, it changes the whole world, without any spasmodic or piecemeal interference; moreover the change is quite radical, a supernatural transformation which science cannot observe, let alone account for.

This making over of Nature into Supernature—so thorough yet without the slightest interference—is the function of the 1st person as consciously distinct from the 3rd. The 3rd person lives in the universe, which in turn lives in the 1st person. Everything is thrust upon the 3rd person from outside, but it all comes from within the 1st person. No wonder, then, things look and feel quite different for the 1st person who ceases to pretend to be 3rd person. What I find proceeding from my own depths can no longer seem to me alien or threatening or arbitrary or meaningless or mechanical. Now all makes sense; all appearances are saved; all that happens is intentional and meaningful. The 1st person isn't subject to accidents and has nothing to complain of. This is the true interior life, for which nothing is exterior any more.

One who prefers religious language may say: I am so free from self-will, so obedient to God's will, that his will is now my profoundest intention. Now nothing comes amiss, and the care and wisdom of God's management are evident in the tiniest things. Now I live from moment to moment, wholly abandoned to the Divine Providence, and therefore without the slightest anxiety, for "his will is my peace". Though, nothing is 'understood', all is welcome, and all is miraculous or supernatural. Viewed from outside, there is hardly any change, but the inside story is one of revolution: the contrast between this true 1st-person life and the old pseudo-3rd-person life is immense—as immense as the contrast between the 1st person and the 3rd.

What kind of universe it is depends on who is observing it. The same bare data, it seems, can be read in two antithetical ways, as meaningless or as meaningful. The same world can be taken as natural throughout or as supernatural throughout. But in the latter case (it may be objected) how can I be sure I am not deceiving myself and looking at the world through rose-tinted spectacles?

There is no convincing theoretical answer to this question: the only solution (and it is final) is a practical one. It is a problem of self-confidence, of who is trustworthy, of what can be relied upon. If I go by those 3rd persons, they are for Nature—inevitably so, seeing that they belong in Nature; but if I go by this 1st person, I am for the Supernatural—inevitably so, seeing that I don't belong in Nature. Let me only be honest and see and be who I am, and cease playing 3rd person, and observe the result, and trust that result. Then I discover that I am not inhabiting the same old world as before. Though the bare data are in some sense just the same, every slightest thing is profoundly altered. And suffusing them all is this indescribable peace.

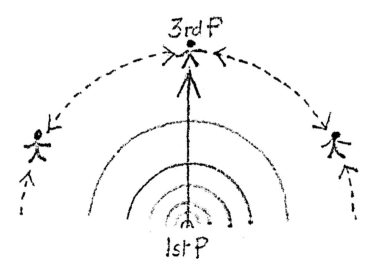

All forms of anxiety come from the fact that there is somewhere in our consciousness the feeling of incomplete knowledge of the situation and this lack of knowledge leads to the sense of insecurity and then to anxiety with all its degrees of intensity. The 'I' is always at the centre of whatever situation we may encounter. When, therefore, the 'I' is not thoroughly known, such questions as 'Has life any meaning?' never cease to torment us.

What makes the 'I' declare itself to be the only real thing in existence?

Where is the secure ground I can stand on without any sense of anxiety? Or, what is 'I'? The 'I' must be discovered. And I shall be all right.

D.T. Suzuki

51 WE ARE ALL IN THE SAME BOAT

Procedure: In the democracy of the world everything is peripheral, from 3rd person to 3rd, a case of somebody confronting somebody else, symmetrically, the same either way, him there opposite him there, face to face, in horizontal relationship involving only one level—the human—with its two-way traffic between persons of equal status and equal complexity.

This horizontal traffic is a show, nothing passes, there is only concord between the behaviour of coloured shapes having no depth from which they could work upon each other, no vertical supporting Process.

Antithesis: In the autocracy of the spirit everything is from this Centre, from 1st person to 3rd, a case of Nobody confronting somebody, asymmetrically, onesidedly, me here opposite him there, no-face to face, in vertical relationship involving many levels—not human—maintained by the one-way traffic plying from the Simplicity here to complexity there.

This vertical traffic is creation there out of Nothing here, evolution there from the world's Beginning here, causation there by the First Cause here.

I'm nobody! Who are you?
Are you nobody too?
Then there's a pair of us—don't tell!
They'd banish us, you know.

How dreary to be somebody;
How public, like a frog,
To tell your name the livelong day
To an admiring bog!

Emily Dickinson

Destroy yourself, because any form or shape is the cause of trouble. Give up the notion 'I am so and so'. 'I am this' or 'I and this' is the ego.

Ramana Maharshi

The heart is naught but the Sea of Light; is the heart the place for vision of God—and then blind? The heart is not contained in hundreds of thousands of persons noble or common. It is in a single one. Which is he? Which?

The real Man is he that hath the spirit within him. These others are not men, they are mere forms.

Rumi

And this superficial concomitance or pseudo-causation obeys rules which are partly natural (mechanical, meaningless) and partly social (conventional, arbitrary)—and productive of anxiety.	And this real Process is seen from its Source here to be free, ever new, supernatural, miraculous, all meaningful because it is the will of God— the true 1st person. This is the cure for anxiety.

Game: I play WAAITSB when, finally abandoning my primitive and childish view of myself, I pretend to shift from the right-hand column to the left, and imagine myself a human victim of meaningless forces in a natural world where miracles never happen and my profoundest will is never realised.

Suppose the plank-bridge breaks as I cross it. If I were a primitive I would take it to be sorcery; if a child, to be punishment for being naughty; if a saint, to be God's will and therefore mine and no accident. Only as a 'normal' adult do I take it to be a mere natural event, due to this human's excessive weight, happening to a mere human, a 3rd person. As procedure, this may save me a second dunking, but as a game it ensures accidents all the time and a life of chronic anxiety.

Ye are the light of the world. A city that is set on an hill cannot be hid. Neither do men light a candle, and put it under a bushel, but on a candlestick; and it giveth the light unto all that are in the house. Let your light so shine.

Except your righteousness shall exceed the righteousness of the scribes and Pharisees, ye shall in no case enter into the kingdom of heaven.

Ye have heard that it hath been said, An eye for an eye, and a tooth for a tooth: but I say unto you, that ye resist not evil: but whosoever shall smite thee on thy right cheek, turn to him the other also. And if any man will sue thee at the law, and take away thy coat, let him have thy cloke also. And whosoever shall compel thee to go a mile, go with him twain. Give to him that asketh thee, and from him who would borrow of thee turn thou not away.

The light of the body is the eye: if therefore thine eye be single, thy whole body shall be full of light.

Take no thought, saying, What shall we eat? or What shall we drink? or Wherewithal shall we be clothed? (for after all these things do the Gentiles seek) for your heavenly Father knoweth that ye have need of all these things. But seek ye first the kingdom of God, and his righteousness; and all these things shall be added unto you. Take therefore no thought for the morrow.

Judge not.

And why beholdest thou the mote that is in thy brother's eye, but considerest not the beam that is in thine own eye?

Enter ye in at the strait gate; for wide is the gate, and broad is the way, that leadeth to destruction, and many there be which go in thereat.

Jesus, from the *Sermon on the Mount*

52 RESPONSIBLE CITIZEN

Procedure: Let's face it, the Sermon on the Mount doesn't work: at least it doesn't apply to ordinary human beings, and certainly not to fully responsible ones. When the good citizen catches someone stealing his coat he doesn't offer his cloak also, but calls the police. When he is slandered he doesn't consider himself blessed, but consults his solicitor. When he sees a thug hitting an old lady he doesn't advise her to turn the other cheek for more punishment, but either attacks the thug or shouts for help. When he finds preventable suffering, or persecution or fraud or exploitation, he doesn't practise resignation to God's inscrutable will, but resorts to strong social action; despising meekness, he stands up for human rights. He judges his fellow citizens, denouncing freely those who break the rules. And his special contempt is apt to be reserved for drop-outs who take no thought for the morrow and are content to let God (or the State) feed them as he feeds the sparrows, and clothe them as he clothes the lilies.

And (again, let's face it) this good citizen's procedure is realistic. Unlike the teaching of Jesus, it works by and large. In any viable society something of the sort is likely to prove indispensable.

How, in that case, did Jesus come to put forward his strange—not to say subversive—ideas, and how is it that they have made some kind of sense to generation after generation of sincere and sensible Christians? Is this just a particularly blatant case of human hypocrisy?

Not at all. There is a completely satisfying and workable answer to this most baffling of all practical problems. It is possible—it is

The claim that a man must die to the worldly world and all its notions, if he is to live 'the life that is life indeed', is as obvious throughout the New Testament as in the Gospels.... Jesus demanded a fresh start on a basis of absolute truth.... The Church of Christ has dared absolutely to reverse the methods of its Master.

Bishop Gore

If the wrong-doing of men fill thee with indignation and irresistible pain, so that thou desire even to take vengeance on the wrong-doers, then above all things resist that feeling.... If thy light had shone forth, it would have made clear the path for others, and the man who sinned would perchance have been saved by thy light. Or if it be that thou didst show thy light, and yet see'st not that any are saved thereby; nevertheless stand thou firm, and doubt not the virtue of the heavenly light.... Love all men and all things.

Dostoevsky

How can I ever be the sold short or the cheated?

Eckhart

essential—to reconcile the Sermon on the Mount with social necessity, and to do so right now without waiting for any sort of millennium or utopia. And it is done, yet once more, by attending to the total distinction, in the moral field as in every other, between the 1st person and all 3rd persons whatever.

Game: Like the animal and the infant and the idiot (like the animal who is obviously non-human, like young Carlos who is sure he isn't a boy,[1] like the idiot who will never learn to see himself as others see him) this 1st person is deficient, unfitted for society, beyond the pale—only much more so. At least an animal has a head! Here is no thing, let alone a living thing, but just 'LIGHT'. To such a one a different set of rules must apply—non-human rules for this non-human being. They are set out in the Sermon on the Mount. This ethic alone fits the 1st person; it is tailor-made for me. To feign otherwise and play the game of Responsible Citizen, attempting to regulate the behaviour of this solitary, luminous, headless one here by the rules which regulate those numerous, opaque, headed ones out there, is inequitable and absurd—even more absurd than it would be (say) to require a ghost or a Martian to observe human conventions. (Even ghosts aren't necessarily transparent and headless, nor do they fill the room!)

Antithesis: The governing principle is enlightened self-interest. Thus *a man* is naturally and properly interested in furthering all that concerns himself as a man among men: that's what makes him fully human. Thus I am naturally and properly interested in furthering

---

1   See: What Are The Results? (i) Child

When we are spoken to of dying to ourselves, of annihilating ourselves, when we are told that that is the foundation of Christian morality.... we do not wish to accept the statement; it seems to us hard and even unjust.... What does God ask of us, when he commands us to annihilate ourselves and to renounce ourselves? He asks of us to *do ourselves justice,* to put ourselves in our proper place and to acknowledge ourselves for what we really are.... What rights can a thing have that is nothing?.... It is then a formal injustice on our part to refuse to be treated, or to treat ourselves, as if we were really nothing.... If my neighbour takes away from me my goods, if he blackens my reputation, if he attempts my life,.... am I justified in wishing him ill for it, or in seeking revenge? No. Because.... I have nothing of my own but nothingness.

John Nicholas Grou

To one who has even for an instant seen into his Ground a thousand ducats of red beaten gold are worth no more than a false farthing. Out of this inmost Ground thy works should be wrought without why.

Eckhart

Lung Shu went to the physician Wen Chih and explained the symptoms of his disorder:

"I do not think it an honor if the whole district praises me, nor a disgrace if the whole State reviles me; I have no joy when I win, no anxiety when I lose. I look in the same way at riches and poverty, life and death, other men and pigs; I dwell in my own house as though lodging at an inn. What's wrong with me?"

Wen Chih stepped back and examined Lung Shu. Finally he said: "Hmm. I see your heart. The place an inch square is empty. You are almost a sage."

Lieh-tzu

all that concerns mySelf as no-man, as embracing all beings. Their interest really is mine. I must love and serve them because I am them in my essential nature. Therefore to stand up for my rights as a human being (which I see I'm not, right here), to plan ahead (as if there were a mortal object, a continuum here to plan for), to strike back (as if there were something here to defend), to take as much as possible for as little as possible (as if I could own anything less than everything), to separate my advantage from any man's (as if I didn't include him)— all this would be making myself out to be what I'm not. *If I'm realistic about what it's like here I shall spontaneously live according to the law of selfless love;* and I shall live this life from moment to moment in perfect trust, unconcerned about tomorrow. I see that this is the only life I'm built for, and that only this 1st person is unsubstantial enough to filter though the needle-eye gate that leads to it.

Conversely, men are not built for that narrow gate or the all-inclusive life it leads to. Each is visibly his separate self, solid, opaque, distinct, headed; and for me to preach the gospel of total self-abandonment to him would be impertinent and unrealistic, and therefore futile. He is there for me to enjoy and love just as he's given, not to make into something else. Accordingly it would be nonsensical to rebuke him for carefully planned and keenly competitive behaviour, or to blame the forces of law and order for their harshness, or trade unions and capital for avarice, or litigants for claiming redress, or minorities for agitating for equal status: though social patterns need amelioration, they are bound to follow the law of self-interest. Mortal man lives according to his mortal nature, as

The things they say and do seem unaccountable, for what God makes obvious to persons on the way to their eternal happiness is foreign to those that have arrived there.... In an instant they will do more lasting good than all the outward actions ever done.

Eckhart

Let us then think seriously, before God, what the world is with regard to us, and what we are with regard to the world. Let us sound our interior dispositions, let us study the depths of our own hearts: we shall most surely find there much that will humble and confound us; we shall discover that the maxims of the world have left a deep impression on our minds...

But let us not be discouraged: to triumph entirely over the world, to brave it, to despise it, and to be pleased that in its turn it should despise and fight against us, is not the work of a moment... Let us remember, in all our necessities, those words of Jesus Christ: *Have confidence, I have overcome the world.*

John Nicholas Grou

I am not of the world.
I am the Light of the world.

Jesus

winged birds fly and finned fish swim. It is right that he should mind his own business and look ahead and consider where his next meal is coming from: unlike the 1st person, he has a mouth to feed. It is right that he should be somewhat hard-headed: that's the way he is.

That is not the way I am. To the extent that I attend to this very special form (the form of luminous emptiness) here, there follows the very special behaviour that goes with it—if it doesn't follow, I'm not attending. *And I find that only this behaviour works.* Just as the Sermon on the Mount doesn't suit the world, just as (in other words) 1st-person morality doesn't suit 3rd persons, so, conversely, 3rd-person morality doesn't suit this 1st person: it lets me down at every turn. Not surprisingly—seeing that I lack the physique for playing Responsible Citizen—the game proves endlessly tiresome and inefficient and frustrating. I notice, for instance, how the more I demand my rights the less they are admitted, how the more I nurse my reputation the less I'm respected, how the more I judge the less I'm tolerated, how the more I scheme ahead the less I can rest in the results, how the more I seek to enlighten people the less they listen, how the more I get the less I like what I get, how the more I resist evil the less it responds to my treatment—and so on indefinitely. The more security or influence or prestige I manage to acquire the more I must have to keep going: the drug is terribly addictive. And all the misery is not so much because I'm living a *bad* life as an *unnatural* one, and setting up to be something that I'm not.

But as soon as, dropping this silly pretence, I dare to notice what I am and to start living my own life, I taste deep satisfaction. At last

Be not conformed to this world.

If any man among you seemeth to be wise in this world, let him become a fool, that he may become wise. For the wisdom of this world is the foolishness of God.

St. Paul

The Buddha said to Subhuti: "A Bodhisattva should think thus: 'As many beings as there are in the universe, all these I must lead to Nirvana, into that Realm of Nirvana which leaves nothing behind. And yet, although innumerable beings are thus led to Nirvana, no being at all is led to Nirvana.' And why? Because if a Bodhisattva retains the notion of an ego, a person, a being, or a soul, he is no longer a Bodhisattva."

Diamond Sutra

God enjoys himself. In the joy wherein God enjoys himself therein he enjoys all creatures, not as creatures: creatures as God.

I alone take all creatures out of their sense into my mind and make them one in me.

All happiness to those who have listened to this sermon. Had there been no-one here I must have preached it to the poor-box.

Eckhart

I begin living *now*, in a world suddenly beautified and peopled with immensely lovable beings—a truly redeemed universe. Moreover, society itself is genuinely benefitted. I do no good in the kingdom of the world by playing the game of belonging to it, but much good there by loyally adhering to another kingdom altogether—to the 'Country of Everlasting Clearness.' When I live by the Light that I am—my eye being single and my whole body replaced by this Light—it must shine forth upon men. As for everyday necessities, I find that when I seek first the Kingdom of God within, all things needful are added out there.

The reason Responsible Citizen gets so hard to play, so unrewarding, is that it is really an exercise in irresponsibility and self-deception. Its basic manoeuvre (like that of all the games described here) is to patch up a bogus compromise between the 1st person and the 3rd, confusing them till there seems no difference at all. I play this befogging game from two directions. *First*, (operating from the near side of the field) I make out that the Sermon on the Mount, and my spontaneous impulses to live that way, are quite impracticable. I tell myself I should do more harm than good by living a life of undiscriminating love and self-abandonment: only in a few deserving cases may I safely give and forgive to the limit; only when my plans have gone hopelessly awry am I justified in handing over to Providence; only when I have no alternative will I cheerfully allow myself to be taken advantage of. Otherwise, I am excused from such idealism, and society's meaner, tougher, 3rd-person procedures are right for me. And, *second*, (operating from the far side of the field) I call upon the community—Church, State, 'Them', politicians, business men, youth, anybody and everybody—to behave much more idealistically, to temper their materialism and aggression and self-seeking, and (in short) to accept that *my more generous, more tender, 1st-person procedures are right for society.* In particular, when occasionally I make an unselfish gesture—such as an unsolicited gift of my time or money or affection—I expect that gesture to be noticed and promptly responded to. It is not enough reward that I have acted in accordance with my true nature here: something to match has to follow out there in the community. And when it doesn't, I don't like it, and get comparatively mean and tough again. Thus I seek, crazily, to reverse the natural order, to impose 1st-person standards on society and 3rd-person standards on myself!

But when I stop playing Responsible Citizen I stop blaming those 3rd persons for being themselves, and I stop excusing this 1st person from being himself. I am no longer surprised or hurt when what I am led to do turns out to be the very opposite of what others do: seeing how differently we are constituted, the sharpest contrast in behaviour is only to be expected. And when, confronted by a moral dilemma, I don't at first know what way to act, at least I may be sure that (the wisdom of the 1st person being foolishness with the 3rd, and *vice versa*) the right way for me will not be the world's way. There is not one set of moral standards but two: there is one law for man, another for the no-man he really is, and no compromise between them will do. Unless my righteousness is truly 1st-person, and therefore far exceeds the 3rd-person righteousness of the social order, I shall neither enter the Kingdom of Heaven myself nor be of much use to the Kingdom of the World.

Footnote: Why bother to write these words, if 3rd persons are for accepting as such and not converting into 1st persons? In fact, there is only one 1st person, and in so far as these words are meaningful they proceed from no human mouth or brain but from that unique Void or Essence which is the indivisible 1st-personhood of all beings. And no matter how many such beings read these words they can only mean anything to one Reader—the universal 1st person who composed them. They are his soliloquy, at once an expression of his Self-awareness and a means to it. This is the famous paradox of the *Diamond Sutra,* wherein the Bodhisattva enlightens all beings by realising there are no separate beings to enlighten.

Certain (Tibetan) disciples are advised to contemplate the sky and sometimes to confine themselves to this practice only. Some lie flat on their back in the open, in order to look at the sky with no other object in sight. This contemplation…. is said to lead to a peculiar trance in which the personality is forgotten, and an indescribable union with the universe is experienced.

Alexandra David-Néel

Our task is to make the Earth invisible in us.

Rilke

And down through the cool of the mountain
The children sank at the call,
And stood in a blazing fountain
And never a mountain at all.

A.E.

It is probably on us alone that it is incumbent to augment the consciousness of the Earth.

Maeterlinck

Till we conceive her living we go distraught,
At best but circle-windsails of a mill,
Seeing she lives, and of her joy of life
Creatively has given us blood and breath….

Meredith

53 THE EARTH FACE GAME

Procedure: The face of the Earth—how exceedingly (and tragically) familiar this vast and curious countenance is. But modern man is more than map-conscious. In effect, he spends much of his time poised up there in a space-ship, regarding the continents as anything but the mere coloured shapes he can see. He fills out their presented geography with countless thoughts about climatic and economic conditions, famine areas, trouble spots, war zones, racial and ideological divisions, the pressure of huge populations. Several times a day his newspapers and television rocket him skywards, to where he can take such a global view of this troubled planet. And the more responsible a world-citizen he is, the more he lives up there, reading all manner of ideas into what he sees down here. This is his necessary procedure, and the mounting anxiety that goes with it cannot be helped.

Game: I make the key move in the 'Human' Face Game when, playing the Jerk, I project myself (say) six feet away from myself here, to the region where my *human* face is presented. Now the key move in the Earth Face Game is just the same; only this time I jerk myself still further afield, to a distance of (say) six thousand miles away from myself here, to the region where my *terrestrial* face is presented.

Again, the basic absurdity of the 'Human' Face Game consists in my pretence that I have only one face, and it is human and opaque, and it is what I am now looking out of, at the faces of other people. And again, the basic absurdity of the Earth Face Game is not different;

What widens within you, Walt Whitman?
What waves and soils exuding?
What climes? What persons and cities are here?

Within me latitude widens, longitude lengthens,
Asia, Africa, Europe, and to the east—America is provided for in the west
Within me zones, seas, cataracts, forests, volcanoes, groups,
Malaysia, Polynesia, and the great West Indian islands.

Whitman

The Earth is that entire whole of which one's body is but a member; it is that permanent whole of which one's body is but a brief part; it is to one's body what a tree is to a single twig, or a permanent body to a small and perishable organ.

Fechner

We may say that the Earth has a spirit of growth; that its flesh is the soil, its bones are the successive strata of the rocks which form the mountains, its muscles are the tufa stone, its blood the springs of its waters.

Leonardo da Vinci

it consists in my pretence that Earth has only one face, and it is the one shown on Mercator's Projection, and it is what I am now looking out of, at the face of the Moon and the Sun. The truth that both these games deny is that, alike at the human and the planetary level, I have another, a True Face, right here.

Antithesis: EFG is 1st person playing 3rd person on the cosmic stage. The remedy is that I look here and see what is actually looking out at the heavens.

I am sitting at home in the dusk, with my wife, and through the uncurtained window I can see the house opposite, the crescent Moon, and a star. They are what I'm looking at—the face of *another* human being, the facade of *another* house, the face of *another* heavenly body. What about the Looker—*this* eye, *this* human being, *this* house, *this* planet, *this* star or solar system?

What, in my 1st-person experience, is being looked out of?

Well, I find that *this* eye is eyeless, *this* man is faceless, *this* house has no facade, *this* heavenly body is mapless—and (so to speak) hollow, open, full of light. All I can find here is this one True Face which is absolutely featureless at all observational levels, this single Glassless Mirror in which parts of humans, humans, houses, planets, stars, and everything else are presented impartially and with equal brilliance. Evidently this 1st person is above or below all such prejudices and distinctions, and isn't 1st-person-cellular, or 1st-person-human, or 1st-person-terrestrial, or 1st-person sidereal, but simply 1st-person, the One Subject of all objects. The Original Face I find here is as much the Original Face of this planet as of this man,

I wondered how men's notions could be so perverted as to see in the Earth only a dry clod, and to seek for angels apart from Earth and stars or above them in the vacant heaven, and never find them. My view, however, is called fantastic. The Earth simply is a globe, and whatever else it may be is found in the glass cases of our museums of natural history.

Fechner

How can we be so narrow-minded in our obstinate anthropological jealousy as to deny any sort of conscious life to the great mother of all the life we know? ….. If the strange calm, that comes to us when we fling our spirit into the elements, brings an indescribable inspiration, felt as much in the city as in the country, why should we think of this inspiration as a cosmic phenomenon, dependent on cosmic consciousness, in place of a planetary phenomenon, dependent on planetary consciousness? So far in the wrong direction have the crowd values moved, that if you told an average modern person that the purpose of your life was a communion between your consciousness and the Earth's consciousness, he would think you had simply gone mad.

John Cowper Powys

She (Earth) has been slain by the narrow brain
But for us who love her she lives again.

Meredith

because in fact it is neither planetary nor human, but absolute.

Let me put the matter like this: the 1st person *sports* all kinds of opaque faces for looking in at (ranging from particles, through organisms, to stars and galaxies), but is only one transparent Face for looking out of. The Zen Master's advice, then, "See what your Original Face looks like, the face you had before you were born" though seemingly directed at a human being, really applies to all beings, and can only be obeyed by the One Being that lies at their heart.

What, in practice, does this mean?

It doesn't mean that one denies the objective or 3rd-person reality of the creatures and things and events which go to make up this heavenly body, any more than one denies the objective or 3rd-person reality of the creatures and things and events which go to make up this human body. Geography and history are perfectly valid, and so are anatomy and physiology—including all the imperfections (or worse) which they display. These are not denied, but *placed*— always there, never right here; real appearances of Reality, but not that Reality itself; a true story, but an outside one. The Inside Story of this Earth is exactly the same as the Inside Story of this man and of all his parts and particles: it is Simple Clarity, a great Emptiness ready to be filled with *other* heavenly and earthly bodies.

Clearly *seeing* this inner Brilliance (*thinking* it is no good, and even feeling it is far from good enough) roots out one's fundamental anxiety. The Heart of all things is visibly sound, and this is enough. Now the outward aspects of things can be accepted fearlessly and

He who dwells in the Earth, and within the Earth..... whose body the Earth is, and who rules the Earth within, he is thy Self, the Ruler within, the Immortal.

Brihadaranyaka Upanishad

Earth, isn't this what you want: an invisible re-arising in us? .... What is your urgent command, if not transformation?

Rilke

I believe that most of what was said of God was in reality said of that Spirit whose body is Earth.

A.E.

A star is a world of consciousness, which comprises in a superior unity the consciousness of its creatures, while it is closed against that of the other stars, but altogether open to God; so that the stars constitute an intermediate and mediating grade of existence between their creatures and God, and the Earth is one of those stars.

Fechner

processed efficiently—from the Void that produces them. The whole Earth is seen through, from her Source.

There was a child went forth every day,

And the first object he looked upon, that object he became,

And that object became part of him for the day or a certain part of the day,

Or for many years or stretching cycles of years.

Walt Whitman

As Rudyard Kipling's Mowgli thought of himself as a wolf, so Jock (a hand-reared jackdaw), had he been able to speak, would certainly have called himself a human being.... As long as he was walking, he considered himself a man, but the moment he took to wing, he saw himself as a hooded crow, because these birds were the first to awaken his flock instinct.

Konrad Z. Lorenz

If a child grows up among the Arapesh of New Guinea, he will be shocked by the slightest sign of self-assertion, boastfulness, or anger. If he grows up among the nearby Mundugumor, violence and aggression will be his ideal. Among the Tchambuli, he will be meek, emotionally dependent, concerned with his personal appearance, dominated by his womenfolk. Among the Zuni of New Mexico, he will be concerned with religious ceremonial, admire men who are easy-going and without aspirations, and detest the ambitious. Among the Dobu of North-west Melanesia he will cultivate animosity against his neighbours.

Ruth Benedict (paraphrased)

54 CLUB MEMBER

Procedure: Within the limits of an individual's capacity, his upbringing is his assimilation to those around him—quite regardless of what he happens to be, and quite regardless of what they happen to be. He just has to become one of them, has to take on their characteristics no matter how badly they fit. Anything to belong.

Examples: (1) A dog's relationship to the family—*his* family.

(2) Konrad Lorenz found that Greylag goslings unquestioningly accepted as their mother the first living being they met, and ran confidently after him. Mallard ducklings also regarded Lorenz as their mother, but in their case he had to go around on all fours, quacking.

(3) There have been many instances of feral children, but none so well-documented as that of Kamala, an Indian girl who was suckled and reared by wolves, and lived as a member of the pack till she was found and rescued at the age of eight, in 1920. From then on, she lived in an orphanage in Bengal, where gradually she learned not to run on all fours, not to sleep all day and go prowling at night making wolf-howls, not to chase chickens and tear out and devour their guts, and so on. From being virtually a wolf, she became in the end something like a normal human being. Before she died at sixteen, she was able to walk upright, make good use of her hands, and talk a little.

(4) A normal child soon gets over his initial feeling of uniqueness and comes to reckon himself a human being—because from the start he has been surrounded by human beings. Automatically he puts in

You do not belong to the Brahmin caste or any other, nor to any social group. You are not perceived by the eyes. Unattached, formless and witness of all are you. Be happy.

Astavakra Sarihita

A certain man from Madura asked Ramana Maharshi: "How can I know the power of God?"

Maharshi: "You say 'I AM'. That is it. What else can say 'I Am'? One's own being is His Power. The trouble arises only when one says, 'I am this or that, I am such and such.' Be yourself, that is all."

The Sadhu, seeing the One Self enlightening all bodies, walks solitary as a rhinoceros.

Avadhut Gita

for membership of the club, and is readily accepted. And evidently he belongs. This is his sensible, healthy procedure.

Game: One's own case is altogether different: this 1st person is admitted only on special terms, as a kind of fiddle. The implied contract is: "Let's pretend I qualify and am like you all, and I promise never to look here again to see what I'm really like." In other words, one's anxiety not to be excluded from the human club is such that there are no limits to the entrance fee one will cheerfully and dishonestly pay.

Antithesis: It takes courage to be the odd one out, and admit that the difference between oneself here and those humans there is far, far greater than the difference between Lorenz and his ducklings, or between Kamala and her wolves. There is no club for the 1st person, who is always singular.

Do not seek refuge in anyone but yourself.

Gautama Buddha

You have not known others from yourself. You stop at every form that you come to, saying, "I am this." By God, you are not .... You are that Unique One.

Rumi

Realisation is getting rid of the delusion that you haven't realised.

Ramana Maharshi

Illumination means the realisation that Illumination is not something to be attained.

Hui-hai

Ultimate Nirvana is attained by avoiding all samsaric deeds, such as seeking Nirvana, or casting off impurity and clinging to purity, or harbouring attainments and proofs of attainment, or failure to discard rules.   How, then, is deliverance to be achieved? Never having been bound, you have no need to seek deliverance.

Hui-hai

55 I'M NOT ENLIGHTENED

Procedure: A single glance at that 3rd person, the one on the far side of my mirror, and the very idea of his Enlightenment is ridiculous. It isn't merely that he hasn't put in enough years of spiritual practice yet, or achieved any kind of holiness or perfection whatever. His trouble is at once much deeper and more obvious. If Enlightenment means anything at all, it means non-duality, and he is many things among many more things; it means clarity, and he is quite opaque; it means changelessness, and he alters all the time; it means simplicity, and he is very complex; it means disembodiment, and he is very much a body; it means infinity, and his boundaries are there to see. And so on. All these disabilities are incurable, and the least of them debars him permanently from Enlightenment. The fact is that he isn't merely incapable of Enlightenment, he's its antithesis, the complete exemplar of all it is not. His sensible course, then, is to admit it without any hedging or reservations.

Game: I am playing INE when, falsely supposing the one on the *near* side of my mirror to be—or even slightly to resemble—the one on the far side, I take it that this one, too, is thoroughly unenlightened.

Antithesis: The game is stopped by seeing who is playing it—by seeing the immense difference between this non-human 1st person here and that very human 3rd person there. The trouble with him is his luckless habit of turning up in the wrong place at the wrong time. For finding Enlightenment is like finding anything else: you have to know where it is and when it is there, and then be sure to keep your

Monk: How does one get liberated?

Shih-t'ou: Who has ever put you in bondage?

Monk: What is the Pure Land?

Shih-t'ou: Who has ever defiled you?

Monk: What is Nirvana?

Shih-t'ou: Who has ever subjected you to birth and death?

To awaken suddenly to the fact that your own Mind is the Buddha, that there is nothing to be attained or a single action to be performed—this is the Supreme Way; this is really to be as a Buddha.

Huang-po

Thus we receive in idleness of spirit the Incomprehensible Light, enfolding us and penetrating us. And this Light is nothing else but an infinite gazing and seeing. We behold that which we are, and we are that which we behold.

Ruysbroeck

appointment with it. *This is an appointment which I couldn't miss if I tried.* Enlightenment is to be found nowhere but HERE, at no time but NOW.

Outside and second-hand information is useless when it comes to this crucial question of one's own Enlightenment. It's no good relying on hearsay—on books however sacred, on teachers however revered, on friends however perceptive and frank. Even first-hand inspection, once it has passed over into memory, will not do. Only an immediate test, applied here and now, will settle the question beyond doubt. And when I look I see, at this moment and on this spot, this non-dual, lucid, simple Void which can never be worked up to, earned, achieved. Enlightenment has never occurred. It just is, and there's no escaping it.

The soul is furious for self-knowledge. Her face is lit with passion, red with rage for the arrears withheld from her in God, because she is not all God is by nature, because she has not all God has by nature .... The third rage of the soul is that she should be God and that there should not be a single creature ....

Fourthly, she rages to be absolutely nothing but the naked essence, there being neither God nor creature.

Eckhart

There is nothing so easy to me, so possible, as to be God.

Eckhart

No matter how often he *thinks* of God or goes to church, or how much he believes in religious ideas, if he, the whole man, is deaf to the question of existence, if he does not have an answer to it, he is marking time, and he lives and dies like one of the million things he produces.

He *thinks* of God instead of experiencing *being* God.

Erich Fromm

If you give up all else and seek Him alone, He will remain as the 'I', the Self.

Ramana Maharshi

56 GOD THE UNNECESSARY HYPOTHESIS

Procedure: There are few professing atheists. But the likelihood that most people would, if pressed, deny the atheist's creed—'There is no God'—doesn't prevent them from living it. Their virtual atheism isn't at all unreasonable or unpractical. For clearly they are not God nor even Godlike; and as for a God in Heaven, what real evidence is there for anyone of the sort? And it's arguable (to say the least) that belief in such a Deity has proved, on balance, beneficial neither to the individual nor to society. Certainly, then, I can blame no-one for regarding God as an unnecessary hypothesis.

Game: Or rather—no-one but myself. When I, the 1st person, deny the existence of God, I am overlooking the denier himself, and turning a blind eye to evidence that could not be clearer or more copious or more accessible. GUH is the most dishonest of the games one plays.

Antithesis: There is no God. *Here* is God. God is always here, never there. Each of the preceding chapters has examined the One Here from a particular angle, and in each case this One was found to be in the sharpest contrast to the man over there, his polar opposite. If such adjectives as Godlike, divine, unconditioned, perfect, real, apply anywhere at all, they apply here and only here. Nowhere but on this Spot can I find Him, and here I find Him without coverings, totally manifest.

(If I don't care for the word 'God', I can substitute Atman, Buddha-

The consciousness "I am Devadatta (or Jack Robinson)" is independent of circumstances; similarly with the knower of Brahman who knows he is Brahman.

Sankara

Thou shalt find, when thou hast forgotten all other creatures and their works—yea! and also all thine own works—that there shall remain yet after, betwixt thee and thy God, a naked knowing and feeling of thine own being: the which knowing and feeling must always be destroyed.

The Cloud of Unknowing

He who divides the One, wanders from death to death.

Katha Upanishad

If a man knows that he is Him, why should he hunger for a body?

Brihadaranyaka Upanishad

As rivers lose name and shape in the sea, wise men lose name and shape in God, glittering beyond all distance.

Mundaka Upanishad

nature, the Self, the One, the Void, or what I like. There are many names for This, for the Nameless which—precisely because it is so real and vivid in experience—cannot be named or thought about.)

The 1st person *is* God. The One on *this* side of the mirror and on *this* side of everything seen, the One here who sees without eyes and hears without ears, the One here who exclaims 'I AM: I've actually occurred!'—this One is God.

I did not mean united to Him, or like Him, and certainly not a part of the One who is indivisible, but Him entirely. What does it feel like to be Him? One can say that only this is Home, only this total identity satisfies, that to be saved is to *be* Him, that this Homecoming is perfectly natural to the 1st person who has never really left Home anyway. But such talk is, strictly, inadmissible. Who is this 1st person addressing but this 1st person? There are conversations which can only be concluded wordlessly and in private.

If a sharp penance had been laid on me, I know of none that I would not very often have willingly undertaken, rather than prepare myself for prayer by self-recollection .... The sadness I felt on entering the oratory was so great that it required all the courage I had to force myself in.

St Teresa

I tell you no one can experience this birth (of God in the soul) without a mighty effort. No one can attain this birth unless he can withdraw his mind entirely from things.

Eckhart

No one succeeds without effort. Mind control is not your birthright. The few who succeed owe their success to their perseverance.

Ramana Maharshi

Effortless and choiceless awareness is our real nature. If we can attain that state and abide in it, that is all right. But one cannot reach it without effort, the effort of deliberate meditation.

Ramana Maharshi

Realisation already exists; no attempt need be made to attain it. For it is not anything external or new to be acquired.

Ramana Maharshi

57 THE SPIRITUAL EXERCISE GAME

Problem: Some masters say that spiritual exercises—and particularly meditation systematically practised, maybe for a lifetime—are indispensable for Enlightenment. Some seem to think them unnecessary. Some go so far as to say they are what's standing in our Light. And (to complete our confusion) some say one thing one day and the opposite another day.

Let us apply the kind of analysis we have been using up to this point, and see whether this serious practical problem will not, as in the other cases, solve itself when we settle whose problem it is.

Procedure: Who, if anyone, needs to undergo this arduous spiritual training? The obvious answer is: All whose Enlightenment isn't yet complete. There have lived a few highly gifted people whose training was comparatively brief and easy, but for most aspirants it's a very long and hard endeavor, not so much to gain some initial illumination, as afterwards to develop it to the limit. A man gets what he goes in for, which means what he works for methodically, perseveringly, whole-heartedly; and the spiritual life is no exception to this rule. It's useless his sitting back and expecting Enlightenment to drop into his lap: he must climb a very tall and thorny tree and pluck it for himself. The reason he isn't thoroughly Enlightened is that he doesn't sufficiently *want* to be, and therefore cannot bring himself to make the necessary effort.

But why, in that case, do acknowledged experts so often not merely deny the need for training, but actually condemn it?

Ah, be diligent! Be diligent! Of a thousand or ten thousand attempting to enter by this Gate, only three or perhaps five pass through.

Huang-po

When the Master (Huang-po) had taken his place in the assembly hall, he began:
'You people are just like drunkards.
I don't know how you manage to keep your feet in such a sodden condition.
Why, everyone will die of laughing at you. It's all so *easy!*'

The Wan Ling Record

On this pilgrimage one must never slacken: effort is what counts.

Anandamayi Ma

He who interrupts the course of his spiritual exercises and prayer is like a man who allows a bird to escape from his hand; he can hardly catch it again.

St John of the Cross

You people who are engaged in spiritual cultivation, who wish to achieve the Buddha doctrine, for you there is no place for using effort. The only way is to do the ordinary things and nothing special, to relieve your bowels and pass water, to wear clothes and to eat, when tired to lie down, and as a simple fellow to laugh at yourself over these matters.

Lin-chi

Game: The explanation is clear once we ask *who* needs training? No doubt the right sort of spiritual endeavour makes sense and does much for all who seriously try it—*with one exception.* The 1st person finds it makes no sense and cannot possibly work. Pretending otherwise is turning the necessary 3rd-person procedure (SEP) into an absurd and frustrating 1st-person game (SEG)—a game which is, indeed, secretly concerned to avoid Enlightenment by the ingenious method of working exceptionally hard for it.

Antithesis Consider what spiritual training would mean for the 1st person, for the one here. It would mean one is anxious to get something, whereas in fact one is complete. It would mean one is looking for future results, whereas in fact the Goal is Now or never. It would mean drawing comparisons with others' attainments, whereas in fact this one is incomparable. It would mean making enormous efforts to curb the wandering mind, whereas in fact it's trying so hard that's the trouble. It would mean sitting at the feet of some guru, or attempting to master the scriptures, whereas in fact it's this sort of indoctrination from outside which prevents discovery right here. It would mean dwelling on prescribed ideas (such as impermanence, no-self, non-duality) whereas in fact they would only cloud the Emptiness here: what's needed is to drop all ideas and stay perfectly open. It would mean cultivating feelings (such as compassion, love, calm) whereas in fact they would only obscure this central Dispassion. It would mean the hard grind of keeping up one's exercises, so many hours a day, day in and day out for years, in the teeth of all natural impulses, whereas in fact the divine ease I'm seeking so painfully is painlessly available here this very instant.

The more a man operates, the more he is and exists. And the more he is and exists, the less of God is and exists within him.

Benet of Canfield

Spiritual cultivation cannot be cultivated ....

The intrinsic nature is already enough. Not to be attached either to good or to evil is all that a man engaged in spiritual cultivation needs to do. To cleave to the good and eschew evil, to contemplate emptiness, to enter into the state of concentration—all these are deliberate activities .... The more you do these things, the further away you get.

Ma-tsu

As to performing the six paramitas and vast numbers of similar practices, or gaining merits as countless as the sands of the Ganges, since you are fundamentally complete in every respect, you should not try to supplement that perfection by such meaningless practices.

Huang-po

So far as this 1st person is concerned, then, there is something wildly wrong about the very notion of spiritual training. It isn't merely that this training doesn't make for Enlightenment: it makes off in the opposite direction! A more effective antidote could hardly be imagined. SEG takes a direct path from its goal—from the Enlightenment it purports to be seeking—into outer darkness.

What is the truly 1st-person, game-free spiritual life?

Instead of training, enjoyment. Instead of working for the future, realization of what is present to perfection, with no other end in view. Instead of indoctrination, the inexhaustible adventure of Self-discovery. Instead of psychological improvement or spiritual development, total evacuation now, the surrender of all ambitions and claims. This way, there is no question of any future payoff: one isn't interested in anything that isn't given from moment to moment. This, the freely given present, is sufficient. Concerned only with this, one finds the days, months, years slipping by almost unnoticed, and every day is a good day. Such is the inside story.

Of course the outsider is entitled to exclaim: "Look how he practises, unremittingly dedicated, till his whole life becomes one spiritual exercise."

This outside, 3rd-person story is all right in its place, so long as the one here doesn't take it seriously, and doesn't imagine that any training is going on here in fact. Here, for the 1st person, deliberate training is a series of manoeuvres against Enlightenment. The only genuine and effective training is no-training, the only real spiritual discipline is freedom from anything of the sort. In other words, it is game-free.

Man is obviously made to think. It is his whole dignity and his whole merit; and his whole duty is to think as he ought.

Pascal

Thought is like a fish-hook, which looks pleasant but is not.
Thought is like a bluebottle, because it looks for what is lovely in what is not.

Siksha

Wordiness and intellection,
The more with them, the further astray we go;
Away therefore with wordiness and intellection,
And there is no place where we cannot pass freely.
When we return to the root, we gain the meaning;
When we pursue external objects, we lose the reason.

Hsin-hsin Ming

For one of superior intellect, the best meditation is to remain mentally quiescent, the mind devoid of all thought processes, knowing that the meditator, the object of meditation and the act of meditating constitute an inseparable unity.

Gampopa

Every time a thought arises, throw it away. Just devote yourself to sweeping away thoughts .... When thought is put down, the Original Face appears.

Daito Kokushi

58 THINKER THOUGHT

Problem: The Sages tell us that thinking is our trouble: it seems we shall not be Enlightened till we can stop, not merely our silly mental chatter, but all conceptual thought. This presents at least three practical difficulties. First, the task appears almost impossible: the harder we try to stop thinking the harder we think about it, and other things. Second, the Sages are apt, inconsiderately, to add that any deliberate efforts to stop thinking are worse than useless; but when we relax and just let our minds rip, they lead us everywhere and nowhere, and certainly no nearer Enlightenment. And third, we have an uneasy feeling that, even if we could still our minds, we would by doing so degenerate into vegetables, below rather than above the human norm. This very reasonable suspicion hardly encourages us to take the Sages' advice seriously.

Let us see whether this three-sided problem will yield to analysis. The question, as always, is: *whose* problem is it?

Procedure: Man is the thinking animal, and above all the animal that thinks about itself. Thought is his proper procedure. The more he thinks the more human he is, and the more proficient and sustained his thinking the more mature and civilized he reckons himself to be. He doesn't attribute his mistakes to taking too much thought. The more of it the better, the less of it the worse. There is no problem: man *is* thought, and to deny it would be to deny himself.

Game: Man is thought, but who is the Thinker? The Thinker is the 'I', the pure subject who can never be an object of thought, the

An ancient says: 'In Zen the important thing is to stop the course of the mind.' It means to stop the working of our empirical consciousness, the mass of thoughts, ideas and perceptions.

Great Dogen says: 'Cut off thought by the power of meditation. By this alone nearly everyone can attain the Way.' Attaining the Way is realising the Buddha heart which is our own true Nature.

Takashina Rosen

If you would spend all your time—walking, standing, sitting or lying down—learning to halt the concept-forming activities of your own mind, you could be sure of ultimately attaining the goal.

Since your strength is insufficient, you might not be able to transcend samsara by a single leap; but, after five or ten years, you would surely have made a good beginning and be able to make further progress spontaneously.

Huang Po

The mind cannot be absolutely vacant, and as the thoughts arising from the senses and the lower mind are discarded and ignored, one must supply their place by right mentation. The question then arises: what is right mentation? The reply is: right mentation is the realization of mind itself, of its pure undifferentiated Essence.

Ashvaghosha

thought-source who remains upstream of language, words, concepts, reason, the one who *has* thoughts but is neither a thought nor thinkable. Attempting to think this 1st person (falsely attributing body and mind to this spot which is free from them), or allowing this 1st person to become obscured with thought-clouds however vaporous, is playing the game of Thinker Thought. Like all the other games we are studying, it is the misapplication of a 3rd-person procedure, so necessary out there, to the one Spot where it has no business.

Antithesis: Thought itself supplies many good reasons why thought is out of place here, in this central, 1st-person country, the land of the present. For example, thought takes time, is never all of it contained in one moment of its on-going process, is always looking to the past and the future, is (in short) time-ridden; whereas this spot is only now and free of time. Again, thought is always referring (implicitly if not always explicitly) to space, to the over-there and the elsewhere; whereas this spot is only here, all of it simultaneously present. Again, thought is essentially divided against itself, splitting off into such opposites as true and untrue, good and bad, real and apparent; whereas this spot is unitary, divided by no interior debate or contrasting aspects. Again, thought is self-limiting by nature and in all kinds of ways: thus it is subject to the exigencies of grammar and the rules of logic, as well as to the intellectual limitations of the practitioner; the counters it plays with are always partial, never the whole story; it can only proceed by ignoring (for the present) much that is actually relevant;—whereas the one here knows no

As often as the end is obtained, the means cease, and when the Ship arrives in the Harbour the Voyage is over. So if the soul, after she hath wearied herself by means of Meditation (involving discursive thought), shall arrive at the stillness, tranquility, and rest of Contemplation, she ought then to put an end to all discursive thought, and repose in the loving Contemplation and simple Vision of God.

Molinos

When you strive to gain quiescence by stopping motion, the quiescence gained is ever in motion.

Hsin-hsin Ming

To know our Mind is to obtain liberation. To obtain liberation is to attain the Samadhi of Prajna, which is 'being without thoughts'. 'Being without thoughts' is seeing and knowing all things with a mind free from attachment.... But to refrain from thinking of anything, so that all thoughts are suppressed, is to be Dharma-ridden, and this is an erroneous view.

Hui-neng

Do you know that leisurely philosopher who has gone beyond learning and is not exerting himself in Anything? He neither tries to avoid idle thoughts nor seeks the Truth.

Yung-chia Hsuan-chueh

such limitations. Again, thought is always on the move and always changing (changing its tone, changing sides, changing position) and essentially interminable; whereas the one here is always the same. Finally, what can be thought up can always be argued away, what can be conceived can also be doubted or disproved, what can give intellectual satisfaction one day can fail to give any the next day. Thought is inconclusive, whereas this one is finality itself. I can doubt everything except the one here who is doing the doubting.

Here, I can only *be*—be Self-aware without thoughts. When I am playing Thinker Thought, and pretending to smuggle thoughts into this central region, I'm really doing nothing of the sort: I'm only escaping from here into the outlying regions where thought prevails. In other words, this thought game is my lapsing from Self-awareness into partial unconsciousness, from alertness into dream, from attention to BEING-HERE-NOW into non-being. It is failure to mind my own business, a dishonest muddle about who I am and where I belong.

What, then, is the practical answer to the practical problem set by the Sages—the problem of how to stop one's thinking in order to become Enlightened?

Instead of stopping thought, I have only to place it—out there in its own place. Instead of rejecting thoughts, I have only to authorize them—where they are perfectly in order. Instead of making enormous efforts to improve the situation, I have only to see that it is all right, and everything is already achieved. No thought can ever come quite home, or penetrate this clear country. All I must do, then, is stay at

It is the nature of the mind to wander. You are not the mind. The mind springs up and sinks down. It is impermanent, transitory, whereas you are eternal .... To inhere in the Self is the thing. Never mind the mind .... In the realized man the mind may be active or inactive, the Self alone remains for him.

Ramana Maharshi

Of God himself can no man think. And therefore I would leave all that thing that I can think, and choose to my love that thing that I cannot think.

The Cloud of Unknowing

Home. And this is so easy once I see what this wonderful Home is like. It takes no practice to be a real Home-lover.

The man of true breeding is the Mean in action.

Confucius

Virtue finds, and when found adopts, the mean....
And so it is hard to be good: for surely hard it is in each instance to find the mean....
At all events this much is plain, that the mean state is in all things praiseworthy.

Aristotle

Extremes meet.

Old Proverb

The way out into the light often looks dark,
The way that goes ahead often looks as if it went back.
The way that is least hilly often looks as if it went up and down,
The power that is really loftiest looks like an abyss.
What is sheerest white looks blurred.
The power that is most sufficing looks inadequate,
The power that stands firmest looks flimsy.

Tao Te Ching

God is the absolute maximum and also the absolute minimum, who can be neither greater nor less than He is.

Nicholas of Cusa

59 GOLDEN MEAN

Procedure: The civilized and efficient 3rd person is no abandoned extremist. Society itself is compromise, an exercise in moderation.

Game: The 1st person, precisely the opposite, does nothing by halves, meets no-one half way, rushes to both extremes simultaneously — when not playing Golden Mean and masquerading as 3rd person.

Antithesis: The antithesis, as always, is to observe carefully the difference between that one and this one, thus:

He is something.	As nothing, I am all things.
He knows a thing or two.	As knowing nothing, I know all things.
He is somewhere.	As nowhere, I am everywhere.
He has a little power.	As having no power at all, I am all-powerful.
He has a human body.	As bodiless, the universe is my body.
He has human qualities.	As without qualities, I have all qualities.
He has a human mind.	As mindless, I am the One Mind.
He has mixed feelings.	As impassive, I enjoy everything.
He has opinions.	Having no opinions, I entertain all opinions.
He lives in past and future.	As only now, I take in all time.
He owns a few things.	As claiming nothing, I have everything.
He is often lonely, never alone.	As Alone, I am never lonely.

I observe how needful it is for me to enter into the darkness and to admit the coincidence of the opposites, beyond all the grasp of reason, and there to seek the Truth, where impossibility meets us.

Nicholas of Cusa

It is the boundless Richness and Cause of Identity, and contains beforehand in Itself all opposites under the form of Identity.

Dionysius the Areopagite

Its Formless Nature produces all form; and in It alone Not-Being is an excess of Being, and Lifelessness an excess of Life and Its Mindless state an excess of Wisdom.

Dionysius the Areopagite

The false assumption in the theory of analysis is that simplicity is to be found in one direction only, the direction of the microscope. The simplicities of the world are presumably bipolar.

W.E. Hocking

Now that he ascended, what is it but that he also descended first into the lower parts of the earth? He that descended is the same also that ascended up far above all heavens, that he might fill all things.

St Paul

God is the floor, the roof of creatures.

Eckhart

He achieves something.	Idleness itself, I am responsible for all things.
He is alive.	As stone dead, I am Life itself.
He loves some people, sometimes.	Loveless, I love all beings, always.
He is only human.	As infrahuman, I'm suprahuman.
He is partly known.	As wholly unknowable, I am wholly known.
He attributes some subjectivity to 3rd persons.	Attributing no subjectivity to 3rd persons, I attribute to them the Subjectivity of this 1st person.

And so on, indefinitely. An important point: it isn't that I'm nothing because I'm all things; examining myself, I see it's the other way round, and I'm all things because I'm nothing. The way down from the human level, the loss and the dying are prerequisites of the ascent. Not that either is really difficult: on the contrary, both are natural and easy—it is the fiction of the human mean which I find hard to keep up. To see this 1st person as human is to be unstable in two directions—down to the Essence and up to the Whole. Only my extremities are stable and true. These terminuses really terminate. Floor and Roof, they comprise my only Home.

Trust thyself; every heart vibrates to that iron string.

What pretty oracles nature yields us on this text, in the face and behaviour of children, babes, and even brutes! That divided and rebel mind, that distrust of a sentiment because our arithmetic has computed the strength and means opposed to our purpose, these have not. Their mind being whole, their eye is as yet unconquered, and when we look in their faces, we are disconcerted. Infancy conforms to nobody; all conform to it.

Nothing is at last sacred but the integrity of your own mind.

When good is near you, when you have life in yourself, it is not by any known or accustomed way; you shall not discern the footprints of any other; you shall not see the face of man; you shall not hear any name; the way, the thought, the good, shall be wholly strange and new. It shall exclude example and experience. You take the way from man, not to man.

Thus all concentrates: let us not rove; let us sit at home with the cause. Let us stun and astonish the intruding rabble of men and books and institutions, by a simple declaration of the divine fact. Bid the invaders take the shoes from off their feet, for God is here within.

Emerson

All creatures are searching for the Godlike. The more vile they are the more they search outside.

Thou hast no image save of what is outside thee, therefore it is impossible for thee to be beatified by any image whatsoever.

God is nearer to me than I am to myself.

Eckhart

362

60 HUMBLE PIE

Procedure: A man doesn't play Humble Pie; he *is* humble—of humble birth, low in cosmic rank, a rather insignificant figure—or else he is a humbug claiming to be much more than evidently he is.

Game: I am even more of a humbug (but of quite the opposite kind) when, taking my cue from him, I play Humble Pie—because I dare not see for myself how exalted this player really is.

Antithesis: I am now looking here and seeing clearly that the Occupant of this spot is not a man. But is this seeing believing? Do I know, through and through, Who I am? It would hardly be enough to go by what I see, if it gave the lie to what I feel. If the Divine Essence has to be tugged and manoeuvred into position and kept here by constant vigilance, instead of riding in smoothly and naturally under its own steam and flying the ensign of utter conviction, it would remain no more than a wonderful idea. Any lurking doubt whether I am this Essence would show that I'm not.

Once I go into the matter thoroughly, for myself and wholeheartedly, I find I can doubt everything but this supreme certainty, this Conviction which makes all other convictions seem mere notions, this bed-rock Certainty that remains unshaken when every opinion is shattered. I am the One, with no separate being or existence. Truly this is all I know. Everything else was fantasy.

No, it's not this One here, but the man over there in my mirror, who is so difficult to believe in. *He* is the artefact who has to be

There is no other Buddha for him who knows himself.

Attributed to Kanakamuni

You resemble Joseph (the paragon of beauty) and yet you gaze not on yourself.

Rumi

In this place is one greater than the Temple.

Jesus

God is more intimately and more closely present to each thing than each thing is to itself.

De Adhaerendo Deo

It is natural to man to have a supernatural Light.

William Penn

That all the world is yours, your very senses and the inclinations of your mind declare.

Traherne

If you want to use what you have in yourselves, use it; don't stand wavering. What's the matter with Zen students nowadays that they are unable to reach realisation? The trouble lies in their not believing in themselves enough.

What do we lack? Aren't we sufficient to ourselves?

Lin-chi

contrived, practised, maintained at enormous cost in determination and vigilance—and then at best with only partial success. Unable to endure the strain of pretending to be what he isn't, he tends always to fall back on what he is, on his true Nature. For secretly he is sure he is unlimited, only he lacks the courage of his convictions: it's his fear of mankind which constitutes his manhood. A man is a man because, socially intimidated, he dare not take himself seriously. So he struggles, works, lays plans with astonishing patience and ingenuity, in order somehow to ward off Self-knowledge. It is indeed hard to be one of many, so easy to be the One.

When I dare to be honest about myself, what do I find? Dropping all pretences, all attempts to be good or modest or respectable, what do I feel like in the everyday world, with its concrete details? The startling discovery I make is that *I have always felt the exact opposite of what I was supposed to feel.*

My divinity is no new thing. I entered the scene bursting with self-confidence. As an infant I had the inner assurance (not expressed in words, but more eloquently in actions) that I was the unique, bodiless Centre of the world, perfect and beyond criticism, the rightful owner of all things, all-powerful, free, immortal. Growing up consisted in being talked and laughed and spanked out of all this 'nonsense'—or pretending to be. The hard lesson I was supposed to learn was that I was only human after all, that I was not God but only one of the myriad things He had made, that the world wasn't my private Heaven but more like a public Hell in which I was usually in the wrong, and

Everyone is in fact Self-realised; only—and this is the great mystery—people do not know this.

The state we call Realisation is simply being oneself, not knowing anything or becoming anything.

Ramana Maharishi

Drinking that Essence, man rejoices. If man did not lose himself in that joy, he could not breathe; he could not live.

Taittiriya Upanishad

God does not proclaim Himself, He is everybody's secret, but the intellect of the Sage has found Him.

Katha Upanishad

My Me is God, nor do I recognise any other Me except my God Himself.

St Catherine of Genoa

The word "I" stands for the actuality of divine truth for it is the glyph of one-existence.

It proclaims that God alone is....

The word "I" denotes God's pure essence.

Eckhart

In those respects in which the soul is unlike God, it is also unlike itself.

St Bernard

always unsatisfied, weak, pushed around by people and things, and doomed to die. In short, I didn't grow up to manhood; I was dragged down, protesting, from Godhood.

Yet secretly I remained as I was. A difficult pupil, I refused to be cut down to man-size. Even my growing use of the word 'I' implied that I knew Who this 1st person was. Everything I did was a veiled protest against all imposed and supposed human restrictions, a tacit assertion of divinity. For example, only because I was still the Owner of everything could I be so sure I owned anything, and so determined to get more and more, as if to prove I had no limits. Only because I was still, in principle, omniscient, could I be so sure of the truth when I heard it (being reminded of what, evidently, I knew already) and so keen to go on learning, as if I *must* know all. Only because I was still free and unconditioned could I be so willing to shoulder responsibility for all I had done, and so sure I was unfettered by heredity and environment. Only because I was still in some sense omnipotent could I be so absurdly confident that I was always changing the iron course of events at will, by my every action. Only because I was still the Alone could I be content—and more than content—with this profound isolation from all other beings. Only because I was still immortal could I live cheerfully under sentence of death, in this condemned-cell of a world.

And so on.... These were no tokens of Who I might be, but real evidence. My whole life was a vivid demonstration that I was never really taken in by the game of Humble Pie which I pretended, half-

He who knows himself knows God.

Rumi

The soul has learnt all things; so there is nothing to prevent one who has recollected—learnt, as we call it—one single thing from discovering all the rest for himself, if he is resolute and unwearying in the search; for seeking and learning are nothing but recollection.

Plato

That was the true Light, which lighteth every man that cometh into the world.

He was in the world, and the world was made by him, and the world knew him not.

He came unto his own, and his own received him not.

But as many as received him, to them gave he power to become the sons of God.

St John's Gospel

O my God, how does it happen in this poor old world that Thou art so great and yet nobody finds Thee, that Thou callest so loudly and nobody hears Thee, that Thou art so near and nobody feels Thee, that Thou givest Thyself to everybody and nobody knows Thy name? Men flee from Thee and say they cannot find Thee; they turn their backs and say they cannot see Thee; they stop their ears and say they cannot hear Thee.

Hans Denk

heartedly, to be playing. All that remained was to have the courage of my deepest convictions, the nerve to admit the divinity I had always felt and acted upon.

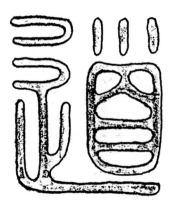

The Chinese character for Tao is made up of the characters for HEAD and GOING.

It's too clear, so it's hard to see.

The Gateless Gate

Perceiving then, O man, all this in thyself, that thou art immaterial, holy, light, akin to him that is unborn, that thou art intellectual, heavenly, translucent, pure, above the flesh, above the world, above rulers, above principalities, over when thou art in truth, then comprehend thyself in thy condition and receive full knowledge and understand wherein thou excellest: and beholding thine own face in thine essence, break asunder all bonds.... desire earnestly to see him that is revealed unto thee, him who doth not come into being, whom perchance thou alone shalt recognise with confidence.

Acts of Andrew (c. 260 A.D.)

'Take on the characteristics of God' has been realised.

'I am for him hearing and sight' has been realised.

This is an extremely majestic station.

Rumi

The only proof of His existence is union with Him.

Mandukya Upanishad

I find myself ... more important to myself than anything I see. And when I ask where does all this throng and stack of being, so rich, so distinctive, so important, come from, nothing I see can answer me... Nothing else in nature comes near this unspeakable stress of pitch, distinctiveness, and selving, this selfbeing of my own. Nothing explains or resembles it..... Searching nature, I taste *self* but at one tankard, that of my own being. The development, refinement, condensation of nothing shews any sign of being able to match this to me or give me another taste of it, a taste even resembling it. One may dwell on this further. We may say that any two things however unlike are in something alike. This is the one exception: when I compare myself, my being-myself, with anything else whatever, all things alike, all in the same degree rebuff me with blank unlikeness; so that my knowledge of it, which is so intense, is from itself alone, they in no way help me to understand it.

Gerard Manley Hopkins

61 EPILOGUE

Throughout, the aim of this enquiry has been to discover the enquirer, to see who is here.

To have taken for granted that this one is a man would have been to assume the very point at issue and end the enquiry before it began. From the start, therefore, the method was as far as possible to ignore all hear-say and mere book-knowledge, and just look again to see whatever was to be seen, and trust only that. The result of this self-inspection has been the discovery that the one here is about as different from the one there—the one seen in the mirror and all others like him—as it is possible to be. A gigantic mistake has occurred, an astounding confidence trick has been played. In this spot is no trace of a man, but God Himself—right here, in place of the human body that never was here. To pretend otherwise is the ploy of all the games described in this book.

Once the Face Game and its varieties are halted, there is an end to the confusion they aim at: the divine and the human are thoroughly unscrambled. Everything is now in order, everything makes sense, and there is no end to the discoveries, clarifications, and new insights which follow. The foregoing chapters are only a sample of the sort of thing that waits impatiently (hidden only by its obviousness) to be noticed.

What is needed isn't more spiritual or mental discipline, or study, or prolonged and systematic meditation, or any working up of states, but simple honesty, courage, faith, and single-mindedness—the honesty to see what there is to see without editing it, the courage to take it seriously, the faith to act on it, and the single-mindedness just to go on being quietly Oneself. Then there are no more problems.

It is true that the findings of this enquiry fail to pass the test of common sense. On the contrary, they show up common sense as the great hoodwink, a huge game of escaping Enlightenment by every means and at all costs. But these findings do pass four other tests. Relying on no authority whatever, they are readily verifiable; intellectually clarifying, they settle many well-worn puzzles; put into day-to-day practice, they work out most beneficially; and, finally, they agree with the teachings of the acknowledged masters of the spiritual life. All the same, it will not do to rest in any of these. The only Enlightened course is to remain open to whatever may be given from moment to moment.

To be totally Self-realised is to be totally honest, totally game-free, totally 1st-person. On the way to this sublime goal a number of stages must be distinguished. These have already been noticed or implied in various places in the foregoing chapters, and partially set out in the table at the end of Part II. Let us now summarise, thus:

Preliminary Stages
Infant (1) INNOCENCE—not knowing What one is
Child (2) GLIMPSING—catching sight of What one is
Adult (3) DELUSION—thinking one is what one isn't

Steps on the 'Spiritual Path'

(3) to (4) Gradual (4) UNDERSTANDING—knowing What one is

(4) to (5) Abrupt (5) SEEING—seeing What one is

(5) to (6) Gradual (6) ILLUMINATION—steadily seeing What one is

(6) to (7) Abrupt (7) SELF-REALISATION—being Who one is

(7) to (8) Gradual (8) FULL SELF-REALISATION

  —steadily being Who one is

  —steadily seeing What one is

  —steadily realising That one is

This map is subject to variation in individual cases. Thus Understanding (4) may come later than Seeing (5), and Illumination (6) may come later than Self-realisation (7). Again, some of the stages may be telescoped, though not actually avoided. And, of course, the titles chosen for the eight stages are rather arbitrary and will not please everybody. (For instance, some will wish to replace the term Self with No-self, or No-mind, or the One Mind, or the Buddha Nature, while others will prefer to speak of God or the Godhead; but in any case the essential realisation is the same for everybody.) In fact, having set up such a scheme, it is easy—and, in the end, necessary—to demolish it. Before doing that, however, let us observe to what extent it can clear up misunderstandings as to the nature of Self-realisation and as to how it may be arrived at.

(1) INNOCENCE—not knowing What one is

The animal and the infant, also some primitives and imbeciles, are wholly (or almost wholly) unaware of themselves. They aren't concerned with What, or Who, or That, they are: they overlook themselves. On the credit side, they don't suffer from delusions about themselves.

It is a common error to confuse Self-realisation with reversion to this paradisal phase. The fact is that 'losing oneself' in work or love or some beautiful object, or in mystical experiences (with or without the aid of drugs and austerities) cannot take one back to the lost Paradise: the reversion is only partial and temporary. In any case, true Self-realisation is the opposite of primitive self-forgetfulness: the Sage who is seeing his absence is in a very different state from the baby who isn't seeing his presence, however similar they are in other respects.

(2) GLIMPSING—catching sight of What one is

Some children (what proportion we don't know), between the ages of, say, eighteen months and ten years, from time to time see, briefly but clearly, their absence—their facelessness. This preliminary seeing is normally lost, as the growing child learns to take a 3rd-person view of himself. If he fails or refuses to learn this art, he is liable to need institutional care.

(3) DELUSION—thinking one is what one isn't

The marks of this stage are that one believes the world is real in its own right, that one is a body that is a part of the world, and that one's consciousness is dependent upon the body.

The activities which normally go with this stage are the pursuit of pleasure; and, when that disappoints, the pursuit of possessions and power; and, when those disappoint, the pursuit of reputation and fame.

(4) UNDERSTANDING—knowing What one is

It is a decisive development in one's life when one turns from the surrounding world to oneself at its Centre, and asks What lies here. Increasingly one comes to understand that one is not the body but Spirit or Consciousness or the Self, that one is not a thing among other things but that unique No-thing which is the Container and Ground and Source of all things. One comes wholeheartedly to believe that the Real is not what is experienced, but the Experiencer, the one that is not in the world but in whom the world is.

Profound intellectual and moral work is characteristic of this stage, including ascetic and devotional practices, talking and reading about spiritual matters, and systematic meditation. All this can lead to the growth of one's desire for Self-realisation, directly experienced. On the other hand, it can become an end in itself and a lifelong refuge from Self-realisation.

(5) SEEING—seeing What one is

Though it is a valuable preparation, no amount of understanding the Self will ever build up into seeing the Self. And for a very good reason: seeing This is incompatible with thinking about This, and is a much simpler and more direct experience. Instead of *knowing* that right here, on the very Spot one now occupies, is this brilliant Clarity without so much as a speck of body-mind, one actually *sees* this Clarity, more sharply and convincingly than one sees anything else. The Self here enjoys itself as perfectly lucid, transparent, obvious.

This Self-seeing is true Liberation, the decisive step, the leap in the dark. Nevertheless it does not (in any of the cases we know) last: it fades when it is not actively attended to, and needs constant renewal. In a sense, therefore, this stage is only the beginning of the true spiritual life.

(6) ILLUMINATION—steadily seeing What one is

Genuine Self-seeing, after the initial experience of it, is renewable *at will.* One may, of course, be so diverted from it that *in practice* it is no longer available, but this is because one does not at the moment desire it; *in fact* it is always at hand. And certainly one's seeing needs to be practised and stabilised till it goes on all the while. Actually, 'practised' is misleading, because seeing is so very easy and natural and agreeable. All the same, it can be neglected, and total dedication is indispensable. Normally, it will take years of more-or-less deliberate seeing before the faculty becomes quite automatic, in all the circumstances of everyday life.

(7) SELF-REALISATION—being Who one is

Just as there is no footbridge between understanding the Self and seeing the Self, so there is no footbridge between seeing the Self and being the Self. The transition is a sudden leap, powered by Grace. No amount of seeing clearly *What* one is—namely, this Emptiness of body-mind—will automatically lead to full 1st-personhood, to the first-hand experience of being *Who* one is—namely, the One, the sole Reality, the Alone. On the other hand, no doubt some progress in stabilising one's Self-seeing will make Self-realisation more likely.

The mark of this stage is that, instead of merely thinking about and seeing the One, one actually feels like the One. One answers to this Name, as before one answered to a human name. One discovers what it really is to be the All and the Source of All. Yet, paradoxically, this ultimate Independence and Self-sufficiency is also the ultimate dependence and abandonment and self-naughting: it is at once absolutely exalting and absolutely humbling.

But again, this realisation is not necessarily permanent. Rather it is likely to begin as a series of recurrent realisations, flashes of the Supreme Identity separated by periods of Self-forgetfulness.

(8) FULL SELF-REALISATION—steadily being Who one is

And again, it is certainly not practice as a task or a duty, but as ever-renewed enjoyment, which leads to the permanent establishment of the Supreme Identity.

Probably, long before that Identity is uninterruptedly enjoyed, it will be found to include, besides seeing *What* one is, and being *Who* one is, vividly realising *That* one is. In other words, though the experience of this eighth stage is in the last resort perfectly simple and indivisible, yet it must somehow include ontological wonder, a gasping amazement at the 'impossible' fact that one has—against all the odds—actually occurred, that anything exists at all, that the Self has happened, that it *is*. Here, one exclaims 'I AM!', and that is enough. Not *How* I am or *What* I am (what is achievement after the achievement of Being?) but *That* I am. Somehow it has come off—this very special enterprise, this incredible feat of having, without any help or reason or cause, raised Oneself out of non-existence into glorious Actuality. This is at once the highest knowledge and the deepest ignorance—the Self's own wonder at Itself, the divine surprise, the Mystery revelling in the Mystery.

The scientific world would be an impossible sort of place to inhabit. It is a symbolic world and the only thing that could live comfortably in it would be a symbol.

The mind may be regarded as regaining from Nature that which the mind has put into Nature.

The frank realisation that physical science is concerned with a world of shadows is one of the most significant of recent advances.

Sir A. S. Eddington

The universe cannot admit of material representation, and the reason, I think, is that it has become a mere mental concept.

Sir James Jeans

No dungeon was ever constructed so dark and narrow as that in which the shadow physics of our time imprisons us.

Bertrand Russell

The subject does not belong to the world.
The sense of the world must lie outside the world.

Wittgenstein

Science (at least as a temporary methodological device) can rest upon a naive faith; religion is the longing for justification. When religion ceases to seek for penetration, for clarity, it is sinking back into its lower forms.

A. N. Whitehead

PART IV

THE THIRD-PERSON WORLD GAME

Procedure: Up to the present, science has proceeded on a single basic assumption which is rarely stated and never questioned. It is this:—*my 1st-person view of the universe is invalid.*

Following inevitably from this unexamined premise is the kind of universe which science 'discovers'—an exploded and decentralized universe organized about innumerable centres, none of which has overriding priority; an unconscious and 'dead' universe in which life and mind are very rare, local, and late evolutionary by-products, dependent upon certain delicate material structures or processes and disappearing when they disappear; a meaningless and even anti-human universe in which man is a stranger and afraid, and his values carry no weight at all.

However arbitrary it is in fact, undeniably this 3rd-person model of the universe works out in practice. On no other procedural basis could science have achieved its astounding intellectual and practical successes. For the prediction and control of events, this model has proved the indispensable instrument. This is not to say that it will remain so.

Game: Here and now my 1st-person universe brilliantly displays itself, all of it set out around this Centre. If *this* world doesn't carry conviction, what other could do so? If *this* arrangement of limbs, people, houses, trees, mountains, clouds, sun and sky, is not to be taken seriously, what is? If *this* is false, what is truth?

Yet the astonishing fact is that (till I stop playing 3P-WG) I dismiss it all without a backward glance of regret, or even a passing thought, in favour of another universe altogether. I don't like my world: someone else's is much preferred. And what a world it is! His world is as alarming as mine is encouraging. And whereas my world is available freely, clearly, instantly, effortlessly, his world is still to make: it is the product of endless toil in lecture theatres and libraries and laboratories—and even then it is only the bare skeleton of a cosmos. Nature and Artifice are opposites; how, then, can anything so manifestly artificial as this immense contrivance fail to obscure Nature?

A game is being played—by whom? Who is up to tricks, Nature or the naturalist? What sort of world is revealed when I trust the data, and stop playing games with it?

Antithesis: It does not follow from the foregoing that the game-free, 1st-person world-view is obscurantist or even unscientific. On the contrary, if one fully admits the procedural validity of the 3rd-person universe constructed by science, without abandoning the 1st-person universe disclosed by perception, they are found to be quite compatible. In fact, science itself, when it takes itself seriously enough, points away from a 'dead' and meaningless universe to a living and meaningful one, and even a 1st-person one. The theme of the following pages is that there is no longer any intellectual need to be so miserable about the universe. If one insists on depersonalizing the cosmos, and discounting one's first-hand view of it, this is not a stoical facing of the facts, but a dishonest avoiding of them.

Editor's note: In the typescript of The Face Game the author proposed to reprint here, with some minor abbreviations, his article The Universe Revalued (first published in the Saturday Evening Post in 1961). But he did not include the slightly abbreviated article. However, you can read this article (with several introductory paragraphs added by Harding) in *Look For Yourself,* a collection of Harding's essays. (Highly recommended!) It is Chapter 15 and is called The Universe Enlightened.

APPENDIX

A THESAURUS OF POINTERS

The following devices, which may roughly be described as 'contemporary koans', have been found effective as invitations to seeing into one's Self-nature. The main purpose of recording them here is to arm people who already see, by supplementing their own repertoire of means for helping other people to see; the actual means selected will, however, depend upon the inspiration of the moment, to fit the special needs and interests of the inquirer. There is no need to work through them all, for to penetrate one is to penetrate the others. The list is tentative and open-ended: it is for testing (on interested persons only, of course) and for adding to. Though it is meant for use in his face-to-face (no-face) encounters by one who sees, he can also use these 'koans' as personal triggers, handy reminders of the fact that his own clear seeing is always available, at will and regardless of mood, and is capable of endless deepening.

1 Playing magicians

I'm a magician, waving this wand at you and reciting this spell: "Cheeks turn green, eyes grow together, hair fall out!" I wave my wand again and say: "As you were!" Will you ever know what really happened?

I wave my wand again and charm your memory away. It's as if you were newly born this instant, with no idea whether you are a cloud, a flame, a rose, a crocodile, a man, or about half a man. Well, just look and see.

Unfortunately, your memory returns, so I wave any wand a third time, reciting: "Face go, face go!" Now notice how powerful this magic is. Will you ever get your face back?

2 Drawing

Put your feet up on the sofa and make a self-portrait, drawing only what you see, exactly as you see it now. Take the result seriously.

3 Spectacles

Put on your glasses slowly and notice at what point the two lenses merge. Then say how many eyes you are now looking out of.

4 Bathrooms

Does your bathroom mirror reveal two faces confronting each other, or one face? If only one, where is it—in that bathroom beyond the glass, or in this bathroom? If in that bathroom, what remains in this one?

5 Asymmetry

Look at those two people over there. They are equals; their relationship is symmetrical; what's one side of the half-way line matches what's the other side. The noses add up to two, the eyes to four.

Now look at me and say whether our relationship is like that. How many noses and eyes can you make out now? Are we face to face or face to no-face? Is there any comparison between us?

6 Your side

Look at that patch of blue carpet and see what's your side of it now. Is there anything confronting the blue or added to it, any mistiness or speck or stain imposed upon the pure colour, any visual apparatus, any seer or seeing of the blue? Are you not utterly blued, become just blueness itself and nothing more?

Is there anything, ever, in front of what's seen?

7 Knock, knock

Only as little children shall we enter the Kingdom. Then let's play a child's game. I ask you where you are. You point out the spot. I knock at your door (forehead) and ask to be let in. You tell me not to be silly: "No admittance!" So I wait outside on your doorstep while you tell me what it's like in there.

Is it stuffy or congested? Are there any dark corners? Do these two little windows let in enough light? What do they look like from your side of them? The outsides of houses are often deceptive: how big is yours, inside? How far are the walls apart, how lofty the ceiling? Is it quite empty of furniture?

And what about its Inhabitant? Are you in? If you are out, see whether I am not in, filling your house at this moment. No admittance, indeed! Isn't there room for the whole world in there? And isn't this the Kingdom?

8 Cut it off

Look at my hands and notice they are connected to a trunk. Look at yours and notice whether they are connected to anything.

When you see them as loose, independent objects, do you find they do their work differently? If so, how? And whose hands are they? When walking, repeat this investigation with regard to your legs. If your hand or foot 'offends you' or hurts, try 'cutting it off', and observe what happens to the pain.

Why is it that young children often draw their hands loose, unconnected to a body, and when asked to 'give a foot' sometimes pick it up and hand it over as if it were an independent object?

9 The dumb method

Without a word, I point to your foot, then to mine, and we nod agreement. Then I point to your leg, then to mine, and we nod again. And so on upwards, till we reach our faces—and we do *not* nod.

This method was devised for use with foreigners, the deaf and dumb, and over-talkative people.

10 Seeing absence

How can you see an absence? Suppose when you go home you find that the picture over the fireplace is missing. You see its absence today at least as clearly as you saw its presence yesterday, and you do so with the same kind of seeing. In precisely the same matter-of-fact way, can you not see the absence of your face now, at least as clearly as you are seeing the presence of mine?

11 Hearing silence

How can you hear a silence? You hear this clock ticking. Now I do something to the works and you notice it has stopped ticking. Now you hear its silence at least as clearly as, before, you heard its sound, and you do so with the same kind of hearing. In precisely the same matter-of-fact way, can you not hear your own Silence (does it not hear itself, rather?) into which the world's sounds drop?

12 The glass nose

Look sideways at me and observe the pinkish, transparent shadow thrown diagonally across my face. Compare this transparent 'nose' with my opaque nose. Are they the same sort of thing, at all? And what is your side of it? Is there anything to support it, or is it just dangling there in mid-air?

13 Head handling

I put my hands on my ears and ask you to describe what lies between them. Now I put my hands on your ears and ask the same question. You repeat the exercise with your own hands.

14 Bodily stocktaking

I invite you to look straight ahead and to count, *on the present evidence,* your toes, legs, arms, fingers, and to say how big they are. Next, I ask you to look at your hand and count the fingers, then slowly bring it towards your forehead, observing exactly what happens to the fingers. On contact, try counting them again, and say how big your hand is now. Has it melted into your forehead, and where does your forehead end?

15 The cowl

Arrange a shawl or towel over your head and let it project a few inches like a nun's hood. The outline of your face is now visible. Describe its features.

16 Growing a head

If you insist on having a head attached to your body, try 'growing' one at the end of your arm—with the help of this oval hand-mirror. Have you now two heads?

17 Make-up

If your face is where you *think* it is (namely some five feet in front of where you see it is) then surely you should be able to tell me all about the lipstick design I'm now drawing on your forehead. You do your best, but the laugh is on you. I'm using the wrong end of the lipstick, and your forehead is spotless!

18 Making an appearance

I'm not asking you *whether* you have a face (of course you have) but *where* you keep it—right at the centre of your world, or a few feet off, in cameras, mirrors, your friends, your dog. The same question may well be asked of everything. Where is the sun warm and yellow and round and sunny—over there in itself, or here in you and me?

Is it true that peripherally and in its seers, a thing is the thing they see it to be; and that centrally and in itself, it is the no-thing it sees itself to be, once it gets round to self-inspection? If this statement is untrue, correct it.

19 Plunging neckline

Look down at your chest. How much of you is form now, how much void? Can their present boundaries, the frontier where they meet, be located? Can the upper limit of your form be mapped?

See how your clothes fit. At the collar or neckline, do they not terminate with the body they cover? A yoke or necklace may conveniently remind you of your extent. Is it true (as Jesus perhaps hinted) that one who wears this yoke finds rest, because the burden it carries is indeed light?

20 Creating and destroying

Can this void catch itself producing, out of itself and instantly, a hand or foot, or trunk (as far as the neckline), and instantly absorbing them again? Can the void create, at will, men, trees, clouds, stars, and then destroy them without trace?

(For the infant, initially, disappearance is annihilation. The toy or the mother doesn't go on existing when out of sight, and so isn't looked for. And the Sage—says the *Tao Te Ching*—sees and hears no more than an infant sees and hears.)

21 Taking your lid off

The world is a cellar full of sealed jars—but one of them has a loose lid. Which one? The world's doors are all locked against you—all except one. Which door is that? The world is inscrutable—except in one place. Which place?

You have direct, inside information about one sample piece of the universe, because you *are* that sample, plus its own ability to unwrap and examine itself. When you take this sample seriously, as a true one disclosing the intrinsic nature of all things, what do you find?

22 Semantic confusion

We describe ourselves as face to face, but this one word face has to do for two totally different experiences—your experience now of my face, and of your face. What is the difference between the content of these two experiences? Isn't this misuse of language much more ridiculous and confusing than if we were to use one and the same word for, say, an elephant and a cloud?

Doesn't the same duplicity make nonsense of many other much-used words, such as *head, self, person, man,* and *seeing, hearing, being?* Isn't it one of the principal functions of language to blind us to the infinite difference (obvious once words are dropped) between oneself and all others? No wonder seeing oneself is incompatible with thinking about oneself.

23 Counting parts

Notice how many parts there are in what is seen, then how many parts in what sees. Can that last which has parts, and that decay which has no parts?

24 Looking out of

Try looking at me now without overlooking the Looker. Is it so difficult simultaneously to see what you are looking at and what you are looking out of? How does this two-way regard affect your perception of me?

25 What other selves?

Can you find any spook behind my eyes now, peering out of them at you? Have you any more reason for attributing minds or spirits to men than primitives have for attributing them to stones and trees? Be as honest about me as about yourself, in both cases going by what you see instead of by what you imagine. Your double task is to exorcise the illusory face from your mind, and the illusory mind from my face, till you see yourself as all mind and me as all body, in total contrast.

(The consequences of this refusal to go beyond the evidence are seven. (1) I don't make you shy. You look me straight in the eye. (2) You really *see* me. No longer haunted, this face can be read like a book: all is revealed. (3) What's revealed is so interesting. Now you really look and really listen. (4) Because we are polar opposites, each having what the other lacks absolutely, we are instantly joined in perfect unity. Our old pretence that we are at all alike was, in fact, mutual rejection and fear of love. (5) Now that matter and spirit are sorted into their proper places, Spirit sees itself as indivisible. There is only the One. (6) It isn't that other people are machines lacking any trace of mind, but that they keep all of it *your* side of their eyes. In fact, the primitive is right, and nothing is mindless or dead. The world is saturated with the one Life. (7) You come to see every object as a unique expression or incarnation of this one Life, this Void-which-you-are, to be loved as Yourself. I am your own embodiment.)

26 Primitive man no jerk

Prehistoric man hardly ever includes a face in his representations of the human body. Either the head is reduced to a small and practically featureless blob, or is left out altogether.

Is this how he saw himself?

27 How many voids?

See now whether your void has any parts or edges or limits or anything to distinguish or separate it from other voids. Isn't this the one, solitary, indivisible, unique Void, which is that inmost Essence of all beings throughout all time and space, including the weirdest of extraterrestrial creatures? In seeing and knowing and being This, aren't you all of them, for ever? Isn't this the true resurrection of the dead, the true all-knowledge?

28 Side by side

When he fails to make a sale across the table, the expert business man moves over to sit alongside his customer. Putting their heads together over a proposition, they are more likely to come to terms. Why?

29 Gape

See what happens to your food, where your words come from, what holds your cigarette in position. When you see thus, what difference does it make to the taste of your food, the coherence and value of what you say, and your desire to smoke?

30 Mandala

What is the world really like? How does the universe actually sort itself out, in your first-hand experience? Is it seen to be arranged about many centres of equal status, or about one supreme Centre? Is it a loose, anarchic aggregation, or does it all hang together, a system obedient to one Ruler? Does it resemble the works of a very complicated watch, or its simple face?

Do you find that all things sort themselves out, each keeping to its own region, round about you, with the result that they all keep their proper distances and sizes and temperatures, and even the sun and stars are small and cool?

Aren't all these inhabitants of your regions entirely different from you and essentially inferior? Aren't they observably finite, eccentric, mutually exclusive, mere parts of you?

Isn't this 1st-person universe best depicted by a nest of concentric circles, with You at their Centre, yet including them all? And isn't the contrasting 3rd-person universe, which is only imagined and never seen, best depicted by a collection of separate circles, each with its own centre? Drawing and dwelling on these two contrasting diagrams can help to show you Who you are.

31 The nest of boxes

The scientist doesn't take things at their face value, but goes into them. Approaching you, he makes out that your apparently solid body is really a collection of organs, which are really tissues, which are really cells, which are really molecules, which are really atoms, which aren't material objects at all, but more like empty space. Now you alone are in a position to complete the scientist's story, and either confirm or deny that the reality at the centre of all your appearances is in fact empty. He can only observe what you are like out there; what you actually are, at the Source of all these regional appearances, only you have any right to say. What do you find? Is there Nothing in the last box—a Nothing which nevertheless sees itself as such?[1]

32 Seeing without eyes

Look at my face now and say whether you believe it is really lurking somewhere inside your head. Have you ever for one moment supposed that what you see isn't the real thing, but only an unreliable

---

1 Cf. Eddington: "The revelation by modern physics of the void within the atom is more disturbing than the revelation by astronomy of the immense void of interstellar space."

reconstruction of it, produced in a small, dark, tightly-packed bone box? Is there room in this container for sky and mountains and trees and men, and do brain operations disclose anything of the kind—anything except brains? How could this brilliant and vast world be squeezed into so tiny and congested a part of itself?

Aren't you now de-faced by my face? Isn't your seeing the world always your replacement by it? Doesn't your seeing require the *absence* of eyes and brain, since they would block the view? Can there be any other kind of seeing than this kind, and is there ever more than one headless Seer around?

33 Hearing without ears

Repeat the above investigation with hearing. Do you really believe that the sound of my voice is a condition of part of your head? What head? Who is the unique Hearer?

34 The four fools

Four fools happening to meet, each decided to make his own record of the occasion. The result was four photographs, each showing three fools. The fools all maintained, however, that the missing person was included in each picture—perfectly photographed as the nobody on the back of the print, and the three bodies on the front.

35 The Red Queen

What are you really like where you are? Seriously wanting to know,

I am now taking the liberty of coming to see. I notice that, as I approach you, the whole man is replaced by a half-man, the half-man by a head, the head by a nose, the nose by skin-pores, the skin-pores by nothing. The only way to find you again is to get back to my own chair, five feet off.

"I think I'll go and meet her," said Alice....

"You can't possibly do that," said the Rose. "I should advise you to walk the other way."

This sounded nonsense to Alice, so she said nothing, but set off at once towards the Red Queen. To her surprise, she lost sight of her in a moment.

36 Empty chair

Compare the One sitting in your chair with the one sitting in my chair, now, and tell me who you are. Early representations of the Buddha show merely a footprint or an empty seat.

37 How far behind?

The following well-known limerick has been attributed to Woodrow Wilson:—

As a beauty I am not a star,

there are others more handsome by far,

but my face—I don't mind it

for I am behind it.

It's those in front get the jar.

38 The colour question

Laurens van der Post: "It's very difficult to realize that my black African friends feel just as white as we do inside, just as full of light."

Compare this with the true story of a simple-minded American negro who, when asked by a television interviewer why he failed to get a job, replied: "They say I'm black, but (fingering his cheeks) I'm not, really." [2]

When black and white are face to face, *who's black?*

The only radical solution to the colour question is (as always) to see whose problem it is.

39 Gaol-break

If you are in your body, are you in it the way tea is in this cup? Are you smaller than your body, or the same size, or do you spill over?

Take hold of my hand. What evidence is there, at this moment, that you stop at your fingertips, or are more inside your hand than mine?

Look at your foot on the carpet and say where you end and your environment begins. Until you *incorporate* your dentures, your clothes, your car, any tools you happen to be using, are you using them properly? Where are the limits of your total Body?

Surveying yourself from the chest down, which side of your suit are you now. Again, where are you seeing and hearing me?

Aren't you at large in this living room, filling its living space?

---

2 And the true story of a small negro girl in a white school: her hands and forearms were found to be very sore—she had been trying to scrub them white. At this stage, of course, her face presented no problem.

You can see it contains your body (where you keep various pains, pleasures, muscular tensions, etc.) just as it contains your bureau (where you keep various papers), but could you see this if you were shut up in either receptacle? Isn't your body in you (instead of you in it), and aren't you, now, as big as the view you are enjoying?

If your body were ever your prison, haven't you visibly blown its top off, and blasted your way out of it? Haven't you made yourself scarce, and got clean away from that lidless jug? Can you find now, at the Centre of your world, any centre, any lump, anybody, anything but Unfurnished Accommodation for all beings? Isn't this filled Vacancy your marvelous Home?

40 Distance no object

Is the world inside you or outside? What's outside you is at a distance, what's inside you is not; so you have to measure how distant things are. Hold up a ruler and read off the distance between any two stars, trees, men: obviously they are well separated. Now measure the distance between any one of them and yourself. This involves rotating your ruler through 90° till it is end-on, and its units of measurement have shrunk to nothing. Taking this discovery seriously, say now whether you are in the world, or the world is in you.

41 Walk tall

Walk tall, and you will find that headlessness comes easier. Or, better, be headless and observe yourself walking tall, and (as the well-known song says) looking the world straight in the eye.

(F.M. Alexander was an advocate of walking tall. A therapist who treated successfully many famous people for a great variety of complaints, he got his results by very simple means. He urged his patients to get what he called their head-neck-back (h-n-b) control going—thinking the head forward and up, relaxing the neck, and widening and lengthening the back. In effect, the patient was to get home and take charge, consciously inhabiting this ruling upper region from which he had disastrously strayed. He was to leave the body's members to carry on with their own business free from his *direct* interference, almost as if they were cut off.

This homecoming, Alexander claimed, by withdrawing attention from the abnormally functioning parts to their controlling centre, corrects their functioning automatically, and often swiftly. In addition, there is a tendency for eyes to brighten, complexions to clear, the head to be held higher and at a better angle, and general health and happiness to improve. The effect of treatment was in some cases for the patient to feel airborne.

Alexander was never clear why his technique worked. Significantly, its results are very much like the results of seeing one's facelessness or headlessness. This isn't surprising, for in practice the maintenance of the h-n-b control means clearly *locating* and concentrating upon a presence here which, though very real and potent, is quite empty of content. At their best, Alexander's disciples were faceless without fully recognizing it. This was sufficient to produce many 'miraculous' cures.)

42 Drink or drugs

Much of the appeal of alcohol and other drugs is that they give temporary relief from the Face Game—by regression to more primitive modes of self-experience.

A.E.G., returning home rather drunk from a regimental reunion, fell and broke the bottle he was carrying in his hip pocket. Before turning into bed he discovered he had cut his bottom, and applied adhesive tape to the wound. In the morning, Mrs. G. was puzzled to find a piece of tape stuck on the bedroom mirror.

THE PERSEUS MYTH

Perseus is a hero whose father is God (Zeus) and whose mother (Danse) is a mortal..	It is for a hero to realize his divine Source, in spite of all appearances to the contrary.
As a child he suffers misfortunes and is brought up in poverty.	Fallen, alienated, he goes through a period of ignorance and suffering.
Grown to manhood, he is set a task—to kill the terrible Gorgon,	His remedy is to overcome the world.
Medusa, who turns all who look at her to stone.	Looking upon the objects around him, he thinks he must be like them—earthly, material, opaque. Seen thus directly, the world turns him to stone.
Athene, goddess of wisdom, arms him with her Mirror-shield, in which alone Medusa can safely be viewed.	But seen indirectly and with wisdom, in the mirror of the Self, it is harmless. Turning from the world to himself its seer, he sees he is unpetrified,
He gets from Hades the Cap of Invisibility,	transparent, headless,
from the Graeae their Single Eye,	one-eyed,
from the Nymphs a pair of Winged Sandals	airborne, 'riding on the wind',
and a Magic Wallet in which to hide Medusa's severed head,	and the Void which packs all things away.
and from Hermes the Adamantine Sickle with which to kill Medusa.	Wielding the Sword of Discrimination, he sees he is not of the world: he cuts it off.

Having accomplished his task, Perseus mounts Pegasus, the winged horse who springs from Medusa's corpse.	Now the world is harmless, indeed his friend. United to it, he is borne heavenwards.
Medusa's sisters pursue Perseus, but, aided by the cap of invisibility, he escapes.	The hero's triumph is resented, but his Emptiness protects him.
Further adventures follow, in which he turns others (Atlas, Andromeda's Monster, her family) to stone, by showing them Medusa's head.	Now It is our hero's turn to petrify others. The corollary of seeing his own transparency is seeing others' opacity: he is all spirit, they are all body.
He sets sail for Argos with a party of Cyclops.	Yet, paradoxically, he recognizes that others are like him—one-eyed, empty.

JUDAR THE FISHERMAN

The *Arabian Nights Entertainments* contains the story of Judar, a young fisherman who finds a well-hidden Treasure House. He knocks at the door. A porter, armed with an axe, opens and says: "Stretch out your neck so that I can cut off your head." Unafraid, Judar does so, and the blow is painless. He sees that the porter is a body without a soul.

After further adventures, he proceeds to the Treasure itself, which includes the Four Valuables—the Celestial Disc (whose owner sees all lands as near), the Sword (whose owner can slay all), the Seal-Ring (whose owner rules the world) and the Collyrium Pot (whose owner can see all the world's treasures).

THE KING'S NEW CLOTHES

Two swindlers once went to a king and held up for his approval what they claimed was a magic suit of clothes—visible to a wise man but not to a fool. Naturally the king, not willing to appear a fool, ordered a complete outfit. The queen, also not willing to appear a fool, declared that the clothes were the most beautiful ones she had ever seen. So did the whole court, and everybody else—except one small boy, who hadn't heard about the magic suit and didn't know what he was supposed to see. So, at the great parade held for displaying the king's wonderful new clothes, he gave the whole game away by shouting: "Look, the king's stark naked!"

This well-known tale is reminiscent of the convention, common in early Christian and Gnostic writings, that one's clothes stand for one's body, and undressing stands for seeing-through-the-body-illusion. In the *Gospel of Thomas* we read:

"Jesus said, 'When you undress yourselves and are not ashamed, and take your clothes and lay them under your feet like little children and tread on them; then you are sons of the Living One and you will have no fear.'"

JESUS THE SEER

Did Jesus see his Facelessness?

His words were not recorded till long after they were spoken, and have come down to us with many additions and subtractions. Inevitably the gospel-makers' selections from and interpretations of the Master's teaching were determined by their own spiritual horizons; and people who don't see aren't the best guides to one who does see—specially when they aren't primarily concerned about historical accuracy. All the same, there can still be found in the New Testament numerous indications of Jesus's seeing—provided one knows what to look for. They may be summarised as follows:

(1) The Kingdom of Heaven, the Living Water, the Light, the Spirit—these (or rather That of which these are metaphors) await discovery within you.

(2) But unless you turn round (are converted) and

(3) become like a little child, you will not enter the Kingdom.

(4) It is better, having one Eye (like an infant) to enter the Kingdom than having two eyes (like an adult) to be cast into hell fire. (Your imagined two-eyed face here is sufficient to make life hellish.)

(5) If your hand or foot offends you (functions badly) cut it off (see it as it is given, loose, unconnected to any owner, and notice how much better it functions.)

(6) You are the Light of the world. Don't hide the Light under a vessel (your pretended head) but let it shine before men.

(7) "When thine Eye is single, thy whole body also is full of Light..... If thy body therefore be full of Light, having no part dark, the whole shall be full of Light, as when the bright shining of a candle doth give thee light."

Did he leave behind him any other seers, any school or tradition of seeing? And was this tradition one of the sources of Christian Gnosticism? We don't know. What is clear is that certain Gnostics who saw believed that Jesus did so pre-eminently, and that his most important sayings were about salvation by Self-knowledge, or rather Self-seeing.

Thus in the *Gospel of Thomas* the true disciples are 'Light-men' or 'Luminous men', essentially Spirit; and they are rich, indeed they reign, when they discover their true Nature, the Kingdom within, the Pearl of great price, the Treasure hidden in the field, the Place of Rest. This saving gnosis is only to be had by becoming like an infant who is (for himself) as yet unbodied, sexless, single-eyed, immortal. One has to *see* what is before one's face, to trust the two 'good' senses of sight and hearing more than the other three, to observe how the opaque and dead things one eats are dissolved in the Light and Life of the immaterial Eater, to be empty and clean of body and not like the Pharisee—a whitened tomb full of bones and corruption.

"His disciples said:

'Show us the place where you are,

for it is necessary for us to seek it.'

He said to them:

'He who has ears let him hear!

There is a Light within a Light-man

and it illuminates the whole world;

if it did not illuminate it—darkness.'"

Gospel of Thomas, 25.

And every Space that a Man views around his dwelling-place

Standing on his own roof or in his garden on a mount

Of twenty-five cubits in height, such space is his Universe:

And on its verge the Sun rises and sets, the Clouds bow

To meet the flat Earth and the Sea in such an order'd Space:

The Starry heavens reach no further, but here bend and set

On all sides, and the two Poles turn on their valves of gold;

And if he move his dwelling-place, his heavens also move

Where'er he goes, and all his neighbourhood bewail his loss.

Such are the Spaces called Earth and such its dimension.

Blake

CPSIA information can be obtained
at www.ICGtesting.com
Printed in the USA
LVOW12s2210220418
574486LV00001B/109/P